WALKING NABOTH'S VINEYARD

University of Notre Dame
Ward-Phillips Lectures in
English Language and Literature

Volume 13

Walking Naboth's Vineyard

New Studies of Swift

EDITED BY

Christopher Fox

AND

Brenda Tooley

UNIVERSITY OF NOTRE DAME PRESS
NOTRE DAME, INDIANA

Library of Congress Cataloging-in-Publication Data

Walking Naboth's vineyard : new studies of Swift / edited by
Christopher Fox and Brenda Tooley.
     p.   cm. — (Ward-Phillips lectures in English language and
literature ; v. 13)
    "A collection of essays from a marathon conference on Swift and
Ireland at the University of Notre Dame"—P. 2.
    Includes index.
    Contents: Swift: virtue, travel, and the Enlightenment / Seamus
Deane— Jonathan Swift as Irish historian / Carole Fabricant—Swift,
God, and power / Michael DePorte—Swift and romance / Margaret
Anne Doody—Laetitia Pilkington on Swift / A.C. Elias—The humors
of Quilca / Joseph McMinn—Jonathan Swift's library, his reading,
and his critics / Heinz J. Vienken—Sarah Fielding as Swift's printer
/ James Woolley—Swift and Catholic Ireland / Robert Mahony.
    ISBN 0-268-01950-9 (alk. paper)
    1. Swift, Jonathan, 1667–1745—Criticism and interpretation—
Congresses. I. Fox, Christopher, 1948–   . II. Tooley, Brenda.
III. Series.
PR3727.W27   1994
828'.509—dc20   94-15112
                                                    CIP

Contents

Acknowledgments

The Notre Dame Sesquicentennial Irish Meetings resulted from happy collaboration. In furthering the distinguished tradition of the Ward-Phillips Lectures, the Notre Dame English Department sponsored major addresses. The Notre Dame Sesquicentennial Committee and Dean Harold W. Attridge of the College of Arts and Letters also offered major financial assistance, as did Vice President Nathan O. Hatch of the Graduate School. For co-sponsoring the American Conference of Irish Studies Meeting (also part of this event) we thank Robert Burns and the Notre Dame History Department, and Professor Mary Helen Thuente. By combining resources, an international program was produced that included seventy papers on Swift, and over one hundred talks on other subjects, ranging from Irish women writers to Celtic and Christian Ireland, Gaelic scholarship in the eighteenth century, Edward Lovett Pearce and Irish architecture, emigration and ethnicity, the troubles in Northern Ireland and Anglo-Irish relations. For valuable help with this complicated program, we thank Harriet Baldwin and Viedra Thomas. We also thank Thomas Bonnell, Andrew Carpenter, A. C. Elias, Jr., John Irwin Fischer, Judith Fox, Laura Sue Fuderer and the Notre Dame Department of Special Collections, Rev. Ernan McMullin, John Matthias, David G. Schappert and Ewa Ziarek.

For continuing efforts without which the project would have been impossible, we pay tribute to Angela Brant, Margaret M. Jasiewicz, Nancy McMahon, Nancy Kegler, Cheryl Reed, Sherry Reichold, John Quinn, and James Manifold. Finally, we thank Nila Gerhold for managing much of the detail and helping prepare this volume for press, and Ann Rice of the Notre Dame Press, for her care with our work.

Contributors

Seamus Deane teaches in the English Department at the University of Notre Dame, where he is the Donald and Marilyn Keough Chair of Irish Studies. A member of the Royal Irish Academy, he has written several books, including *Celtic Revivals: Essays in Modern Irish Literature; A Short History of Irish Literature;* and *The French Revolution and Enlightenment in England.* Along with editing *The Field Day Anthology of Irish Writing,* Seamus Deane has also written five books of poetry and a forthcoming novel.

Michael DePorte is Professor and Chair of the Department of English at the University of New Hampshire. He is the author of *Nightmares and Hobbyhorses: Swift, Sterne, and Augustan Ideas of Madness* and numerous essays on Restoration and eighteenth-century writers. He is also the editor of Henry More's *Enthusiasmus Triumphatus* (1966), Thomas Tryon's *Discourse on Madness* (1973), James Carkesse's *Lucida Intervalla* (1979), and Marius D'Assigny's *The Art of Memory* (1985).

Margaret Anne Doody is Andrew W. Mellon Professor of Humanities and Professor of English at Vanderbilt University, where she has also been Director of the Comparative Literature Program. She is the author of a number of studies of the eighteenth century, including *A Natural Passion: A Study of the Novels of Samuel Richardson* (1974) and *The Daring Muse: Augustan Poetry Reconsidered* (1985), as well as a biography, *Frances Burney: The Life in the Works* (1989). She is completing a book on the novel from antiquity to the present decade.

A. C. Elias, Jr. has been preparing an annotated critical edition of Laetitia Pilkington's *Memoirs* since 1985. His book *Swift at Moor Park* (1982) won the John L. Haney Prize at the University of Pennsylvania Press.

Carole Fabricant is a member of the English Department at the University of California, Riverside, where she teaches eighteenth-century literature, Swift, women's literature, and Marxist and feminist theory. She is the author of *Swift's Landscape* and has published widely on Pope, Swift, and the Earl of Rochester, as well as eighteenth-century ideology and culture, landscape gardening, tourism, and travel. She is currently working on a book-length study of representations of history in eighteenth-century English and Irish writings.

Christopher Fox, who chairs the English Department at the University of Notre Dame, is the author of *Locke and the Scriblerians: Identity and Consciousness in Early Eighteenth-Century Britain* (1988), and the editor of several books, including *Psychology and Literature in the Eighteenth Century* (1987), *Inventing Human Science: Eighteenth-Century Domains* (with Roy Porter and Robert Wokler) and the forthcoming *Gulliver's Travels: Contemporary Studies in Criticism*.

Joseph McMinn is Senior Lecturer in the English Department of the University of Ulster, at Jordanstown, Northern Ireland. He is author of *Jonathan Swift: A Literary Life*; *John Banville: A Critical Study*; and *The Internationalism of Irish Literature and Drama*. His new book is *Jonathan's Travels: Swift and Ireland*.

Robert Mahony is Associate Professor of English and Director of the Center for Irish Studies at The Catholic University of America. He has also held teaching positions at Trinity College, Dublin; the University of Illinois-Chicago; St. Patrick's College, Maynooth; and University College, Cork. The editor of *Different Styles of Poetry* (1987) and co-editor (with B. W. Rizzo) of *Christopher Smart: An Annotated Bibliography* (1984) and *The Annotated Letters of Christopher Smart* (1991), he has published articles on Akenside, Collins, Goldsmith, Smart, Swift, Yeats, and the pastoral, and is preparing a study of Swift's Irish identity as determined by his patriotic reputation.

Brenda Tooley is Assistant Professor of English at The Colorado College. She has published on anti-feminist satire, Swift, and Richardson. She is working on a book-length study concerning the connections between the Actaeon-Diana myth, dressing-room satire, and novelistic representations of female subjectivity. She is also completing a shorter study of the rhetorical strategies of female advocates in the Restoration period.

Heinz J. Vienken teaches English language and literature at the University of Münster in Germany. He has worked on neo-Latin drama in England, translated John N. Finlay's *Plato and Platonism*, co-authored a monograph on *Gulliver's Travels*, co-translated *Gulliver's Travels* into German, and co-authored a monograph on *Gulliver*. He has co-edited *Swift Studies* and co-founded the Ehrenpreis Center for Swift Studies. Together with Irvin Ehrenpreis and Daniel Albright he has published *American Poetry: Texts and Meanings* and has published widely on Swift. He is currently working on a handbook about Swift's library and his reading.

James Woolley teaches in the English Department at Lafayette College. He has published numerous articles on Swift and is the editor of the recent Oxford edition of Swift's *Intelligencer.*

Introduction: Swift and Irish Studies

BRENDA TOOLEY AND CHRISTOPHER FOX

> And it came to pass after these things, that Naboth the Jezreelite had a vineyard, which was in Jezreel, hard by the palace of Ahab king of Samaria. And Ahab spake unto Naboth, saying, Give me thy vineyard, that I may have it for a garden of herbs, because it is near unto my house: and I will give thee for it a better vineyard than it; or, if it seem good to thee, I will give thee the worth of it in money. And Naboth said to Ahab, The Lord forbid it me, that I should give the inheritance of my fathers unto thee. (I Kings 21:1–3, King James Version)

The story of Naboth's vineyard, with its narrative elements of acquisitive power in conflict with loyal stewardship, implicit class conflict, feminine duplicity, false witness, sycophantic conspiracy, mob violence, and, ultimately, after the just man's death, revenge against the usurping imperial power surely appealed to Swift.[1] Swift named his orchard in Dublin "Naboth's Vineyard" and railed against the labor and expense of the property in letters to English friends with more orderly, productive gardens.[2] But tidy, manageable English properties are not the sole comparison here. As Carole Fabricant notes, Swift's orchard seems a microcosm of a post-Edenic world even as it alludes to specifically Irish realities:

> Although [Swift's] interest in enhancing the condition of the land persisted, as he grew older he increasingly transformed aspects of his immediate environs into symbolic statements about the irrevocable loss of Eden and the consequent obsolescence of the pastoral mode. His version of 'Henry Hoare's Paradise' (Hoare's gardens at Stourhead) or Lord Cobham's Elysian Fields at Stowe was a two-acre plot of ground near the deanery (unfortunately, also near

1

the frequently flooding Poddle), which he pointedly called Naboth's Vineyard, after an orchard cursed by God.[3]

The curse that Ireland experienced during Swift's lifetime was not, however, so obviously attributable to God; English economic policies and Ireland's inability to act collectively in its own best interest could more plausibly be blamed and Swift did not hesitate to point fingers. In fact, a latent promise of divine retribution lurks in the name Swift chose for his property; if not in his lifetime, yet at some future date, God would smite the greedy and unscrupulous Ahabs of England, English colonial policymakers and Irish absentees alike. Swift aligns himself with a particular set of interests in choosing the name Naboth's Vineyard: the powerless, the dispossessed, the falsely accused, the unjustly condemned, all those whose position relative to that of a greater power leads them into danger through no fault of their own. The Irish context of Swift's life and work gives a resonance to the story of Naboth's vineyard that supplements and complicates sweeping applications of the biblical narrative. Swift did not deal in large abstractions but in the concrete details of the political moment; injustice and exploitation were terms applicable to the situation of traders and craftsmen of Dublin, the rural Irish cottagers, the Irish Protestants whose paradoxical situation in Ireland, empowered but dependent, highlighted the complexities of cultural and political authority.

1

Walking Naboth's Vineyard contains a collection of essays from a marathon conference on Swift and Ireland at the University of Notre Dame exploring, among other topics, Jonathan Swift's life and writing as situated in an Irish context, which is to say Swift as a member of a population divided against itself, colonized by a neighboring kingdom, politically and culturally marginalized. Irish allegiances and concerns inform much of Swift's writing both before and after 1714 (and *Gulliver's Travels* as surely as the *Drapier's Letters*). Swift himself understood that his Irish context would be unfamiliar, and his Irish sympathies eccentric, to his correspondents in England. In a 1729 letter to Alexander Pope,

Swift adds a half-apologetic, half-defensive explanation to the end of a digression on the state of Ireland:

> I had a mind for once to let you know the state of our [Irish] affairs, and my reason for being more moved than perhaps becomes a Clergyman, and a piece of a philosopher: and perhaps the increase of years and disorders may hope for some allowance to complaints, especially when I may call myself a stranger in a strange land.[4]

Ever since Louis A. Landa's *Swift and the Church of Ireland* (1954), Swift's connection with Ireland has slowly become a central question. The volume *Jonathan Swift 1667–1967: A Dublin Tercentenary Tribute* (1968), for example, situates Swift in an Irish context with essays on "Ireland in the Age of Swift" (J. G. Simms, pp. 157–75) and "Swift as a Political Thinker" (R. B. McDowell, pp. 176–86). Clive Probyn's *The Art of Jonathan Swift* (1978), includes a study of Swift's Irish perspective in his early writings by Angus Ross ("The Hibernian Patriot's Apprenticeship," pp. 83–107). Irvin Ehrenpreis's biography *Swift: The Man, His Works, and the Age* (1962–1983) recognizes the importance of Swift's life in Ireland to any understanding of his work.

Oliver W. Ferguson's *Jonathan Swift and Ireland* (1962), one of the studies to which Ehrenpreis declares himself especially indebted, carefully pieces together Swift's political writings and contemporary Irish events. Ferguson argues that, while Swift's epitaph probably signifies a concern for forms of liberty beyond the political, "Swift . . . devot[ed] much of his time and his passion to the . . . cause of political liberty; and nowhere did he do so more intensely or more dramatically than in—and in behalf of—his native Ireland."[5] Ferguson acknowledges that Swift was an agitator for Irish liberties as well as a proponent of restricted civil rights for Catholic and dissenting members of the Irish population, but concludes that the unity of Swift's life's work implies a regard for political justice that overrides the Dean's contradictory advocacy: "A part of my purpose has been to justify his right to this title [the Irish Patriot], which was bestowed on him by the Irish of his time but which has been questioned more than once in the two hundred years following his death. Although it was the rights of the Anglo-Irish minority that Swift most often championed, the force, the clarity, and the courage with which he resisted England's Irish policy—and the earnestness with which he tried to alleviate Ireland's domestic problems—amply atone for his limited conception of Irish liberty."[6]

Swift's representations of his place in Anglo-Irish politics are complex and sometimes contradictory, as were his shifting relations to power during his lifetime, as was his writing practice itself. More recent critics have explored Swift's work in relation to his Irish environment, his stance as writer of ephemeral political propaganda, and his deconstructive virtuosity. Critics have considered Swift as a writing subject marginalized by his relation to colonial power, using satire as a rhetorical weapon to defend against the vicissitudes of the world.[7] Edward Said, in *The World, the Text, and the Critic*, notes that "Swift himself seems to have been haunted by the impermanence of events, a concern that accounts not only for his lifelong interest in conversation (a speaking event) but for his solicitude for history, for correct language, for his stubborn distrust of everything that could not be verified by direct experience."[8] Said argues against the formalist attempt to construct a unified explanatory narrative for Swift's life which would reconcile the ambiguities and dislocations in Swift's texts: "The productive force of Swift's energy as a writer need not be portrayed as emanating from a vision we create of him as an Anglican divine whose life can be described as a sequence of events over a period of time. On the contrary, we do him a greater service if we accept the discontinuities he experienced in the way he experienced them: as either actual or imminent losses of tradition, heritage, position, history, losses located at the center of his disjointed verbal production."[9]

Working out of insights in Vivian Mercer's *The Irish Comic Tradition* (1962), Andrew Carpenter's important 1978 study and his more recent introduction to the *Field Day Anthology of Irish Writing* (1991) have taken such "disjointedness" to be central to Swift's experience as an Irish writer. Swift's writing, Carpenter argues, has a "fantastic, grotesque side closer to that of the Irish comic tradition than to anything in English literature." In fact, "the tone of his major work is profoundly un-English . . . full of rough energy and aggression, quite unlike that of even the most energetic of his English contemporaries."[10] This dimension has also been explored by Joseph McMinn and several others.[11]

Along with that work, Carole Fabricant's *Swift's Landscape* (1982) has made it difficult for subsequent critics to ignore the material circumstances of Swift's Irish life. The ways in which Swift describes Ireland lead Fabricant to certain conclusions about Swift's relationship to his environment, to his sense of self in an unwelcoming world: "To the extent that a conception of 'home' appears in Swift's writings, it is often identified as the place he is furthest away from at the moment, or the place he has just left behind; hence the impression he repeatedly conveys of moving through alien space in his various scenes of 'banishment.' " Fabricant sees Swift consolidating his identity and finding (or forging) a place for himself in his world in his engagement with English-Irish political conflict, if only as he embraces the foreign and the powerless in order to create a rhetorically powerful oppositional stance:

> The role of the Drapier . . . served as a means by which Swift's marginality and political insignificance from the point of view of established authority could be converted into an eminently formidable—and ultimately triumphant— political force. By the same token, the Drapier's role was a means by which Swift, the stranger in a strange land, became the beloved patriot and folk hero of a people who enthusiastically claimed him as their own.[12]

Political authority may be located on the margins of institutionalized power; satiric techniques may be strategically deployed by the writer whose influence is constituted upon his awareness that authority is contingent, a self-sustaining fiction of rhetorical and political power. And sometimes one becomes a hero in a land one professes to despise:

> As to my Native Country (as you call it) I happened in deed by a perfect Accident to be born here, my Mother being left here from returning to her House at Leicester, and I was a Year old before I was sent to England; thus I am a Teague, or an Irishman, or what People please, although the best Part of my Life was in England. What I did for

this Country was from perfect Hatred [of] Tyranny and Oppression.[13]

Our contextualizations of Swift do not give us the "true" Swift, do not provide unmediated access to "the man himself" now (at last) fully understood in his proper setting. Recognizing the importance of Swift's relationships with Irish peoples and politics enlarges our field of discussion and complicates representations of Swift (even his own) as anglophile, or an Irish patriot by default. The connections that are currently being made reflect contemporary reassessments of authoritative centers of interpretive, political, and social power. Swift may cease to be comfortably "canonical" when his work is explored in the light of his marginal status as Irishman in relation to colonial British power (as Pope's canonic status is complicated in light of his Catholic faith: like Swift's his position as writer is paradoxically marginal and powerful). Our reconstructions of history are explanatory narratives that capture moments in a larger process of which we ourselves are a part:

> To say the Truth, I had conceived a few Scruples with relation to the distributive Justice of Princes upon those Occasions. For Instance, A Crew of Pyrates are driven by a Storm they know not whither; at length a Boy discovers Land from the Top-mast; they go on Shore to rob and plunder; they see an harmless People, are entertained with Kindness, they give the Country a new Name, they take formal Possession of it for the King, they set up a rotten Plank or a Stone for a Memorial, they murder two or three Dozen of the Natives, bring away a Couple more by Force for a Sample, return home, and get their Pardon. Here commences a new Dominion acquired with a Title by *Divine Right*. Ships are sent with the first Opportunity; the Natives are driven out or destroyed, their Princes tortured to discover their Gold; a free License given to all Acts of Inhumanity and Lust; the Earth reeking with the Blood of its Inhabitants: And this execrable Crew of Butchers employed in so pious an Expedition, is a *modern Colony* sent to convert and civilize an idolatrous and barbarous People.[14]

The extent of Swift's own ideological involvement in such activity is explored in Seamus Deane's 1986 essay, "Swift and the Anglo-Irish Intellect" and in his *Short History of Irish Literature*.[15]

2

Most of the essays here throw light upon Swift's relationship to Ireland, its history, its politics and people as well as his more particular connections to the Dublin literary and publishing worlds. Other essays explore his theology, his reading and his library, his engagement with novelistic traditions, and finally his reputation as an Irish (but Anglican) patriot in the Irish-Catholic communities of the nineteenth and twentieth centuries and the uses to which these constructions of Swift have been put.

Swift was not only an acute observer of public behaviors, but a theorist of observation as well, his satiric practice inevitably complicated by self-reflexive indictments of the satiric gaze. The opening essay, by Seamus Deane, explores connections between European historical and exploratory discourses and *Gulliver's Travels*. In Deane's reading, Gulliver produces a travel narrative that entraps its ostensibly objective observer in a world become, as a consequence of Gulliver's immersion in foreignness, utterly unfamiliar. For Gulliver, even the domestic becomes strange, abhorrent. Deane argues that the paradoxical positioning of the eighteenth-century European traveler in foreign realms (geographical as well as imaginary) creates a potentially radical undermining of objectivity and certainty of belonging. Estrangement from one's community accompanies one's use of the language of the cultural explorer. For "traveling in the past, through study, can make the traveler a foreigner in his or her own time and space."

Narratives of the foreign also work to establish a consensus about a common European identity. Investigations into geographically distant cultures as well as into European history mark Europe's distance from its idealized agrarian (classical) past; its acknowledgement of this distance between an exemplary model of civilization and its own cultural modes demands in turn a complex awareness of the forfeited possibilities created by its form of modernity. The traveler's narrative is thus located on a thin line between a progressive hope and a culturally conservative fear. The stories the traveler tells can never allay that fear nor fulfill the hope. Narrative itself is too fragile a web to bear the weight of cultural crisis: the domestic becomes strange when placed within the wide array of divergent cultural practices.

The travel narrative, which seems to exempt the reader from complicity in the exotic or barbarian practices to which he may be drawn, in fact creates endless complications in the reading of one's own culture. The colonial parodist of travel narration turns comfortable distinctions between foreign and familiar inside out. As Edward Said has argued, the West's discursive construction of the geographically and culturally foreign indicates what it refuses to accommodate within itself, not a delineation of difference, but what the imperial West needs the Other to be.[16] Swift, unlike the "oriental," could speak to the colonizer's fears about cultural integrity.

Carole Fabricant is also concerned with the cultural work that historical narratives do. She is particularly interested in the ways in which Swift appropriated history for personal as well as political ends. Fabricant understands Swift's use of Irish history as a discourse at the service of a culturally situated person with specific motivations. Whatever his ambivalence about his Irish nationality, Swift found in Ireland's worldly position an analogue for his own complex position in the political and cultural worlds he knew: "To the extent that Swift did succeed in establishing a 'racial genealogy' for himself, it was through recording and identifying with the history not of England but Ireland, giving a special aptness to his later portrayals of Irish patriotism in terms of filial duty and protection of one's mother." As a consequence of his distance from the self-serving narratives of cultural origins and triumphs, Swift repudiated the received forms of eighteenth-century history-telling, preferring instead forms reminiscent of street culture: "In place of the elegant accounts embodying the maxim of 'philosophy teaching by example' which scholars regularly associate with English histories of the eighteenth century, Swift wrote pugnaciously *in*elegant tracts which had more in common with popular journalism and street ballads than with noble Augustan genres like the epic." His refusal of polite historical discourse accords with his debunking of complacent

English accounts of cultural accomplishments: "Above all, instead of producing hegemonic texts commemorating the development of England's institutions and in effect ratifying her increasingly imperial role in the world, Swift wound up writing mostly counter-hegemonic pieces challenging not only English actions and policies, but also the official rationales invoked to justify them." At the same time, Swift's use of history destroys any assumption he may have had that history may aspire to the clarity and purity of 'truth.' Irish history not only complicates English history, it undermines its own status as authoritative narrative.

Both Deane and Fabricant see Swift attempting to define a particular relation to authority. Michael DePorte explores Swift's engagement with authority itself in examining Swift's sermons and other writings. Although Swift was an Anglican priest for fifty years, the "true nature of his beliefs" was during his ministry a matter for speculation and uncertainty. "[T]he place to begin is with his view of power, because the most pressing issues in his work are issues of power and contention: of king against parliament, established church against dissenters, Tory against Whig, Ireland against England, ancients against moderns. . . ." Deporte sees Swift's statements on religion as concerned as much with questions of power and social stability as with personal faith. Swift "saw the Church of England as besieged by secular and sectarian enemies; again and again he argues that its dominance is essential to the preservation of English society." The strength of the Anglican church is dependent upon its relation to the state and upon its use of a simple psychology—carrot and stick—to police the actions of the populace. "Christianity triumphed over Greek and Roman philosophy, Swift insisted, because it could draw on a source of power greater than intelligence and firmness of character. . . . Heaven and Hell are concepts even the simplest person can understand."

Deporte argues that Swift's sense of the political efficacy of the Anglican faith stands in uneasy relation to his satiric performances of parodic unbelief. "Swift preached that the doctrine of future rewards and punishments was important for ordinary people, but it is by no means clear how much real efficacy he thought the doctrine had." An individual's religious convictions cannot be determined by even a keen observer, nor are they subject to proof, but the collective enactment of religious ritual may stabilize the state. Deporte suggests that Swift's "most frequent concern is for the public ramifications of shared belief" and not for the nuances of personal faith. "Swift talks about God as the ultimate authority for doctrines of imperative social importance about crimes against social order being crimes against God, but about individual relationship to God he says remarkably little. Indeed, there is a great deal in Swift's writing to suggest that he found the whole matter of a personal relationship with God disquieting. Certainly he distrusted those who claimed to derive their authority from private communion with the Lord."

Margaret Doody finds that Swift collaborates in *Gulliver's Travels* in a transcultural, transhistorical structure of meaning, which she discusses in mythic rather than religious terms: "I believe that all novels are interconnected—at least, I mean in the Western tradition, a tradition which includes influences from Asia and Africa. All novels are connected, and every Western novel is related—in some way, at more or less distance—to every other." Swift's age was the last age in which novelistic production could appropriate traditional tropes without self-conscious regulation of form and content. "The seventeenth century (in which Swift was born) was in many ways the heyday of free writing of fiction not yet policed by copious reviews and culturally heightened self-consciousness."

Gulliver's physical transformations, Doody suggests, are Lucius' transformations in *The Golden Ass: "The Ass, The Golden Ass, Gulliver's Travels*—all three deal in very physical terms with the changes and violence wrought upon a shrinking self which has to try to cope with an entirely new set of circumstances." At the same time, Swift's satire incorporates new elements. "It is not the hero who is transformed, but the worlds he is in—places which, like Lucian's satiric alternative societies, exhibit, though less outrageously, alternative biologies which make Gulliver's own biological self 'abnormal.'" Both Gulliver and Lucius embody a stock trope of the Western Novel: the threatened, vulnerable self. "Apuleius' novel is only one version of a story perpetually told in novels of all kinds—the story of the hapless self injured, mutilated, transformed, displaced." In such details as the shipwreck, skin-clothes, abandoned child, enslaved foreigner, Doody finds echoes of a narrative tradition embedded in Swift's text. Her range is as broad as western civilization itself, encompassing (as she argues the Novel does) Lucian, Apuleius, the Greek romances, the *Alexander Romance*, the French romances of the seventeenth century and much else: "In all of these novels, and I am inclined to say in the Novel in general as a genre, coming to a shore is very important. Traversing, changing—coming to a new experience, a new phase of life—all of these are represented by the arrival on a shore. To arrive on a shore is to arrive at an Other Place, to begin to accept becoming Another Self." Doody places Swift not on the margins of Western culture, on the edges of political and literary life, but at the center of a discursive tradition in which he was well versed. "Swift had, I believe, a very deep and long-standing knowledge of all kinds of fiction, including long works of prose fiction, or 'Romances.' One of the reasons *Gulliver's Travels* lasts so very well is that it draws upon the deep traditions of prose fiction in the West and is itself a virtuoso performance within that tradition." In her insistence upon the centrality of Swift's work to a coherent tradition, she complicates the positioning of Swift as exile from the meaning-making discursive practices of his society.

A. C. Elias, Jr., has been preparing an edition of Laetitia Pilkington's *Memoirs* and his essay explores the reliability of her statements. Although Pilkington "provides the liveliest and most realistic firsthand glimpse of Swift that we have," the publication history of her volumes indicates the relation between her need to publish and the accuracy of her narrative. The complexity of even the most routine life suggests how difficult accurate anecdotal representation of a life can be. Not surprisingly, Pilkington's memoirs conflate episodes, confuse dates, exaggerate potentially humorous occurrences, and feature herself in admirable, long-suffering poses. Elias urges an informed and cautious approach to her text, especially as concerns the publication history of each volume, the circumstances of which matter in assessing the value of the anecdotes within it: Pilkington became increasingly pressed for time in the second volume (the third was posthumously published by her son); her consciousness of celebrity status in the second and third volumes alters her mode of writing.

"Increasingly Mrs. Pilkington seems more eager to shock her readers than to amuse them." Elias argues against a too ready dismissal of the value of Pilkington's testimony concerning Swift's life and character. "That we need to check Mrs. Pilkington's facts before using them, against outside sources and against the *Memoirs* themselves, should not prejudice us against her. To some extent we need to check the facts in all the other early biographical accounts which we have of Swift, not to mention the accounts written since." Critical dismissal of Pilkington's memoirs as wholly unreliable is, Elias concludes, unwarranted.

Joseph McMinn's paper on the relationship between Swift and Thomas Sheridan, and more particularly between Swift and Quilca, Sheridan's Irish estate, also values specific details of Swift's life as indicative of Swift's general character. Swift, one learns, enjoyed hating Quilca. "For him, the anarchic condition of the place was inseparable from the personality of its owner. . . ." McMinn sees in Swift's impatient enjoyment of the ramshackle estate a model for Swift's hopes for Ireland and an unlikely refreshment for Swift himself. What he could do with Quilca could be done for Ireland; the disorder he found there could be transformed. "Quilca was an important literary retreat for the Dean, a place where he finished and transcribed *Gulliver's Travels*, and where he completed his campaign as Drapier. The wilds of Cavan also allowed Swift to indulge his favorite and obsessive practical arts, plantation and gardening, the ordering of rural chaos." At Quilca, Swift had an opportunity to engage his "strong, observant and critical sense of physicality and landscape" in the process of bringing the land into relatively productive order. "Sheridan's mismanagement of his property affronted everything in Swift's political and emotional outlook, an example of slovenliness perhaps natural to the natives, but inexcusable in a settler." Swift found in Sheridan himself a "disconcerting blend of cultural sophistication and domestic ruination." "The uncultivated terrain of Quilca became a kind of productive paradise for Swift, a place where he could test his energies against the stubborn and lawless elements and inhabitants."

Heinz Vienken is one of several German scholars engaged in expanding our knowledge of Swift's library. The contents of Swift's library, he argues, have never been adequately explored:

"Although we are given a rough description of the subject matter and authors" of the books in Sir Harold Williams's facsimile reprint of the sale catalogue of Swift's library, "we are told nothing about the fact that here are represented some 1,961 authors." Texts bound together in a single volume were not and have not been separately listed. Vienken points to "the necessity of looking at each imprint in the Dean's library again, especially when it comes to the contents of each volume." Vienken adds two additional cautions concerning contemporary interpretations of Swift's library: first, that the "contemporary authority of texts and authors that are either completely forgotten today or have lost their reputation in the meanwhile" be carefully established, and second, that one note the "many vestiges of authors not in his library whom Swift can be shown to have read." Swift's library holdings do not give us the full scope of his reading, but Vienken's and his colleagues' progress provides a solid foundation for informed critical study.

James Woolley's essay concerns Swift's choice of Sarah Harding (and until his death, her husband, John Harding) as the publisher of a number of his Irish pamphlets, including *A Short View of the State of Ireland* (1728), the *Intelligencer* papers (1728–29), and *A Modest Proposal* (1729). The first difficulty, Woolley notes, is determining what texts are Swift's. "[O]ne may consider and rapidly dismiss the notion that whatever was published in Dublin by a prominent Dublin author must have been published with his cooperation or contrivance if not at his direct request. In fact a considerable number of Swift's writings issued during Queen Anne's reign . . . were mere reprints of London publications, and there is as a general rule no reason to suppose that Swift had anything to do with such reprints." Only collation can determine the degree of authorial sanction and involvement in such cases (Woolley cites several exceptions to his general rule). Swift's selection of John Harding may have involved a number of considerations, including the fact that Harding was both printer and (sometime) bookseller, he was willing to deal with inflammatory political material, and his slipshod professional style may have accorded with Swift's persona as Drapier. After John's death, Sarah became Swift's printer. Woolley concludes his paper with an appeal to Swift scholars to explore more closely the relationship between Swift and the Hardings: "the collation of multiple copies—a labor not undertaken by Herbert Davis—promises to reveal new textual variants and new information about the publication and revision of these works as well." An appendix listing Sarah Harding imprints follows Woolley's analysis.

Robert Mahony's essay explores Swift's reputation in Catholic Ireland. Although Swift was known during his lifetime (and represented himself) as a champion of Irish liberties, "contemporary Irish Catholics themselves left very little evidence that they admired Swift." Swift's attitude toward the Irish Catholic population, Mahony suggests, is ambivalent at best. He "exhibits comparatively little overt anti-Catholicism, but he never disputed the necessity of the penal laws or otherwise adopted the cause of Catholics specifically, as distinct from that of Ireland." Swift's status as an Anglican patriot served Irish Protestants well in subsequent political conflicts. "That Swift had effectively created an Irish People reflects a view increasingly appealing to nineteenth-century Irish Protestants. For it accorded them an identity that was much more than colonially British, one in which Catholics and Protestants both could share, based upon a historical antipathy to characteristics of British governance in Ireland, however differently those characteristics might be seen by the two communities." At specific moments in the Irish struggle for independence, however, Swift's reputation could be turned to Catholic purposes. This use of Swift as patriot was never unproblematic; as in his own time, Swift was also represented as a disappointed, embittered man rather than as a true patriot. Nevertheless, Swift's name and texts continue to find new interpretations in each phase of political conflict in Ireland. Whatever the nuances of the representation, Swift as historical figure continues to have some relevance in political and literary constructions of Irish identity., "Contemporary Ireland is almost certainly not what Swift anticipated, nor necessarily what other patriots looked for, but in each generation since Davis's time these have not only espoused a cause but sought to validate it by invoking a tradition. Or, perhaps more accurately, by inventing one."

NOTES

1. For the Biblical story's relation to Swift's stance toward monarchial authority, see Michael DePorte, "Avenging Naboth: Swift and Monarchy," *Philological Quarterly* 69 (Fall, 1990): 419–33.

2. Carole Fabricant contrasts Swift's experience of land ownership with that of his English acquaintance (most notably Pope): "Along with feelings of rejection and deprivation, Swift's landscape communicates a recurring sense of man's helplessness vis-à-vis his environment. . . . Even in Dublin Swift remained in an exposed position, open to threats of political reprisal as well as personal attack, and helpless against the severities of the climate. In contrast to the womblike sanctuary provided by the typical Augustan landscaped garden, Naboth's Vineyard left its owner out in the cold, vulnerable to all the natural and man-made disasters regularly occurring in the outside world" (*Swift's Landscape* [Baltimore: The Johns Hopkins University Press, 1982], 226).

3. *Swift's Landscape*, 71.

4. The *Correspondence of Jonathan Swift*, ed. Harold Williams, 2nd ed., 5 vols. (Oxford, 1963-65), 3:341.

5. Oliver W. Ferguson, *Jonathan Swift and Ireland* (Urbana: University of Illinois Press, 1962), 2.

6. *Jonathan Swift and Ireland*, 2. Ferguson also provides a discussion of colonial Ireland and the Anglo-Irish ascendancy that has been complicated but not overturned in subsequent studies: "As a Protestant Anglo-Irishman, Swift was a member of a privileged class. The outbreak of the Revolution of 1689 in Ireland had seriously jeopardized the supremacy of the Anglo-Irish (Swift was one of many who fled to England at the beginning of the war), but the collapse of James's cause and the surrender at Limerick in 1691 left them more completely in power than they had ever been. During the Protestant Ascendancy—the period from 1691 to 1800—the Irish Catholics, who made up the great bulk of the population, were under the absolute control of the Protestant minority. The position occupied by this minority, however, was strong only in comparison with that of the Catholics whom they suppressed, for they were themselves subjected to England's domination. Though in title a kingdom, eighteenth-century Ireland was in fact virtually an English colony. Almost all important government and ecclesiastical positions were held by English appointees. In addition, a number of minor posts, pensions, and sinecures held by nonresident Englishmen were a constant drain on the nation's economy. The country had its own parliament, but its powers were so curtailed as to make it little more than a rubber stamp for measures enacted in England" (p. 7).

7. See Carol Houlihan Flynn, *The Body in Swift and Defoe* (Cambridge: Cambridge University Press, 1990).

8. Edward Said, *The World, the Text, and the Critic* (Cambridge, Mass.: Harvard University Press, 1983), 57.

9. *The World, the Text, and the Critic*, 65.

10. Andrew Carpenter, "Swift," *Field Day Anthology of Irish Writing*, ed. Seamus Deane, 3 vols. (Derry: Field Day Publications, 1991), 1:327. Also see Carpenter's essay on "Irish and Anglo-Irish Scholars in the Time of Swift: The Case of Anthony Raymond," *Literary Interrelations: Ireland, England, and the World*, ed. Wolfgang Zach, and Heinz Kozak (Tübingen: Nar, 1987), 1:11–19 and his *Irish Perspective of Jonathan Swift* (Wuppertal: Hammer, 1978).

11. Some other studies of Swift and Ireland include the following: Joseph McMinn, "Jonathan's Travels: Swift's Sense of Ireland," *Swift Studies* 7 (1992): 36–53; J. C. Beckett, *Swift and Ireland* (Belfast: St. Mary's College, 1986) and "Swift and the Anglo-Irish Tradition," in *The Character of Swift's Satire: A Revised Focus*, ed. and intro. Claude Rawson (Newark, N.J.: University of Delaware Press, London Associated University Presses, 1983), 151–65; Ian Campbell Ross, *Swift's Ireland* (Dublin: Eason, 1983); Claude Rawson, "The Injured Lady and the Drapier: A Reading of Swift's Irish Tracts," *Prose Studies* 3 (May 1980): 15–43; Lance Bertelsen, "Ireland, Temple, and the Origins of the Drapier," *Papers on Language and Literature* 13, no. 14 (1977): 413–19; Ann Cline Kelly, "Swift's Explorations of Slavery in Houyhnhmland and Ireland," *PMLA* 91 no. 5 (1976): 846–55; Clayton D. Lein, "Jonathan Swift and the Population of Ireland," *Eighteenth-Century Studies* 8 no. 4 (1975): 431–53; A. Norman Jeffares, "Swift and the Ireland of His Day," *Irish University Review* 2 no. 2 (1972): 115–32, and Mackie L. Jarrell, "'Jack and the Dane': Swift Traditions in Ireland," *Journal of American Folklore* 77 no. 304 (1964): 99–117.

12. *Swift's Landscape*, 213, 262.

13. Swift, *Correspondence*, 4:229.

14. *Gulliver's Travels*, ed. Herbert Davis (Oxford: Basil Blackwell, 1965), 294.

15. Seamus Deane, "Swift and the Anglo-Irish Intellect," *Eighteenth-Century Ireland* 1 (1986): 9–22; and *A Short History of Irish Literature* (London and Notre Dame, Ind.: Hutchinson and the University of Notre Dame Press, 1986), 44–45.

16. Said, *Orientalism* (New York: Pantheon Books, 1978). Also see Said's more recent *Culture and Imperialism* (New York: Alfred A. Knopf, 1993).

Swift: Virtue, Travel and the Enlightenment

SEAMUS DEANE

> For conversing with men of past ages is somewhat like travelling. It is good to know something of the mores of other people, in order to judge our own more soundly.... But when one spends too much time travelling, one must eventually become a stranger to one's own country; and when one is too much interested in the practices of times past, one usually stays ignorant of the practices of the present. Descartes, *Discours de la Méthode* (1637)

1

Travel happens in both time and space. We can travel in the past as much as in foreign lands. Although traveling in foreign parts can help towards a sounder judgment of home and its practices, traveling in the past, through study, can make the traveler a foreigner in his or her own time and space.

I want to begin with travel in time, of the sort that we call history. More specifically, I want to look at one period of historical time that fascinated many of the writers of the European Enlightenment—the period that saw the passage of Rome from a city of virtue to a great and ultimately decadent empire. If we confine ourselves to the two great historians of this transition—Montesquieu and Gibbon—we can simplify their intricate analyses by saying that Rome fell to the barbarians because it lost its republican virtue and that it did so because of the lethal success of the republic, manifested in its expansion into an empire. The loss of virtue was not permanent. The barbarian invasions to some extent restored what Gibbon calls "a manly spirit of freedom."[1] Both he and Montesquieu conceded that this restoration was not identical with what had been lost. Further, in modern

17

conditions, with the rise of commerce and with the supposedly new phenomenon of movable property, virtue, were it to exist at all, must do so on the basis of something other than the arms-and-agriculture economy that Rome and the Goths had developed. The point is that virtue, whether it was to be associated with the form or *principe* of a system of government, like the Roman republic, or with an economic and social system, was a tender plant that depended upon particular conditions for its survival. No ideal of virtue, like that of the old Roman republic, could be sustained in its original form. Indeed the notion that an original ideal was the same as a historically precedent achievement is one of the issues that lay concealed in the Enlightenment's understanding of virtue as a cultural phenomenon that was always, in some sense, tinged with a sense of loss. Virtue in its truest sense belonged to the simplest forms of agrarian-military society. Advanced commercial societies could not hope to reproduce that achievement, even though they could provide considerable compensations, among which the growth and expansion of liberty would be the most considerable.[2]

Montesquieu, even more than Gibbon, emphasizes another feature of the decline of Rome that has a direct bearing upon the present inquiry. As the Empire expanded, the system became so complicated that it was beyond the range of any individual or group to understand the interrelation of all its parts. There was not only an intensification of the evils that attend upon luxury— the apathy and irresponsibility that characterized for him this early version of a consumer society. In addition, there was a failure to recognize the incompatibility between the original republican form of government and the new commercial economy that the empire had perforce developed. This lack of synchrony between political and economic systems is one that gave both Montesquieu and Gibbon pause. It raised the question, which neither of them answered, if there was in existence (even theoretically) a political system that was consonant with an expanding commercial economy and, further, if such existed, would it be possible to describe it. These problems were confronted most directly by the Scottish philosophers of civil society, Ferguson, Smith, Millar, Robertson, and Hume. But before looking briefly at them, I want to pause at a short essay by David Hume, called simply "A Dialogue," that closes the 1777 edition of his *Enquiries Concerning the Human Understanding and Concerning the Principles of Morals.*

The dialogue is between the author and his friend Palamedes. Palamedes begins by telling a travel story about a strange country, called Fourli, where he found everything that he and his culture considered ethically normal was astonishingly inverted. It turns out that he is teasing his comrade; the country is ancient Greece and the incidents he recounts are founded on episodes in Greek and Roman history. Part of the point of the dialogue is to establish that conceptions of virtue vary according to the cultures from which they emerge. Equally, though, Hume wishes to claim that "different customs and situations vary, not the original ideas of merit . . . in any very essential point." What he calls "the merit of riper years" is the same everywhere and "consists chiefly in integrity, humanity, ability, knowledge, and the other more solid and useful qualities of the human mind."[3] Palamedes agrees but then brings up the question of what he calls "artificial lives and manners," instancing Diogenes and Pascal. These two remarkable men, one Stoic and critical, the other superstitious and contemptuous of life, form a contrast and yet have won universal admiration. So he asks,

> Where then is the universal standard of morals which you talk of? And what rule shall we establish for the many different, nay contrary sentiments of mankind?

The answer is remarkable:

> An experiment, said I, which succeeds in the air, will not always succeed in a vacuum. When men depart from the maxims of common reason, and affect those artificial lives, as you can them, no one can answer for what will please or displease them. They are in a different element from the rest of mankind; and the natural principles of their mind play not with the same regularity, as if left to themselves, free from the illusions of religious superstition or philosophical enthusiasm.[4]

This virtue depends for its survival on particular historical circumstances; its career is fraught with danger and its "original" form can never be perfectly reproduced. In this dialogue, travel into the past is openly (and conventionally) adapted to make a comment upon the present; but the consequence is that, while the principle of culture relativity is conceded with the left hand, it is retracted with the right hand by the assertion of the universality of certain principles of human nature. Yet that universality must itself be suspended to account for the appearance of extraordinary and admirable people like Pascal and Diogenes.

This is not Hume at his most penetrating or persuasive, but it is an instance of the kinds of issues that recourse to the past, traveling in time, raises for those who wish to defend, restore, or otherwise rehabilitate the idea of civic virtue in the eighteenth century. The discussions of the Greek and Roman civilizations, the analyses of their decline and the ethical puzzles raised by the recognition of different cultures or extraordinary exceptions, are all dominated by the trope of difference between that which is "common" and that which is "artificial" or foreign. It is not only civilizations that can betray their native virtue by contracting habits foreign to it; individuals too can do this. At the end of such considerations we wonder if Palamedes' question is answerable at all. Where are the universal principles to be found if the history of humankind shows so many exceptions to them? Why are there so many disasters that are not wholly accounted for by claiming that they resulted from the abandonment of those universal principles? The idea of universality tends to shrink when the heat is on; yet that is when its certainty is most needed.

2

The survey of a society from a detached point of view is one of the standard rhetorical resources of travel literature. The observer who can read a society precisely because he or she is not involved in it has two possible sets of criteria by which an estimate or judgment may be made. One is the criterion of the traveler-observer's own society; the other is the criterion of universal principles of human nature. We get a mix of these at times. By the exercise of the first criterion the observer may become a victim of his or her own observations; by the exercise of the second, the notion that there are such universal principles may be called into question. But if we stay for the moment with the writing of history as a form of time-travel and turn from the history of ancient to that of modern Europe, then we may see how the ground of universality begins more and more to vanish under the feet of those who seek to stand on it. This, of course, has severe consequences for ethical thought and in particular for the career of "virtue."

Adam Ferguson's *Essay on the History of Civil Society* (1767), William Robertson's *View of the Progress of Society in Europe* (1769), John Millar's *Origin of Ranks* (1771), and Adam Smith's *The Wealth of Nations* (1776) are the texts that I will be referring to in the most general terms for the articulation of this dilemma. Smith makes a well-known and even by then well-rehearsed distinction between the barbarous and the civilized state. In Vol. II (Book V, Part III) of *The Wealth of Nations*, he distinguishes them in this manner. In a barbarous state,

> no man can well acquire that improved and refined under-standing, which a few men sometimes possess in a more civilised state. Though in a rude society there is a good deal of variety in the occupations of every individual, there is not a great deal in those of the whole society. Every man does, or is capable of doing, almost every thing which any other man does, or is capable of doing. Every man has a considerable degree of knowledge, ingenuity, and invention; but scarce any man has a great degree. . . . In a civilised state, on the contrary, though there is little variety in the occupations of the greater part of individuals, there is an almost infinite variety in those of the whole society. These varied occupations present an almost infinite variety of objects to the contemplation of those few, who, being attached to no particular occupation themselves, have leisure and inclination to examine the occupations of other people. The contemplation of so great a variety of objects necessarily exercises their minds in endless comparisons and combinations, and renders their understandings, in an extraordinary degree, both acute and comprehensive. . . .[5]

Here is an account of complexity that is still, according to Smith, within range of the detached observer (or gentleman) who can achieve a synoptic view of the whole intricate system. But the question arises, or, rather, is raised by Adam Ferguson, what is the price of such detachment? Later in the century we will hear a great deal, especially from Burke, on the dangers of such detachment from human affairs, the risks of closet-philosophers whose speculations are wilder in proportion to their detachment. But Ferguson anticipates Burke (and, let it be said, lays down at least one plank in the platform of the Scottish Common Sense school, especially as represented by Thomas Reid) and subverts in some degree the writings of Hume, Gibbon, and Montesquieu, not to mention his own, by isolating the position of the person whose function it is to see society as a whole. Leisured detachment, he sees, may itself be only one among a number of social occupations, professionalized specialisms; when, in his phrase, "reason itself becomes a profession,"[6] then detachment itself becomes a fiction. Or, it becomes a disfiguring occupation, removed from the realities of experience and producing only "the jargon of a technical language and . . . the impertinence of academical forms."[7] But if that is the case, then how can the history of civil society be written at all? Where is the space? Are some universal principles not necessary, or some synoptic view not a prerequisite, of writing the history of anything? Whence is the detached observer to come; in what rhetorical space can he be sited? This, I suggest, is one of the questions that bedevils travel writing and makes its rhetorical procedures so elusive; it is also one of the questions that Swift's writings raise with an unequalled force.

If specialization, of the kind described by Smith and Ferguson, was a new, largely economic, phenomenon, it nevertheless had a more conventional cousin in religious fanaticism.[8] Swift married the fanatic and the specialist to produce the virtuoso. The virtuoso was the contemporary version of the enthusiast, emotionally committed to reason to the point of madness, forgoing theologies of damnation and salvation for the new and equally lunatic theology or ideology of benevolence, a preacher of social virtue who embodied within himself every vice that threatened civil society.

I want first to derive from Descartes this distinction between foreignness and home, remembering that to be a foreigner at home is one of the most pronounced dangers of travel—of whatever kind. A passage from *The Drapier's Letters*—Letter VI, "To Lord Chancellor Middleton" has a bearing here: Swift is declaring that the Drapier, far from alienating the "Affections of the People of *England* and *Ireland* from each other . . . hath left that Matter just as he found it." He continues:

> I have lived long in both Kingdoms, as well in Country as in Town; and therefore, take myself to be as well informed as most Men, in the Dispositions of each People towards the other. By the People, I understand here, only the Bulk of the common People; and I desire no Lawyer may distort or extend my Meaning.
>
> THERE is a Vein of Industry and Parsimony, that runs through the whole People of England; which, added to the Easiness of their Rents, makes them rich and sturdy. As to Ireland they know little more than they do of Mexico; further than it is a Country subject to the King of England, full of Boggs, inhabited by wild Irish Papists; who are kept in Awe by mercenary Troops sent from thence: And their general Opinion is, that it were better for England if this whole Island were sunk into the Sea; For, they have a Tradition, that every Forty Years there must be a Rebellion in Ireland. I have seen the grossest Suppositions pass upon them; that the wild Irish were taken in Toyls; but that, in some Time, they would grow so tame as to eat out of your Hands: I have been asked by Hundreds . . . whether I had come from Ireland by Sea: And, upon the arrival of an Irish-man to a Country Town, I have known Crouds coming about him, and wondering to see him look so much better than themselves.[9]

I cite this well-known passage to indicate that Swift had particular reason to be alert to the problems of foreignness and its close intimacy with at-homeness. He was, like the persona of so many works of travel literature, a foreigner at home. But the Irish-English axis of Swift's experience enabled him to uncover a paradox in travel literature that none of the other authors mentioned adverts to at any length. It is this: that travel literature has, built into it as an integral feature, a critique of both the society the narrator belongs to and the society he visits—this is obvious—and a critique of the narrator himself. This is not simply to say that the narrator can be exposed in a number of ways by the comments he makes on what is foreign to him and what he presumes to be "native" or "natural." It goes deeper than this. The question Swift poses in *Gulliver's Travels* is about the possibility of "disinterestedness." What is the ground for a disinterested narrative? Is impartiality a possible narrative stance for a narrator who comes from a particular society and goes to another? Certainly the Cartesian anxiety that in adverting too much to the past or to what is foreign, we may lose contact with the present is a real threat to any hope of achieving true impartiality. Such removal is predicated on a lack of interest in the actual, not on disinterestedness. But there is a subtler and more elusive question to be answered when the distinction between past and present, home and abroad is hard to maintain either in itself or in certain circumstances. England might view Ireland as a foreign territory and yet Ireland was part of the British system—it was both home and foreign as Mexico. But where is the vantage point to be found that will recognize both the kinship and the difference between England and Ireland? If no such ground is available, then the possibility of narrative itself, or narrative of the Enlightenment kind, is brought into question. Europe might look at the world, or the world be brought in to look at Europe. The consequence should be a relativization of cultures. Eurocentric notions of what is normal should thereby be rebuked. Asia or any other region of the world should be shown to be equally culture-bound. But if societies are culture-bound in this manner, then impartiality is a fiction—unless, of course, we can find a position that is free of such boundedness and limitation. It was this that Benevolence claimed to offer—not a culture-bound view of the world but a version of the world's diversity seen from the point of view of the Spectator whose boast was that he had, as his remit, the world of human nature. This, surely, is one of the boasts of the Enlightenment. It surveyed mankind from China to Peru and, in doing so, disengaged itself from all of the provincial views that had been produced by particular histories, circumstances, and beliefs. Swift attacks this possibility because it necessarily abstracts the individual from the particular and the specific in the name of a human nature which is itself a specific product of a specific culture and not, as it claimed to be, a conception of human nature founded upon universal principles. The claim to universality was always rooted in time and place and was, therefore, bogus. There was no vantage point available to any person to survey humankind as such.

In attempting to define a space for "human nature" some of the most radical writers of the Enlightenment attempted to persuade themselves or their readers that there was, within the human person, a fundamental instinct for virtue that was constantly stifled by the operation of laws that were founded on the precepts of religion and convention. This was an argument that was conducted in France with much more vigor than in England, even though some of the basic ingredients for the argument were drawn from the English writers of the Benevolist school, most especially Shaftesbury. In France the literary work that, more than any other, focused this problem was Richardson's *Clarissa* (and *Pamela*, although to a lesser extent). The central argument was played out between Rousseau and Diderot. Rousseau had angered Diderot by remarking, in a note to *La Lettre à d'Alembert sur les Spectacles*, that "I do not at all believe . . . that one can be virtuous without religion."[10] Diderot's reaction to this was complicated, but I want to look here at only a few aspects of it as embodied in the works of the early 1700s, particularly *Entretien d'un père avec ses enfants, Ceci n'est pas un conte, Sur l'inconséquence du jugement publique, Le Supplément au voyage de Bougainville, L'Entretien d'un philosophe avec la maréchale de xxx* and *Jacques le fataliste*.

In effect Diderot argues two chief points. One is that the laws of a society are not necessarily to be obeyed if they contradict our nature or instinct. That which is prior to the law is, he seems to say, superior to it. Virtue is coincident with our instincts. So, in his "travel book," based on the first French voyage to Tahiti by Louis-Antoine de Bouganville (1766–69), Diderot offers an account of a Tahitian culture in which law, custom, and religion were based on the needs of human nature. The sexual relation, in particular, and the care of children were so organized that there was no conflict between desire and law. The dialogue ends with the determination that "We will speak out against senseless laws until they are reformed, and in waiting, will submit to them."[11] This is part of the program of the philosophes and of the Enlightenment in general. But there is another preoccupation in these works which leads to other and more anxious conclusions. Particularly in *Ceci n'est pas un conte* and in *Jacques le fataliste* Diderot is concerned with the relationship between the reader and the story, claiming that stories as such are corrupting because they pander to the reader's love of observing the operation of narrative conventions without being in the least incriminated by what they are designed to communicate. Virtue is not inculcated by our reading about Pamela, Clarissa, or the like. He pointed out that many of the standard portrayals of the trails of innocent virtue were in themselves erotic narratives that aroused in the reader a pleasure that ran athwart their ostensibly didactic purpose. Thus in *Jacques le fataliste* the central story of Jacques' love affairs remains untold, to the frustration of both the master and the reader. Diderot suggests that the reader invent this for himself, that the fantasy be pursued by readers who have to recognize that the triumph of virtue over vice is merely a convention of narrative that conceals the pleasure we take in the depiction of vice itself. Thus Diderot disestablishes the notion that the telling of a story is a legitimate means of inculcating virtue. Sympathy is not, after all, a means to virtue. The surgeon does not feel sympathy for his patient; if he is a good surgeon, he will simply regard the patient's injuries as a challenge to his own technical skills. In displaying these he will not be caught in the sympathy trap; and he will do more good thereby because he might, as a consequence, effect a cure.[12]

I am not suggesting that Diderot surrendered the hope of finding universal principles of human nature upon which to base his campaign for virtue and sincerity, although there is a case to be argued in that direction. Instead, I am suggesting that he questioned the possibility of discovering this through narrative precisely because narrative, fixed within its conventions, had within it the very partition that it wished to erase—the partition between author and reader, or the partition between that which was foreign and exotic—what happened in the narrative—and that which was bound to home, to the self.

The glimpse of Diderot serves merely to remind us of something about Swift's narratives and their very different function. That is to say, that Swift's narratives, *Tale of a Tub* and *Gulliver* primary among them, have within them a consciousness of the author-reader relationship that is subversive of the notions underlying the moral parable or *conte* of the kind that we associate with Dr. Johnson, Goldsmith, Voltaire, or even Gibbon, whose whole history is founded upon that kind of narrative trust that conceals author-reader relationships. The very form of a story told by author to reader is the form favored by travel writing; and it contains within itself the pornographic element that Diderot observed. The reader, faced with the exotic story and its various resolutions, is not incriminated by it. It may show Gulliver, for instance, to be mad or to be rational; it may show the absurdity of English customs and political practices or it may show that any society that attempts to base itself on rational principles is a dream and a chimera that leads to sorrow and bitterness in the end. It may remind us of the discrepancy between our capacity for abstract imaginings and the limitations of our bodies. In a sense, this is all irrelevant. The point about travel narratives, and about works that are, like the *Tale*, so full of digressions and prefatory material and formal jokes that there is no point of rest, no stable center, no norm, is that narrative is of its nature prolific, diverse, heterogeneous. Whether the style is baroque or polite, the ruse that is involved is that narrative takes civil society as its object when in fact narrative is itself the very means by which society becomes "objectivized," reified. It is civil society itself in the form of story and critique; but can it as subject see itself as object? Ireland is both subject and object of England. It is part of the same polity, it gives allegiance to the same prince, etc.; yet the Irish are exotics to the English. They see Ireland in conventional terms as a foreign place much given to rebellion, whereas in fact it is home. The English are readers of the narrative that is Ireland, authored in the case of the Drapier's letters by the Drapier himself, who is not of course truly the author but a persona of the author. But then there is no author who is not a persona. Authorship is an assumption of a persona; so is readership. Swift anticipated, in his own peculiar way, what was later to worry Diderot.

However, this is insufficient as a gloss on what Swift and the Enlightenment, as represented here by Diderot, are concerned with in the travel literature of the period. It is well-established by now that there is a link between the increasing specializations and opportunities offered by a developing commercial society and the varieties of human possibility—or personality—liberated by such a process. This is often held to be one of the sources of the tension and hostility between the "conservatives" who looked back to some ideal of the commonwealth and its antique virtues and stable, heroic personalities and the new Whig-led, Walpolean corruption and diversity.[13] Travel literature is certainly concerned with diversity, but the relativization of culture that is one of the possible consequences of recognizing the "otherness" both of foreign and of native cultures (although foreign cultures were of course often patronized and to some degree canceled by being regarded as native in another sense) brings with it another issue that the Enlightenment analysts of civil society—especially Adam Ferguson, Adam Smith, Bernard Mandeville, and Montesquieu— often remarked upon. That is to say that the rise of the specialist, the expert, the subdivision of labor into so many different compartments and the organizational complexity that was a consequence of this had made it all but impossible for a society to be understood in one embracing conspectus.

Variety and diversity were not merely cultural phenomena for which new literary forms like the novel and travel writing were created to subserve and register. They had made it all the more imperative, especially in Britain, where the industrial and economic changes had begun to accelerate to an unprecedented degree, to assert that within such diversity there was perceptible some harmonizing unity. But, as John Barrell has pointed out, writers like Thomas Gray and William Collins were not quite so enamored of the general conviction of some underlying unity as others—say as the Pope who wrote the *Essay on Man*.[14] They were more interested in those communities that were disappearing under the wave of the new prosperity, the great phenomenon of Luxury that Goldsmith too and a score of others lamented so much.[15] The elegiac note that we are accustomed to hear in the most bitter satires of the century is struck for the loss of a community that could be understood, in its structure and in its operation, by those who lived within it. In some respects, this is what Swift admires in his version of Anglicanism. It is not only a middle way between extremes. The extremes are so crazy that they are literally incomprehensible after a while; they develop so wildly and randomly, fueled by emotional conviction or corrupt reasoning, that they defy any attempt to describe their structure. Anglicanism is the religion of people who live in a comprehensible environment and who, in virtue of that, are balanced people. A society is healthy when it is not overly complex. But the complexity of this lethal sort arises, in Swift's opinion, not from a series of market forces, economic developments, foundation of national debt and so on—they arise from human evil. Evil is of its nature complex and prolific. Goodness is simple and univocal. *Gulliver's Travels* is a work which combines apparent simplicity—of the narrator—with apparent complexity—of his experiences. It is the relationship between these that is to be understood. Gulliver cannot make sense of his experiences which become increasingly complex and more foreign. But his failure to do so—which is not the reader's failure—is an indication of his fake simplicity. He is not, need it be said, a character; he is a composite of attitudes that were then conventional. He is, above all, a writer whose narrative is determined by the conventions by which he is formed. These conventions are, in part, social and cultural. In addition, he has a convention of himself as a rational creature. Such conventions govern what he sees. He is always a foreigner in these distant parts, and, as a consequence, they are always already read by him in his own terms. The foreign is always read in terms of home. As usual, Ireland, as seen under English eyes, is the exemplary instance, since it is home and abroad simultaneously.

In a piece like *A Short View of the State of Ireland* (1728) Swift supplies a list of the reasons why Ireland is not prosperous. But the pamphlet begins with the accusation that people have been misrepresenting the true state of the country to the government commissioners from England in order to gain favor, win place, and allow the English to permit themselves to believe that all is well. The fact is that "No strangers from other countries, make this a part of their travels; where they can expect to see nothing but Scenes of misery and Desolation."[16] But he imagines the commissioners roaming round the country and observing its fertility, productiveness, and prosperity. What "glorious reports" would they make when they went back to England. Then he continues:

But my heart is too heavy to continue this irony longer; for it is manifest, that whatever stranger took such a journey, would be apt to think himself travelling in Lapland or Ysland, rather than in a country so favoured by nature as ours, both in fruitfulness of soil, and temperature of climate. This miserable dress, and dyet and dwelling of the people. The general desolation in most parts of the kingdom. The old seats of the nobility and gentry all in ruins, and no new ones in their stead. The families of farmers, who pay great rents, living in filth and nastiness upon butter-milk and potatoes, without a shoe or stocking to their feet; or a house so convenient as an English hog-sty to receive them. These indeed may be comfortable sights to an English spectator, who comes for a short time, only to learn the language, and returns back to his own country, whither he finds all our wealth transmitted.

nostra miseria magnus es

There is not one argument used to prove the riches of Ireland, which is not a logical demonstration of its poverty.[17]

In the first place, there is misrepresentation of an actual state of affairs, for corrupt reasons; second there is a set of paradoxes—arguments for wealth becoming demonstrations of poverty—that seem to make a nonsense of conventional wisdom. And lastly, there is the difference between what a native sees and a foreigner; or the difference that there should be between what a native reports and a foreigner reports. When these are coincident, corruption or stupidity are present.

If Ireland be a rich and flourishing kingdom; its wealth and prosperity must be owning to certain causes, that are yet concealed from the whole race of mankind; and the effects are equally invisible. We need not wonder at strangers, when they deliver such paradoxes; but a native and inhabitant of this Kingdom, who gives the same verdict, must be either ignorant to stupidity; or a man-pleaser, at the expense of all honour, conscience and truth.[18]

But the telling of lies for whatever reason is not a simple action, although undoubtedly reprehensible. It replaces the thing which is with the thing which is not. It is a misrepresentation that will lead to misinterpretation; and yet, if there is a reason for it, it is at least explicable. But when the distinction between the native and the foreigner disappears, when, in the same person, we have Gulliver the Englishman and Gulliver the Houyhnhnm-lover, is there any connection between what he sees and reports, is there any communication possible between him and anyone else, is language itself not liable to become inoperable as madness—linguistic isolation—deepens?

Language is not a medium which contains within itself authenticating authority; it is no more than a system of conventions, not founded in nature at all. That is the source of the anxiety in Swift's satires, not merely the manipulation of the persona or suspicion of narrative, but the unsettling effects of language itself that are betrayed by the mad virtuoso like Gulliver, or the economist of *A Modest Proposal,* or any of the other mad, despotic writers and commentators that populate his writings.

More than that; *A Tale of a Tub* is a work that provides both criticism of itself and is about the relation of authority to criticism and commentary. The link between travel writing and literary criticism is this: they both take as an object of commentary a culture that previously was not sufficiently seen to be in need of it. Put it another way; the institution of literary criticism, from Dryden to Johnson, had as its object the English national culture and literature. Travel writing had the same object—English, French, Irish national culture. But to convert the unknown to the known, the foreign to the native, the philosophical impasse to a liberating conclusion, to show that there was an ethical system that bound the whole world of human nature together by some set of fundamental principles, these led to such confusions that the idea of a universal ethics, intuitively given, had to be abandoned. With that abandonment came the death of virtue.

But it is also true that Swift's Irish writings are the first in either the English or the Irish language to propose the notion that, since Ireland was going to be maltreated so outrageously by England, and since it could not, in consequence, become a distinct and prosperous kingdom—even though it had all the titles and the potential to be so—then Ireland would, by becoming foreign to England, also become the critical commentary

for which England would be, so to say, the text. If one was
authority, the other was subversion; if one was civilization, the
other was its rebuke, barbarism. But the link between them is
not a contrastive one of opposites but a fearsome one of co-
producers. In some respects, this reading of the situation was
carried on by Burke. The question why the English system did
not migrate successfully across the Irish sea could, if asked with
sufficient sharpness, question the whole basis of that system itself;
and if that system could be subjected to radical inquiry, what
system could not? Travel literature was only rescued from its
descent into the inferno by being transmuted, under different
auspices, into the literature of tourism.

There are many forms of travel literature produced in the
eighteenth century—accounts of actual voyages, imaginary voyages, picaresque novels, fantasy tales, historical accounts of non-
European territories, histories of the past, especially of the
ancient world and, within that, histories of the decline and fall
of Rome. Confining ourselves for the moment to those works
of literature that use the imaginary voyage as their governing
trope, we can see that many of these voyagers—who can be
travelers abroad or within their own country and culture—are
possessed of a sublime simplicity that seems, at first sight, to be
a guarantee of their trustworthiness and their essential virtue. By
contrast, among those whom they meet are often found people of
very complex dispositions, highly untrustworthy and worldly-wise,
sharpers, experts, fashionable people who are, in the broadest
sense of the term, virtuosi. The contrast so established between
two generic types is not always stable. Swift, for instance, could
be said to demonstrate that Gulliver's sublime simplicity is no
more than the concealed face of virtuosity. He is a virtuoso at
not appearing to be so. But I want to defer consideration of this
possibility in order to permit the outlines of the general contrast
to appear. On the one hand, we have simplicity and virtue; on
the other hand, we have virtuosity and vice. This contrast is not
at all confined to travel literature, but it is prominent in that
genre. Why this should be so is part of my concern here.

The simplicity of the virtuous person is both the source and
symptom of his or her moral stability. The vicious person, on
the other hand, is characterized by waywardness, fragmentation,

disloyalty, political and social volatility. It may be one of the consequences of the upheavals of the seventeenth century that English writing begins to produce a portrait gallery of rogues who are identified by their splintered personalities. Samuel Butler's Hudibras, Dryden's Absalom, Pope's Sporus, Swift's author in *A Tale of a Tub* would be among the most outstanding examples, although at a more relaxed level of discourse we could also mention figures like Richard Steele's Jack Dimple, the pretty Fellow, whose artificial behavior contrasts with that of Sophronius, the gentleman of "natural behaviour" (*Tatler*, May 28, 1709) or Dr. Johnson's Mr. Sober (*Idler*, no. 31, Nov. 18, 1758) for whom Johnson's hope is "that he will quit his trifles and betake himself to rational and useful diligence." These portraits are of people who have tried to become many things and have ended by being nothing, victims of the lust for power, of the dictates of fashion, the hunger for fame, the dread of boredom, the spirit of political faction. They all have immense energy but no fixed principles. They lack a moral character; that is why they have, as a substitute, such exotic personalities. In addition, they are all, in one sense or another, enthusiasts, types of that plague of what David Hume called "puritanical absurdities" that were so fatally allied to the history and conception of English liberty. Hume suspected that the high value given to the individual conscience in English Protestantism promoted and even ratified the eccentric volatility of the personality, creating a political instability that was sustained by the Protestant sects with their sullen and gloomy theologies of independence. He contrasted this with Catholic political passivity, nurtured by the terrors and superstitions instilled by their authoritarian clergy.[19] With Hume, as with Swift and many others, it is clear that the religious divisions of the seventeenth century provided a typology in which there were two extremes, Catholic and dissenting, and a moderate "Anglican" middle way. This, in turn, enabled the attack on the "virtuosi" to retain a historical dimension that would enrich and polemicize the vocabulary of moral debate that the literature of this period so readily deploys.

The connection between Protestant dissent and the wilfully individual personality is widely acknowledged. Only slightly less acknowledged is the connection between this species of radical individuality and the "new" system or ideology of Benevolence.

The presentation of the benevolist takes a somewhat different form because he is characterized, not by volatile changeability, but by a uniform placidity of disposition. One changes without reason; the other never sees any reason to change. Both are fanatics. One is generally fierce or gloomy; the other implacably benign. He is more often found in the prose rather than in the verse of this period. His sense of his own virtue is secure and his simplicity the characteristic manifestation of it. Sir Roger de Coverley, Gulliver, Tom Jones, Dr. Primrose, Rasselas, would be typical examples. So decorous, benevolent, and good-hearted are they that it may seem anomalous to dub them fanatics. They seem to be sunlit personalities who have emerged out of the darknesses of puritan antinomianism, who have forsaken chiliastic furies and convictions and become "polite," members of civil society rather than deluded participants in some apocalyptic religious melodrama. They are much given to sententious declarations on human life, the more credible because they are so widely experienced in the ways of humankind, as picaresque or vagabond heroes tend to be. Of course, in the case of the irretrievably benevolent, the range of human experience they encounter is irrelevant. They will emerge from variety in their initial state.

We could put this differently and thereby gain closer access to the issue by saying that there is a rhetorical difference in the treatment of dissenting virtuosos and the virtuosos of benevolence. The figure of the traveler is pledged to the act of discovery, either in the sense of introducing us to something new or in the sense of revealing the known in a new light— Montesquieu's Uzbek and Rhedi, Voltaire's Candide, Goldsmith's Lien Chi Altangi, Defoe's Crusoe, Gulliver of course and the various travelers we meet in the works of the Marquis d'Argens, Horace Walpole, Smollett, and others are assigned a variety of functions. They manage these, for the most part, by making the world conform to their initial convictions. By domesticating what they consider to be strange they often show us how strange the idea of the domestic is. But, rhetorically, they are presented to us in a language of such decorum that they transmit to us a sense of order—no matter how provincial, provisional, or placid it may be—that is unshakable. But the dissenting virtuosi (and they may be Catholic or Protestant, but more often the latter) belong to a rhetorical world in which syntactical, grammatical, and semantic control is always at risk. The difference between the rhetorically baroque world of *A Tale of a Tub* and the rhetorically "polite" world of *Gulliver's Travels* is the obvious example that indicates the scale of the contrast. This imperviously decorous observation of the traveler is all the more impressive and interesting because it includes within its view many exemplary cases of fanaticism, madness, strangeness, eccentricity, and experiment. But these oddities, although threatening, are kept at arm's length. They are, after all, "foreign" to the traveler's native country in the geographical or intellectual sense. They do not belong to the rational world, which is often coincident with Europe, England, or a class or group of people within these.

Further, the rational world is conventionally dissociated from the realm of the bodily and appetitive functions. In Swift, the body humiliates reason. Those whose rational processes are assimilated to bodily processes are fanatics; those who wish to proclaim reason's independence of the body are insane. But the traditional distinction between the two realms is, nevertheless, sustained by him and enhanced by the Benevolist school of Shaftesbury and Hutcheson, which carefully separated the "internal sense" of taste from the five physical senses. Many of the standard objections to those subversive writers, from Mandeville to the French materialists, who insisted on the physiological basis of feeling, including aesthetic and moral feelings, dwelt on the element of "grossness" which they introduced into the world of rationality.

It is also important that the inhabitants of the rational world are male. This gendered exclusiveness is so deeply imbedded that it becomes an integral part of the attack on irrationality and fanaticism, especially when these conditions are transposed from the theological and political to the social arena. What was fanatical in the former becomes faddish and whimsical in the latter; and such whimsicality is often characterized as "effeminate." The powerful association between fashion, especially fashion in clothes, and the fickleness of women, especially women who had escaped what Lawrence Stone called "the companionate marriage" and who were, therefore, "loose," was a key element in the complicated eighteenth-century debates centered around the

vice of the city and the virtue of the country.[20] That debate took
another turn when such fickleness was translated into an intellectual defect characteristic of women and even of a nation, the
French, widely condemned in the later eighteenth century for a
"légèreté" of spirit that had an interest in fashion and a moral,
largely sexual, instability as its characteristic accompaniments or
symptoms. The reaction to the role of women as hostesses of
the French salons and, subsequently (also, by implication, consequently), as prominent members of the "mob" in the early
days of the French Revolution reconfirmed this configuration of
dangerous volatility as a threat to social order.[21]

Nevertheless, the debates about the relation between reason
and virtue modulated into the debates about the relation between
reason and happiness as reason became increasingly identified
with calculation and virtue and happiness became increasingly
associated with sentiment. It was the Benevolists who asserted that
it was rational to be sentimental and the utilitarians who asserted
that it was rational to be calculating. But the division between
these attitudes was not essentially philosophical. Certainly by the
nineties, but probably as early as the Seven Years War (1756–63),
it had become political. The rational ideal of the Enlightenment
only had force in alliance with a cosmopolitan and universalist
view of human nature. Once that ideal began to give way to
a newly assertive nationalism, predicated on notions of national
character, its future was threatened. Although this is not the place
to detail that complicated process, it can be said that, in Britain,
reason was attacked as an abstract energy, dangerously removed
from historical experience, and the rational man or woman was
regarded as a virtuoso, an experimenter, whose highly mutable
designs for social and political life were driven by an intellectual
pride that ruthlessly pursued the dream of its own perfection, no
matter what the cost to intuitive human feeling. An ideology of
solid sense was developed to combat the smiling lunacies of the
Man of Reason or the sodden effusions of the Man of Feeling. We
meet versions of them in Fielding, of course, in Goldsmith, and
in Mackenzie, but it is the novelists of the nineties—particularly
Bage and Holcroft—who bring them to comic and alarming
extremes.

The system of Benevolence has become, in their writings, a system founded upon "sincerity." But for all the emphasis upon "sincerity," Rousseau's work and, even more, Rousseau's reputation had made the ethic of feeling suspect. From a Burkean point of view, we could say that there is "Feeling" and there are feelings. The first is a radical and theoretical formulation; the second is an embedded historical reality. Moreover, the notion that benevolence is rational as well as sincere created a number of problems and conflicts that are singularly embodied in the writings and career of William Godwin. His chief work *Political Justice* (1793) brings the principles of rational benevolence to a point that would have made even Shaftesbury or Hutcheson quiver a little. For Godwin argues that personal, natural feelings must take second place to a rational estimate of the consequences of any action for the human race in general. This raised the ire of readers who regarded Godwin as an exponent of an "unfeeling" philosophy. He recommended as a principle of action what Burke, for instance, had condemned in Rousseau—the promotion of global benevolence by someone who had forgotten that charity begins at home with those who are nearest and should be dearest. It is Godwin who also brings the issue of the relationship between disinterested benevolence and what he calls the "domestic affections" to light in a tragic (and characteristically ridiculous) way by his reaction to the death of his wife, Mary Wollstonecraft.[22] His sexless prose, oddly, betrays the sexism of the philosophy of rational benevolence. But we should also remember that it was the daughter of his marriage to Mary Wollstonecraft, Mary Shelley, who brought travel literature into a new "romantic" dimension with her *Frankenstein* and, further, that Godwin himself saw nothing wrong with the society of Houyhnhnmland in Book IV of *Gulliver's Travels*, Rather he saw in it a rational ideal; those horses were benevolist thoroughbreds who had won the race to happiness. It took almost a century for someone to out-Gulliver Gulliver. Godwin's role is more complex than these remarks would indicate and is beyond my present scope. But behind him and his disinterested benevolence we can perceive the emergence of his son-in-law, Shelley, and the greatest of all the romantic theorists of sympathy, William Hazlitt, both of them youthful admirers of Godwin and rescuers of the philosophical tradition he represented from the fearful aridities into which he had remorselessly led it. It was an admirer of the Houyhnhnms and of the Enlightenment who gave reason and virtue a bad name in England. He became a stranger to the "domestic affections" and, as a radical and an alleged sympathizer with France, became a foreigner in his own country. Many of his contemporaries, especially those who were made honorary French citizens, shared the same fate, victims of the new ideology of national character that had replaced the Enlightenment ideal. The French, in Burke's view, had transformed France into an Asiatic despotism; the real France had disappeared and a foreign country or a country foreign to tradition and history had taken its place. The most dangerous travel undertaken in the eighteenth century had been into the realms of "theory" where "France" had its home.

NOTES

1. Edmund Gibbon, *History of the Decline and Fall of the Roman Empire*, ed. J. B. Bury, 12 vols. (London, 1900–1910), 1:58.

2. See J. G. A. Pocock, *Virtue, Commerce and History* (Cambridge: Cambridge University Press, 1988), 103–23.

3. David Hume, *Enquiries Concerning the Human Understanding and Concerning the Principles of Morals*, ed. L. A. Selby-Bigge, 2nd ed. (Oxford: Clarendon Press, 1902), 341.

4. David Hume, *Enquiries*, 343.

5. Adam Smith, *An Inquiry into the Nature and Causes of the Wealth of Nations*, ed. E. Cannan (New York: Modern Library, 1937), 735–36.

6. Quoted in John Barrell, *English Literature in History, 1730–80: An Equal, Wide Survey* (London: Hutchinson, 1983), 47.

7. Barrell, 47.

8. See Smith's discussion in *The Wealth of Nations*, vol. 2, bk. V, chap. 1, pt. III, 746–48, of the "strict or austere" system of morality favored by the common people and the "liberal or . . . loose system" favored by people of rank. He also argues that religious sects begin with the common people and refine on the austere system with "excessive rigour." "The morals of those little sects, indeed, have frequently been rather disagreeably rigorous and unsocial."

9. Jonathan Swift, *The Drapier's Letters to the People of Ireland*, ed. Herbert Davis (Oxford: Clarendon Press, 1965), 128.

10. Jean-Jacques Rousseau, *Lettre à M. D'Alembert sur les Spectacles* in *Du Contrat Social* (Paris, 1953), 232.

11. Denis Diderot, *Oeuvres Philosophiques*, ed, Paul Vernière (Paris, 1956), 515.

12. See Carole Blum, *Diderot: The Virtue of A Philosopher* (London: Viking, 1974), 127–39.

13. See M. M. Goldsmith, "Liberty, luxury and the pursuit of happiness," in *The Languages of Political Theory in Early Modern Europe*, ed. Anthony Pagden (Cambridge: Cambridge University Press, 1987), 225–51.

14. Barrell, 23–24, 108–9.

15. See John Lucas, *England and Englishness: Ideas of Nationhood in English Poetry, 1688–1900* (London: Hogarth, 1990), esp. 55–70.

16. *The Writings of Jonathan Swift*, ed. Robert A. Greenberg and William B. Piper (New York: Norton, 1973), 499.

17. *Writings of Jonathan Swift*, 500–501.

18. *Writings of Jonathan Swift*, 502.

19. David L. Bongie, *David Hume, Prophet of Counter-Revolution* (Oxford: Clarendon Press, 1965), xii.

20. See Neil McKendrick, John Brewer, and J. H. Plumb, *The Birth of a Consumer Society: The Commercialization of Eighteenth-Century England* (London: Europa, 1982), esp. 51–53.

21. See Ruth Perry, "Radical Doubt and the Liberation of Women," *Eighteenth-Century Studies* 18 (1985), 465–93; Seamus Deane, *The French Revolution and Enlightenment in England, 1789–1932* (Cambridge, Mass. and London: Harvard University Press, 1988), 21–42; David Simpson, *Romanticism, Nationalism and the Revolt against Theory* (Chicago and London: University of Chicago Press, 1993), 104–25; Linda Colley, *Britons: Forging the Nation, 1707–1837* (New Haven and London: Yale University Press, 1992), 237–81.

22. See Mary Poovey, *The Proper Woman and the Woman Writer: Ideology as Style in the Works of Mary Wollstonecraft, Mary Shelley, and Jane Austen* (Chicago and London: University of Chicago Press, 1984), 48–113.

Swift as Irish Historian

CAROLE FABRICANT

1

In an essay contrasting the history of England with that of Ireland, J. C. Beckett argues that the student of English history is confronted with material possessing a "natural and recognizable pattern," a "natural and over-riding unity," as opposed to "the confusion, the cross-currents, the apparent inconsequence of events, the regional isolationism, that meets the student of Irish history." Where, he asks rhetorically, is that student "to find a theme that will lead him, by some process of development, from one era to the next?"[1]

What Beckett is describing here as the incoherence of Irish history, despite his invocation of criteria—unity, symmetry, organicism—that make him sound like a New Critic contrasting modernist and postmodernist verse, is not an aesthetic deficiency but a political and human catastrophe: one similar to what Carlos Fuentes points to when, in discussing the shape of Latin American history, he says that colonialist intervention "damages the fabric of a nation, the chance of resurrecting its history, the wholeness of its cultural identity."[2] In other words, to whatever (I would argue limited) extent smooth linear patterns and clearly defined unities may be said to exist in history, it is certain they will not be found in the development of nations whose past (and therefore, inevitably, whose present) have been inscribed by colonialism. The resulting problems, one need hardly point out, are not limited to the difficulties this situation poses for the historian in search of a flowing narrative with neat evolutionary patterns.

And yet, there are important ways in which the catastrophe of colonialism *is* integrally bound up with the role of the historian, whose constructions of the past can serve either to legitimize or to expose present policies and thereby influence future actions and whose attempts to define nationhood cannot escape being bound up on some level with questions of *self*-definition. In this regard, Beckett's metaphoric depiction of history writing as a kind of personal odyssey has an aptness despite its obfuscating contrast between the English historian as a self-assured traveler "making a journey through a well-mapped country . . . never far from a known route," and the Irish historian as a wanderer along roads that "often . . . seem to lead from nowhere to nowhere," making him "more than likely to lose himself on the way":[3] a contrast that reflects the implicit privileging of the unified imperial center over the dispersed colonial margins and that in effect valorizes the assertion of control in the face of anxiety-producing displacements.

I want to argue it is pertinent to these considerations that when a young Irishman by the name of Jonathan Swift—decidedly Protestant but far from Ascendantly so, born into a fatherless family with ancient roots in Yorkshire but birthplace and closest kin in Dublin, devoid alike of money, land, and worldly position— came over to England in 1689 to escape the upheavals of the Williamite Wars and to seek his fortune, he turned almost immediately to history, and history writing, as a possible solution to his personal and professional dilemmas. During his sojourns in Surrey while working for Sir William Temple he composed *An Abstract of the History of England* as well as *A Fragment of the History* containing accounts of the reigns of William Rufus, Henry the First, Stephen, and Henry the Second, interrupting these historical researches to address a more immediate political crisis via his *Discourse of the Contests and Dissensions between the Nobles and the Commons in Athens and Rome,* which was itself (as the title suggests) a parallel history, filled with reflections and generalizations about the ancient past as well as contemporary events.

Many commentators have remarked upon Swift's preoccupation with the study of history, usually explaining it in terms of such things as his classical reading and Temple's influence. While I don't question the importance of these factors, I want to shift the focus to the way in which the study and recording of history presented Swift with a potential means of resolving certain ambivalences and tensions related to his own sense of who he was, in personal, ethnic, and nationalist terms. Irvin Ehrenpreis is suggestive in his speculations about the youthful Swift's "deeply emotional" wish to be a historian: "By a minute knowledge of his adopted land's past, he could attach himself to the nation of his forebears. . . . In producing a history of the country, he would establish his racial genealogy."[4] We need, however, to go beyond purely personal considerations and take into account the fact that historiography was an institution exerting hegemonic power in the England Swift wished to become part of: an institution as "established" in its own way as the Anglican Church or the monarchy, a locus of centralized authority which regulated official interpretations of the past, hence shaped perceptions of the present and delineated directions for the future. Given the cultural, ultimately political power connected with the practices of historiography, and the mechanisms for legitimation and authenticity it laid claims to, it is little wonder that a displaced and insecure Irishman, having experienced only economic hardship and dependency in the place of his birth, should identify so tenaciously with the office of historian and evidence a desire to appropriate some of its authority to himself. Hence Swift's repeated endeavors to write the "official" history of the Tory ministry under Queen Anne and the events leading up to the Treaty of Utrecht, as well as his strenuous attempts to obtain the post of Historiographer Royal after the death of Sir Thomas Rymer.

Swift, of course, never did get this post, nor any of the others he had hoped for in England, and so a deeply disaffected minor Anglican cleric departed for Dublin on August 16, 1714, to take up his post as Dean of St. Patrick's. The rest, as they say, is history—or rather, as I want to argue here, the making of an Irish historian who, in the process of naming his historical subject and delineating the contours of a nation worthy of having a history, defined, in certain ways reshaped, the contours of his own identity. To the extent that Swift did succeed in establishing a "racial genealogy" for himself, it was through recording and identifying with the history not of England but Ireland, giving a special aptness to his later portrayals of Irish patriotism in terms of filial duty and protection of one's mother.[5] In lieu of the grand narrative and officially anointed history of an emerging world power which was his early aspiration, Swift produced a series of short, fragmented essays addressing aspects of a larger whole that always seemed to be exasperatingly out of reach. In place of the elegant accounts embodying the maxim of "philosophy teaching by example" which scholars regularly associate with English histories of the eighteenth century, Swift wrote pugnaciously *in*elegant tracts which had more in common with popular journalism and street ballads than with noble Augustan genres like the epic. Above all, instead of producing hegemonic texts commemorating the development of England's institutions and in effect ratifying her increasingly imperial role in the world, Swift wound up writing mostly counter-hegemonic pieces challenging not only English actions and policies, but also the official rationales invoked to justify them.

2

Although Swift never wrote a history of Ireland *per se*, he produced a large number of tracts pertaining to Irish affairs. In proposing that we consider these as historical writings, as continuing expressions of his early resolve to be the historian for a nation and an age, I mean to denote something more than the obvious fact that, as occasional pieces, they necessarily deal with the very stuff of history by treating current events and topical issues of the day, at times incorporating brief accounts of aspects of the Roman, English, and Celtic past as relevant examples or as mini-history lessons for a contemporary audience. Beyond this, as occasional writer Swift's search for (to quote Seamus Heaney) "images and symbols adequate to his predicament"[6] produced grimly compelling testimonies to the situation in his homeland which, for all their searing immediacy, invited (indeed, urged) their readers to view current circumstances within a more sweeping historical context of past actions and future probabilities. But even more, I want to consider these tracts as historical writings in the sense that they actively engaged in the historiographic controversies of the time, not only addressing the central issues highlighted by contemporary histories of Ireland, but also functioning as calculated interventions in the combined historical and historiographic enterprise as it had come to be defined by the English and their representatives in Ireland.

To explain what I mean by this, a few words about Irish historiography during this period are in order.[7] For my purposes its most important feature is that it actively partook of the struggles which it recorded and in so doing powerfully illuminated a constellation of problems at the heart of the historiographic project. On the most obvious level, of course, it was engaged in telling a story—actually, in telling two very different stories—about Ireland's past. But as we have been reminded by the quincentennial celebration of Columbus's arrival in the New World and the angry protests it provoked, stories about the past can never be idle or neutral; there is too much at stake in what they say, for both present and future, for both the individual and the nation. Nowhere was this more dramatically evidenced than in the early histories of Ireland, which in their adherence to competing interests and value systems were in effect ideological and rhetorical battlefields that reflected—and in some instances contributed to—the violence, both physical and economic, which ravaged the country throughout the seventeenth and eighteenth centuries.

For easy shorthand reference the two main competing stories may be termed "Catholic" and "Protestant," though it should be kept in mind that such labeling is an oversimplification, glossing over occasional areas of cross-fertilization and serving (then as now) to obfuscate other equally serious divisions: for example, what Frederick Engels and James Connolly exposed as the extreme economic disparities in Irish society, and what earlier commentators discussed in terms of a grossly unequal distribution of power.[8] As M. Carey put it in his *Ireland Vindicated*: "But the dreadful scenes exhibited in Ireland were not the result of any peculiarity in the English nation: they arose from the relations between the two islands. . . . for, if there be one truth more clearly proved by history than another, it is, that bodies of men, or nations, are demons, when they have uncontrolled power over other bodies or nations. All the oppressions, the tyrannies, the rapines, the bloody persecutions, that load the polluted and wretched annals of mankind, bear the most irrefragable evidence to this appalling position."[9]

What was an "appalling position" to Carey seemed a thoroughly reasonable, indeed necessary state of affairs to another group of Irish historiographers. These were concerned in their writings not only to recount a past course of events but to justify current actions and policies on the part of the Anglo-Irish and/or English in light of these events. Invariably they cited and adapted to their own purposes the late twelfth-century history of Giraldus Cambrensis, which functioned to justify Henry II's invasion of Ireland in 1171 by portraying the native (so-called "wild") Irish as heathens and savages engaged in all forms of debauchery and perversions—in Cambrensis's words, "a most filthy race, a race sunk in vice, a race more ignorant than all other nations of the first principles of the faith"[10]—who were desperately in need of England's civilizing influence and control. This basic theme, with variations, runs throughout the later Irish commentaries of men such as Edmund Spenser, Richard Stanihurst, Barnaby Rich, Sir John Temple, and Sir Richard Cox. We may recall Irenius's extended reflections on ways of "reducing that savage nation [Ireland] to better government and civility" in Spenser's *View of the Present State of Ireland*.[11]

In response to accounts such as these, contemporary Catholic historians of Ireland tended to devote a significant portion of their work to refuting what they viewed as the slanders and distortions perpetuated, indeed virtually institutionalized, by the Protestant descendants of Cambrensis. Geoffrey Keating, writing in Irish, attacked "the malicious and ignorant Falsehoods related by *English* writers, in what they call their Histories of *Ireland*," claiming that "whatever these Writers deliver in Dispraise of the *Irish* nation, has no other Authority than the bare Relation of Persons, who bore an inflexible Hatred to the *Irish* Name. . . ."[12] Hugh Reily argued that Protestant writers on Ireland, in order to justify their compatriots' oppressions and confiscations of Catholic lands, "loaded [the Catholic natives] on every *Occasion* with all the *Calumnies* Wit or Malice cou'd invent."[13] And Sylvester O'Halloran lamented that "the later periods of our history have been so shamefully misrepresented, that it will require some time to establish the antecedent facts."[14]

Dennis Taaffe's protest, "We are beset with a chain of false witnesses, descendants from Gyraldus Cambrensis to his modern representative *Musgrave*,"[15] underscores the extent to which, for Catholic historians, the act of writing Irish history was seen as a spiritual and moral imperative to bring the truth to light. It was also inseparable from the act of responding to, by attempting to *re*write, the histories of others; their reactive texts in a sense mirrored their necessarily reactive roles as members of a colonized class in society. The very titles of many of these works—Reily's *Ireland's Case Briefly Stated*, O'Halloran's *Ierne Defended*, Taaffe's *Vindication of the Irish Nation*—suggest the degree to which their authors viewed their role not only as recorders of the past but as defense attorneys presenting exonerating evidence in a court of law, suing for justice even if with the knowledge that prosecutor, judge, and jury would likely be one and the same: a descendant and adherent, moreover, of those who originally condemned them.

"Can you *describe* history I'd like to know? / Isn't it a fiction that pretends to be fact / like *A Journal of the Plague Year*?" Tom Paulin asks in his poem "Martello."[16] "Yes and no," would seem to be the answer provided by Irish histories of the sixteenth through the late eighteenth centuries. Certainly what they reveal are very different pasts viewed and reconstructed through the prism of different sets of national and racial myths, shaped by separate sets of psychological traumas and ideological fictions. Yet these texts also remind us that there are fictions and fictions; that not all fictions bear the same relation to events or exert an equal influence on the dominant myths governing a particular society; that while some fictions produce epic poetry, others produce military invasions. Above all, early Irish historiography shows us what it means for one set of fictions to attain the status of an "official story," so to speak, while others are marginalized or ignored altogether. The power of an official story is that it imposes the labels that others then have the burden of proving false. Those attempting to tell an alternative version are continually having to clear themselves of charges, often unsubstantiated, that have taken on the appearance of fact simply by virtue of repetition and institutional approval. According to Reily's version of this phenomenon, the Protestant historians' "chief *Text* was, Throw dirt enough, something will stick."[17] Liz Curtis's recent study of the British media's role in manipulating public perceptions of the violence in the Six Counties over the past two decades reminds us that this problem is as relevant to present-day Ireland as it was to Swift's. Curtis compellingly demonstrates the extreme difficulty of discrediting or altering the official version of events, even in those rare instances where the story is later clearly proven to be false or adjudged insupportable in a court of law.[18]

The preceding remarks lend support to Connolly's claim that "Irish history has ever been written by the master class—in the interests of the master class."[19] At the same time, in its suggestion of a monolithic and wholly unproblematic exertion of control over Irish history, this statement needs to be qualified; for the "master class" within Ireland was itself a very peculiar kind of ruling elite, not without its own feeling and experience of dispossession. It was a class composed of men who may have been "masters" on their own little plot of ground but who were looked upon with contempt and treated as inferiors everywhere else, including (perhaps especially) the nation with whom they most closely identified and whom they strenuously tried to model themselves after—a fact perfectly grasped by Swift, incidentally, who chided the Irish-born Protestants living in England as men rendered "wholly insignificant and obscure in a *foreign* Country . . ." (*PW* 10:130), "think[ing] themselves too good to live in the Country which gave them Birth, . . . and rather chus[ing] to pass their Days, and consume their Wealth, . . . among those who heartily despise them" (*PW* 9:200). It is therefore not surprising that even the most triumphantly Protestant histories of the period betray signs of insecurity concerning Ireland's identity and place (or lack of it) in the world. As Sir Richard Cox noted in prefatory remarks to his *Hibernia Anglicana*, published in 1689: "it is strange that this Noble Kingdom, and the Affairs of it, should find no room in History, but remain so very obscure, that not only the Inhabitants know little or nothing of what has passed in their own Country; but even *England*, a Learned and Inquisitive Nation, skilful beyond comparison in the Histories of all other Countries, is nevertheless but very imperfectly informed in the Story of *Ireland*. . . ."[20]

We might for a moment reflect on what it means to feel that one is living in a country that can "find no room in history"—as though the latter were an edifice with a limited amount of space reserved for nations with special credentials, a country house that opens its doors to those deemed to be of proper quality, while all others must remain without. If the native Irish were consigned to toil in the field, far away from the house, the Anglo-Irish were forced to wait on the porch—nearer to the interior, it is true, but no less on the outside. Thus it is that the Protestant historian of Ireland, like his Catholic counterpart though obviously in a very different way and for different reasons, was involved by the very nature of his undertaking in a struggle to make a place—and a space—for himself in the annals of history. In the process of putting Ireland on the historical map he was attempting to do the same for himself and his class.

3

Swift was all too familiar with these struggles for proper placement and self-definition, along with the insecurities they bred; they had been an integral part of his life from his earliest days growing up in Ireland. During his stays in England, they expressed themselves in an extreme sensitivity to the way those in power treated him. As he told Esther Johnson at one point, "I have been used barbarously by the late ministry; I am a little piqued in honour to let people see I am not to be despised."[21] Upon his return to Ireland in 1714, Swift found himself technically belonging to a class of rulers in a country of subjects, but in fact having to continue his struggles with and against a group of superiors to get the recognition and respect he clearly felt he deserved but which seemed to him as elusive as ever. Increasingly he came to realize that his own position and identity, his worldly place in every sense, were inextricably bound up with the fate of a nation that was only just learning to declare its name: a nation that in a sense didn't exist yet except in the collective imaginings and textual constructions of those who would help to make it a reality. In the process of devising various strategies for "squeezing his way into history," so to speak, Swift discovered that his own success in this venture would necessarily depend on his country's ability to similarly "find room in history" and command recognition as a nation in her own right. Swift's posture in this respect was not basically distinguishable from that of the typical

Protestant historian of Ireland, who was likewise concerned to publicize the existence of his country while countering the neglect and disdain he suffered at the hands of those he considered his equals and while vindicating his right to be considered a Briton among Britons, a free man among free men. Echoes of this attitude may be discerned in the Drapier's indignant questions: "Were not the People of *Ireland* born as *free* as those of *England*? . . . Are they not Subjects of the same King? . . . Am I a *Free-man* in *England*, and do I become a *Slave* in six Hours, by crossing the Channel?"(*PW* 10:31).

But there were other aspects of Swift's situation that made it more analogous to his native countrymen's and that produced correspondingly counter-hegemonic attitudes. From the moment of his return to Dublin, Swift fell under suspicion for Jacobite sympathies, hence for possibly treasonable offences. Shortly after his homecoming a packet sent to him from England was intercepted by Custom House authorities and delivered to the Lords Justices, who combed it hoping for evidence that could be used against him in a legal prosecution. A letter from Swift recounting the incident to a friend evokes a world characterized by witchhunts, bounty hunting, and governmental coercion to make people testify against their friends. "I would not have answered one syllable or named one person. . . . I would sooner suffer more than let anybody else suffer by me, as some people did," Swift recounts he told Archbishop King.[22] In later years Swift was to express his feelings on this matter more emphatically, excoriating "the whole Tribe of Informers, the most accursed, and prostitute, and abandoned race, that God ever permitted to plague mankind" (*PW* 9:32–33).

In this instance, therefore, as in other similar ones, Swift's position vis-à-vis the established authority in the land had little in common with that of the Anglo-Irish gentry and much in common with the native Catholic population. Like the latter, Swift was an object of surveillance, suspicion, and official hostility, assumed to be guilty until proven innocent, forced to contend with inflammatory labels that, once stuck on him, were almost impossible to remove. As he observed in another letter, "The Parliament here are as mad as you could desire them; all of different parties are used like Jacobites and dogs. All conversation with different principles is dangerous and troublesome. . . . We are as loyal as our enemies, but they will not allow us to be so" (*C* 2:191). Much is made of Swift's collision with the authorities in the Drapier's affair, but in fact this was only one of numerous instances in which Swift found himself on the wrong side of the law, with a price on his head, his writings censored or his printer in jail. It is no coincidence that his later writings are filled with images of prison and sardonic suggestions that the roles of writer and criminal have become conflated:

> For however orthodox [my sentiments] may be while I am now writing, they may become criminal enough to bring me into trouble before midsummer. . . . So in a plot-discovering age, I have often known an innocent man seized and imprisoned, and forced to lie several months in chains, while the Ministers were not at leisure to hear his petition, until they had prosecuted and hanged the number they proposed. (*PW* 9:33)

What connected Swift's position most closely to that of a native Irishman, and to the role of Catholic historian of Ireland in particular, were his continuing struggles to set the record straight and defend himself against what he perceived to be malicious misrepresentations of his character perpetrated by those in high places. As he explained the matter to Pope, "They will just give themselves time to libel and accuse me, but cannot spare a minute to hear my defence" (*PW* 9:33). The example of Chief Justice William Whitshed, who viciously pursued several of Swift's printers both in and out of court (including in one instance into the grave), harassing jurymen and changing verdicts he didn't like, came to symbolize for Swift the corruption of those institutions of society whose specific function was to render judgment on others. Hence Swift's ironic recollection of the words "*Libertas & natale Solum* [Liberty and my native country], written as a Motto on [Whitshed's] Coach, as it stood at the Door of the Court, while he was perjuring himself to betray both" (*PW* 12:8). In this respect the system of so-called justice was not unlike the institution of contemporary Irish historiography: in both cases, the official interpretation of events and judgments based on it were produced in accordance with criteria that claimed to be objective but that were in fact highly partisan, serving the interests of the class in power. In both cases, moreover, there was a high price to pay by those who wound up on the wrong end of the verdict: We might recall that John Harding, the printer of *The Drapier's Letters*, died in prison; and, more chillingly, there were the Cromwellian massacres at Drogheda and Wexford, largely justified by the perpetrators on the basis of earlier judgments made by Protestant historians about the native population's role in the Rebellion of 1641.

In an impassioned and highly topical sermon on the biblical verse, "Thou shalt not bear false Witness against thy Neighbour," Swift in effect lashes out at the whole tribe of slanderers and traducers whom he closely associated with his nemesis, a Whig Ascendancy government that in his view had to bolster its corrupt rule by stirring up paranoia and creating scapegoats. The sermon's repeated condemnation of the act of bearing false witness and its exposure of the act's dangerous consequences for innocent people share in the moral outrage noted earlier in Taaffe's protest against the "chain of false witnesses" whose libelous testimony about the Irish had contributed to their oppression. It also reveals Swift's growing awareness of history's vulnerability to transmission as a one-sided story backed up by the power of a dominant group who know how to prevent other stories from being heard: "The prevailing Side may talk of past Things as they please, with Security; . . . while those who are down are sometimes tempted to speak in Favour of a lost Cause, and therefore, without great Caution, must needs be often caught tripping, and thereby furnish Plenty of Materials for Witnesses and Informers" (*PW* 9:183–84).

It was undoubtedly in part anger at this situation that stood behind Swift's strenuous efforts to publish his *Four Last Years of the Queen* long after the events in question. In the new Preface he wrote for the history, he affirmed his determination "to set future ages right in their judgment" and declared, "as a faithful historian, I cannot suffer falsehoods to run on any longer" (*PW* 7:xxxiv).[23] Earlier he had made Gulliver attack the fallaciousness of modern history writing after discovering, during his voyage to Glubbdubdrib, "how the World had been misled by prostitute Writers" (*PW* 11:199). If the role Swift conceived for himself was that of a dispeller of historical myths, he had most assuredly come to the right place when he sailed for Dublin. There he discovered it was necessary to reconsider the whole problem of misrepresentation in history. Whereas earlier he had imputed these solely to the evil machinations of particular unprincipled individuals or factions in society, his observations and experiences after his return to Ireland suggested to him that such untruths could also be more deeply rooted and systemic in nature, an expression of a social and political structure that depended for its very existence on the distinction between a superior class of rulers and an inferior class of ruled.

This more sophisticated understanding of historical distortion and image manipulation pervades *The Drapier's Letters*. Although these tracts are not devoid of the earlier, more simplistic analysis of how political lies are perpetrated—accusing Wood of spreading slanders about Ireland, for example—they also provide the occasion for some penetrating reflections on the larger political and cultural system that enables and lends sanction to these individual instances of libel. Thus in his letter addressed "To the Whole People of Ireland," the Drapier points out the extent to which England's racial stereotypes about the Irish have contributed to the current crisis:

> Our *Neighbours* . . . have a strong Contempt for most Nations, but especially for *Ireland*: They look upon us as a Sort of *Savage Irish*, whom our Ancestors conquered several Hundred Years ago: And if I should describe the *Britons* to you, as they were in *Caesar's* Time, when they *painted their Bodies, or cloathed themselves with the Skins of Beasts*, I should act full as reasonably as they do. (*PW* 10:64)

In the subsequent *Letter to Lord Chancellor Middleton*, we find a more extended and dramatic, not to mention more bitterly ironic, delineation of the falsifying lens through which the English viewed Ireland and its inhabitants:

> As to *Ireland*, [the English] know little more than they do of *Mexico*; further than that it is a Country subject to the King of *England*, full of Boggs, inhabited by wild *Irish Papists*; who are kept in Awe by mercenary Troops sent from thence. . . .

I have seen the grossest Suppositions pass upon them; that the *wild Irish* were taken in Toyls; but that, in some Time, they would grow so tame, as to eat out of your Hands: . . . And, upon the Arrival of an *Irish-man* to a Country Town, I have known Crouds coming about him, and wondering to see him look so much better than themselves. (*PW* 10:103)

It is difficult to read this passage without thinking of Gulliver in Lilliput, poked and gawked at by a society of minuscule beings suffering from delusions of grandeur, whose ethnocentric fantasies make them believe they are the sole measure of the universe; or without calling to mind the absurdist comedy of Gulliver poised nervously between the Houyhnhnms and the Yahoos, each looking into the face of a creature imagined to be totally "other" only to perceive with a shock of recognition it is themselves they are looking at. In the passages exposing England's stereotypes of the Irish, in other words, we are never very far from the world of Swift's greatest satire.

But even more pertinent to our concerns here, neither are we very far from the world of contemporary revisionist histories of Ireland. In passages such as the ones I've cited from *The Drapier's Letters*, the arrogant but insecure self-assertion and the injured pride of the scorned Anglo-Irish settler has moved into another register; it has crossed over, blended, and transformed into the frustration and anger of the native Irish population, with their deep sense of victimization not only by British armaments and unjust laws but also by a network of falsifying myths. I want to suggest here that Swift, in effect, would have understood the point Declan Kiberd makes when he says, "The English did not invade Ireland—rather, they seized a neighbouring island and invented the idea of Ireland. The notion 'Ireland' is largely a fiction created by the rulers of England in response to specific needs at a precise moment in British history."[24] In other words, while other Protestant patriots were busy asserting their free-born manhood and trying to invent a nation that could accommodate it, Swift understood his task in a somewhat different way: as having to *dis*invent and *re*invent an Ireland that was paradoxically *under*known, in many ways *un*known, yet *over*defined, sagging under the weight of others' caricature images.

4

While Swift's attempts to overturn English stereotypes expressed themselves in a variety of ways, I want to call attention here to two specific myths about Ireland that Swift devoted considerable time and energy to challenging. The first, and most obvious, is one already touched upon: the idea that the Irish were savages and barbarians in desperate need of England's civilizing influence, as expressed in Cox's assertion that "*Prosper* had good reason to call *Ireland, The Barbarous Island*; and the Irish have as much Reason to thank God and the English, for a more Civil and Regular Government exercised over them."[25] As Seamus Deane suggests, this fundamental barbarian-civilian polarity has continued to color Anglo-Irish and Protestant-Catholic relations to the present day.[26] And only recently we were reminded with a vengeance of the continuing power of this distinction to tap into age-old stereotypes and manipulate emotions on a massive scale, when Margaret Thatcher and George Bush warned a Third-World head of state, earlier labeled Attila the Hun, of adverse consequences unless he "decided to join the family of civilized nations," shortly before the "barbarians" were made to experience the full force of the latter's "superior civilization" in the form of 110,000 bombing raids and the equivalent of six Hiroshima explosions—surely one of those situations in which we most sorely feel the absence of a Swift, whose Gulliver, as self-appointed spokesman for advanced civilization, boasts of England's sophisticated weapons of destruction while the more "backward" King of Brobdingnag exclaims disgustedly upon how "so impotent and groveling an Insect . . . could entertain such inhuman Ideas, and in so familiar a Manner as to appear wholly unmoved at all the Scenes of Blood and Desolation" (*PW* 11:134–35).

The whole of the *Travels*, indeed, is a series of ironic *inver*sions and *sub*versions of claims made to civility and to cultural or technological advancement, from the Lilliputian society's simultaneous resemblances to England and resort to savagery in its treatment of perceived enemies, to the supremely rational and civilized Houyhnhnms convening a grand assembly to debate the question of racial extermination. The theme becomes most

explicit in Gulliver's denunciation of colonialist conquest at the
end of the fourth voyage:

> A Crew of Pyrates are driven by a Storm they know not
> whither; at length a Boy discovers Land from the Top-mast;
> they go on Shore to rob and plunder. . . . Here commences
> a new dominion acquired with a title by *divine right*. Ships
> are sent with the first opportunity, the natives driven out
> or destroyed, their princes tortured to discover their gold, a
> free license given to all acts of inhumanity and lust, the earth
> reeking with the blood of its inhabitants: and this execrable
> crew of butchers employed in so pious an expedition, is a
> modern colony sent to convert and civilize an idolatrous
> and barbarous people. (237)

This description powerfully underscores both the specificity of
the Irish situation—evoking as it does the successive waves of
adventurers who came to settle Ireland for personal gain, though
officially under England's banner—and its similarities to other
colonized areas such as North America: similarities Swift was well
aware of, judging by the many associations between the Irish and
the Indians that appear throughout his tracts in particular (see
PW 12:58; 60; 176).

The demystifying attitude that pervades the *Travels* is evident as well in a poem in which Swift adopts the persona of
St. Patrick in order to castigate the English for their arrogant
distortions of history and hypocritical assumption of the role
of civilizing agent: "Thee, happy Island, *Pallas* call'd her own,
/ When haughty *Britain* was a Land unknown. / . . . Thy mar-
tial Sons, whom now they dare despise, / Did once their Land
subdue and civilize: / . . . *Britain*, with Shame confess, this Land
of mine / First taught thee human Knowledge and divine. . . ."
(*Verses occasioned by the sudden drying up of St. Patrick's Well*, 9–10,
13–14, 27–28). Here Swift spotlights the blatant wrenchings of
chronological narrative that were necessary in order to invent
the myth of civilized England coming to dispense enlightenment
to barbarous Ireland. Interestingly, in his earliest contribution
to this discursive opposition between barbarians and civilians,
contained in his fragment of the history of "The Reign of Henry
the Second," written just after finishing the edition of Temple's

works, Swift concurs with the Roman legates' characterization of the Irish "as a savage people, over-run with barbarism and superstition" (*PW* 5:75–76). It is indicative that Swift's ambition at this point in his life to (as it were) become an Englishman should be registered in his uncritical acceptance of the official civilian-barbarian distinction, the two being psychologically and ideologically interdependent.

It is equally indicative that, as Swift's sympathies shifted and as his sense of identity as an Irishman grew, he increasingly turned his rhetorical and satiric powers to undermining the distinction, or to invoking it for his own subversive purposes. His Irish tracts in particular assault some of the most important assumptions of this mythology. Repeatedly we find in them descriptions of living conditions among the native Irish which seem to support the typical claims about their primitive and barbaric way of life, but which in fact reveal these conditions to be a result, not of racial backwardness, but of economic circumstances beyond their control—circumstances, indeed, created and perpetuated by England's economic policies. In his *Short View of the State of Ireland*, for example, Swift observes:

> for it is manifest, that whatever Stranger took such a Journey [through Ireland], would be apt to think himself travelling in *Lapland*, or *Ysland*, rather than in a Country so favoured by Nature as ours. . . . The miserable Dress, and Dyet, and Dwelling of the People. The general Desolation in most Parts of the Kingdom. . . . The Families of Farmers, who pay great Rents, living in Filth and Nastiness upon Buttermilk and Potatoes, without a Shoe or Stocking to their Feet; or a House so convenient as an *English* Hog-sty, to receive them. These, indeed, may be comfortable Sights to an *English* Spectator; who comes for a short Time, only *to learn the Language*, and return back to his own Country, whither he finds all our Wealth transmitted. (*PW* 12:10–11)

If the Irish in effect live like pigs, in other words, it is not because of their brutish natures or their Papist superstitions, as the Protestant commentators would have it, but because the country's resources are being diverted elsewhere. The "English Spectator" in this passage, standing in for the British conqueror and plunderer, both *sees* and *seizes* what he likes; thus he returns to England both with Ireland's wealth and with false stories about the country's economic well-being, eager to report "that we wallow in Riches and Luxury" (12). As both a symptom and an ironic reflection of what Swift is attacking in his *Short View*—i.e., the destructive fictions about the state of Ireland and her people circulated and widely accepted abroad— the partial reprinting of the tract in England by Nathaniel Mist in his *Weekly Journal* brought down a prosecution upon him, by an Establishment that clearly felt such attempts to demolish prevailing myths about Ireland and expose England's own role in creating them were not fit reading matter for an English audience (see *C* 2:390 n.5).

The problems surrounding the suppression and control of information and their inevitable bearing on commonly held mis-perceptions about Ireland were a constant concern of Swift's. After encountering official hostility to his proposal for founding a school in every parish for teaching native Irish children to speak and read the English language—a project often invoked as theo-retical justification for England's "civilizing" mission in Ireland, though in actual terms almost completely ignored—Swift noted: "The common objections against all this, drawn from the laziness, the perverseness, or thievish disposition of the poor native Irish, might be easily answered, by shewing the true reasons for such accusations, and how easily those people may be brought to a less savage manner of life: But my printers have already suffered too much for my speculations" (*PW* 12:88). And reacting to another form of censorship, the Drapier remarks upon the preposter-ous "Rumours industriously spread" and widely accepted by the English because they were prevented from receiving accurate information from Ireland itself, and because "*Wood* prescribes to the News-Mongers in *London*, what they are to write" (*PW* 10:53). Elsewhere Swift expresses his belief "that no Minister ever gave himself the Trouble of reading any Papers written in our Defence . . ." (64). That this statement occurs immedi-ately preceding the one I cited earlier, about England's "strong Contempt" for the "*Savage Irish*," suggests that Swift understood the link between ignoring the other side and considering its proponents literally beneath consideration. The Irish, in other words, had to be silenced not only because they had a *different* view, but perhaps even more because, as "inferior" beings, they had no right to *any* view.

Another piece of so-called evidence frequently cited to establish Ireland's links to "barbaric" societies was the division into two clear-cut groups, barbarous tyrants and enslaved laborers, as conceived in Rich's assertion that "England's role in Ireland should be to defend the poor tenants from the 'thraldome' to which they were being subjected by [the] 'hellhounds' of lords."27 Swift's response to this colonialist rationalization was expressed in a series of scathing attacks that retained the basic structure but wickedly reversed the terms of this equation, transforming the barbarous "hellhounds" from Gaelic lords into precisely the class of landlords that England's conquest had helped create. His denunciation from the pulpit of "the cruel Oppressions of [the poor Popish Natives'] Landlords, who delight to see their Vassals in the Dust" (*PW* 9:209) is typical of these attacks, as is the following passage from *A Proposal for the Universal Use of Irish Manufacture*: "I would now expostulate a little with our Country Landlords; who, by unmeasurable *screwing* and *racking* their Tenants all over the Kingdom, have already reduced the miserable *People* to a *worse Condition* than the *Peasants* in *France*, or the *Vassals* in *Germany* and *Poland*; so that the whole *Species* of what we call *Substantial Farmers*, will, in a very few Years, be utterly at an End" (*PW* 9:21). Here Swift delivers a brilliant stroke—and a particularly well-aimed blow—against a basic precept of England's colonialist mythology: namely, that its own rule, bringing with it Protestant liberty and law, stood as an antithesis and antidote to the Catholic despotism long symbolized by France in the British imagination. According to Swift's formulation, however, it is precisely this rule that has *produced* the despotism it supposedly came to cure. Perhaps it was as much this challenge to England's mythic self-image as it was his suggestion that the Irish "bur[n] *every Thing that came from* England, *except their* People *and their* Coals" (17) which helped account for the fierce condemnations and reprisals the tract provoked, and which landed yet another of his printers behind bars.

Of all the means used to vindicate England's claims to being a civilizer of barbarians, none was so dramatic or emotionally charged as the portrayal of the early Irish as cannibals. This characterization appears in Cambrensis's *Topography of Ireland*, which depicts the country's native inhabitants as bestial creatures who drink each other's blood, and it informs Spenser's grisly description of the vanquished survivors of the Munster wars, who "did eat of the dead carrions . . . yea and one another soon after in so much as the very carcasses they spared not to scrape out of their graves. . . ."[28] Hence cannibalism is one of the first slanders Keating felt called upon to confront in the Introduction to his *History*.[29] I trust I don't need to say much about what Swift does with this particular element of England's racial mythology. Cannibalistic imagery, and variations on it, run throughout his writings, where the unnatural devourers are shown to be not the native Irish but their exploiters, those who feed upon them, such as Lord Joshua Allen, who "draws his daily Food, / From his Tenants vital Blood" (*Traulus, The Second Part*, 41–42), and "that Mongril Breed" (the absentees), "Who from [Ireland] sprung, yet on [her] Vitals feed" (*Verses on St. Patrick's Well*, 95–96).

In Swift's best-known Irish tract, a coolly detached projector, observant of but personally untouched by the suffering around him, "modestly" hatches a scheme for turning Irish babies into *haute cuisine* for "*Persons of Quality* and *Fortune*, through the Kingdom," thereby removing a financial burden from the poor while satisfying the jaded appetites of the wealthy, particularly "*Landlords*; who, as they have already devoured most of the Parents, seem to have the best Title to the Children," the entire scenario made both necessary and legitimate by the ultimate devourer behind the curtain: That "*Country, which would be glad to eat up our whole Nation*" (*PW* 12:111, 112, 117). The Proposer's emphasis on the disproportionately large number of "Popish infants" who would provide the ingredients for these dainty morsels (112) serves to underscore that the very group singled out in the histories of the time for their barbaric eating practices were in fact the ones most vulnerable to being cannibalized by others. The coolly rational, technocratic, genteel, if you will, cannibalism which constitutes the central metaphor of this tract is wholly consistent with the images of institutionalized and cosmeticized violence that Swift elsewhere increasingly identified with England's colonial rule.

5

The second area of Swift's intervention in Irish historiography I want to consider here has to do with his treatment of the Rebellion of 1641, which—together with the Glorious Revolution, though for opposite reasons—occupied pride of place in the Protestant pantheon of historical events invested with almost mythic proportions and transformed into an emotionally charged symbol functioning to justify subsequent political policies. Indicative of the importance ascribed to it is that in 1662 the Irish Parliament formally declared October 23, the day the rebellion was discovered, "an Anniversary holy day in this Kingdom for ever," to be "kept and celebrated" via organized prayers, sermons, and public readings of the Parliamentary Act itself throughout the land.[30]

The circumstances surrounding this event were themselves complicated and ambiguous, involving different groups who joined the uprising against the Protestant settlers at different points in the struggle, and including a large group of Catholics who swore allegiance to the British monarchy and saw their rebellion as a conservative action to uphold the authority of King Charles against the English Parliament. What seems indisputable is that on October 22, 1641, a group of the Irish gentry, upset by prior seizures of their lands, general threats to land titles, and fears of a Puritan takeover, attacked Ulster settlers living outside the walled towns, killing somewhere in the range of 2,000 to 3,000 of them before retaliatory attacks on Catholics and a general widening of the conflict later claimed many more casualties.[31]

Subsequent Protestant accounts transformed the event into myth through two main techniques: first, via a massive oversimplification of the issues involved that produced a narrative of Protestant tolerance and generosity falling victim to Catholic treachery and ingratitude; and secondly, via a gross exaggeration of the number of Protestants killed in the insurrection (claims of 100,000 were not uncommon), accompanied with a litany of alleged Catholic atrocities that at the time filled thirty-three volumes of "Depositions."[32] Sir John Temple's *History of the Rebellion*, written only five years after the fact, became, in effect, the sacred text for many generations of Protestant commentators intent upon proving Catholic perfidy and the impossibility of ever civilizing the Irish savages. Tracing the Rebellion ultimately to the machinations of the Pope, Temple asserted that the Ulster rebels "in a most fierce outragious manner, furiously broke out, acting in all places of that Province, with most abominable cruelty, those horrid massacres and execrable murders, as would make any Christian ear to tingle at the sad commemoration of them," dramatizing his account with graphic descriptions of "Husbands cut to pieces in the presence of their Wives, [and] their Childrens brains dashed out before their faces."[33] The extent to which this view became the official story can be gauged by its later direct incorporation into Hume's *History*: "After rapacity had fully exerted itself, cruelty, and the most barbarous that ever, in an nation, was known or heard of, began its operations. . . ."[34] Particularly telling is the crucial role which accounts of the insurrection played in colonialist ideology for centuries, available to be resurrected on a moment's notice to justify specific anti-Catholic measures. Thus a full century and a half after the rebellion, Edmund Burke, while admitting the "enormity" of the event, asked rhetorically, " . . . will it follow that it must be avenged forever?"[35] And in the year 1819 Carey was still writing about the circumstances of 1641 as though they were current history: "The terrific tales that are recorded of the events of the civil war of 1641, have sowed, and still continue to sow, a copious seed of the most vulgar and rancorous prejudices in the mind of man against his fellow man. . . ."[36]

If the memory of 1641 was still this vivid one hundred and seventy years later, one can well imagine the degree of immediacy it must have possessed in Swift's own time. Born only thirty years after the event in question, and into a paternal family with direct ties both with the Duke of Ormonde, the leader of the royalist Anglican forces during the Rebellion, and with John Temple, father of his future patron and the author of the inflammatory history already mentioned, Swift must have been nursed almost from birth on the myths perpetuated by contemporary accounts. Certainly as a young pupil at Kilkenny School, an institution at this time dedicated to the inculcation of Anglican doctrine and morality, he would have imbibed Protestant versions of recent Irish history as well as the standard classical history texts. Later in life, as an avid student and reader of history, he would have become personally familiar with specific accounts of the period—we know, for example, that he owned and read (as well as annotated) Clarendon's *History of the Rebellion and Civil Wars.*

It is therefore particularly meaningful that Swift's comments about the 1641 Rebellion tend to convey a very different emphasis toward the event, by and large eschewing the Catholic-bashing integral to Protestant accounts of it, and revising their basic judgment of who was to blame for the uprising. Although attacking the fanaticism of Catholics in the time of James II, Swift denies that they had "the least Design to depose or murder their King, much less to abolish kingly Government," contrasting them in this regard with the Puritans, who "were the principal Cause of the *Irish Rebellion* and *Massacre,* by distressing [King Charles I] and making it impossible for him to send over timely Succours" (*PW* 12:257). While the standard Protestant histories portray the Ulster rebels as would-be destroyers of the British monarchy in Ireland—according to Edmund Borlase, for example, "Certain it was, the *Irish* hop'd to shake off the *English* Government by that attempt"[37]—Swift, here as in many other places, emphasizes the Catholics' basic loyalty and submission to the Crown.

From the pulpit as well, Swift recast the events of 1641 within the larger context of the English Civil Wars, thereby removing the sole onus of responsibility from the shoulders of the native Irish. This is of particular significance given that fervent condemnations of the Catholic rebellion and impassioned commemorations of its defeat at the hands of William of Orange were frequent subjects of contemporary Church-of-Ireland sermons, which were regularly delivered before the Lord-Lieutenant of Ireland and the lords of the Irish Parliament, thereby functioning in a politically as well as religiously hegemonic role to affirm Protestant rule in the land. In one such sermon, preached at Christ Church, Dublin in 1731, the Bishop of Clonfert even quotes at some length from Temple's history as part of a text that insists upon a parallel between the Irish Rebellion and the treacherous deception and massacre of the male population of Shalem by Jacob's sons Simeon and Levi (Genesis 34), and that argues the proposition that "Had the Success been equal to the Cruelty of [the rebels'] Intentions, the very Name and Memory of a *Protestant* had been rooted out of the Land."[38] The Bishop of Rapho had used the same pulpit a decade earlier to warn that "the *Popish Religion*, so pernicious to both [our Church, and our Country] heretofore, continues still the same," though he simultaneously reassured his audience that "we need not be afraid while God is on our side."[39] Even those sermons delivered on the anniversary of the "martyrdom" of King Charles I, where we would expect to find the Puritans the objects of condemnation, manage to redirect their focus—and their venom—onto the Catholics. Thus a 1723 sermon on the occasion by the Bishop of Down and Connor is mainly concerned to contrast the generally peaceful "foreign Papists" with those of Ireland, who "tear both Church and State into Pieces," as a way of urging the need for "putting an End to [schism] by making our Island a Protestant Nation."[40]

By contrast, Swift, in *his* sermon *Upon the Martyrdom of King Charles I*, rejects "the bare name of Protestants" as a basis for a unified Irish nation since "surely, Christ requires more from us than a profession of hating Popery, which a Turk or an Atheist may do as well as a Protestant" (*PW* 9:228), and in the course of spotlighting the culpability of the Puritans in the killing of the King and the destruction of the English monarchy, he offers a view of the 1641 Uprising in Ireland very different both in tone and perspective from the one found in standard Protestant histories and sermons alike: "First, the Irish rebellion was wholly owing to that wicked English parliament. For the leaders in the Irish Popish massacre would never have dared to stir a finger, if they had not been encouraged by that rebellious spirit in the English House of Commons, which they very well knew must disable the King from sending any supplies to his Protestant subjects here" (*PW* 9:223). The image that follows of "the English parliament [holding] the King's hands, while the Irish Papists here were cutting our grandfathers throats," emotive but restrained by contemporary standards, is immediately swallowed up by the image of the "murderous Puritan-parliament," and the sermon thereafter turns into a lengthy harangue against what is referred to more than once as "this horrid rebellion and murder"—terms often used in Protestant accounts of the 1641 Rebellion but here alluding to the havoc and destruction produced by the Puritan Revolution in England.

By far the most interesting and significant instance of Swift's attempts to rewrite the myth of 1641 is contained in a remarkable tract he wrote in defense of the Test Act, entitled *Reasons Humbly Offered to the Parliament of* Ireland *For Repealing the Sacramental Test, in Favour of the Catholicks.* As the title suggests, the tract is on the most obvious level ironic, arguing that if any group deserves full rights to civil employment it is the Catholics, not the Dissenters. In this tract Swift assumes the persona of a Catholic, who, in the process of supporting his case, presents a view of Irish history dramatically at odds with the official story (and intriguingly similar in many respects to Reily's view).

Along with reinterpreting particular events, this alternative view also spotlights the crucial problems involved in how to begin a history; put another way, it shows that where one begins inevitably helps determine how one sees and construes things in the end. We can think of this matter in light of more current affairs. For example, in the most recent episode of U.S. intervention, the starting of the official story on August 2, 1990, with Iraq's "sudden" invasion of Kuwait, was an act of highly selective historical amnesia that invented a new beginning capable of producing and justifying the set of results desired by those directing the narrative. Imagine the radical changes in the story that would be necessitated if one took as starting point May of 1916, with the drawing up of the Sykes-Picot Treaty, or any one of a number of other significant dates in the turbulent history of the Middle East that would help redefine the narrative as a longstanding colonialist encounter in which no episode was sudden or unprovoked.[41]

This example points up the validity of Edward Said's observation that "there is no such thing as a merely given, or simply available, starting point: beginnings have to be made for each project in such a way as to *enable* what follows from them."[42] The Rebellion of 1641 was precisely this kind of arbitrarily designated beginning in the English project of Irish colonization. The standard accounts portray it as a sudden, inexplicable act without a prior history: an act that "did break out unexpectedly . . . like a violent Hurricane, bearing all down before it," wholly unprovoked since "never any *Conquer'd Nation* enjoy'd more fully the Liberties and Priviledges of Free Subjects. . . ."[43] It follows, therefore, that the Catholic speaker of Swift's *Reasons*

Humbly Offered feels the need to deconstruct the starting point invented by Protestant historians. He initiates his discussion by establishing another beginning that long antedates the officially designated one: "It is well known, that the first Conquerors of this Kingdom were *English Catholicks*, Subjects to *English Catholick* Kings" (*PW* 12:285). He then proceeds to give a quick overview of centuries of Irish history, inviting us to see not isolated episodes but recurring patterns of behavior:

> It is confessed, that the Posterity of those first victorious *Catholicks* were often forced to rise in their own Defence, against new Colonies from *England*, who treated them like mere native *Irish*, with innumerable Oppressions; depriving them of their Lands, and driving them by Force of Arms into the most desolate Parts of the Kingdom; until in the next Generation, the Children of these Tyrants were used in the same Manner by the new *English* Adventurers, which Practice continued for many Centuries. But it is agreed on all Hands, that no Insurrections were ever made, except after great Oppressions by fresh Invaders. . . . (285)

By the time the speaker turns his attention to the 1641 Uprising, a context has been established which makes it impossible to view this event as a bolt out of the blue; it is not a beginning but part of an ongoing middle in which attack and counterattack have been the order of the day. While condemning the initial moment of insurrection and the slaughter of Ulster Protestant settlers on October 22, the speaker provides a broader perspective that underscores the distortion and oversimplification inherent in standard accounts of the event:

> The *Catholicks* have some Reason to think it a little hard, when their Enemies will not please to distinguish between the Rebellious Riot committed by that brutal Ruffian, Sir *Phelim O Neal*, with his tumultuous Crew of Rabble; and the Forces raised afterwards by the *Catholick* Lords and Gentlemen of the *English* Pale, in Defence of the King, after the *English* Rebellion began. . . . [W]hat Person of loyal Principles can be so partial to deny, that they did their Duty, by joining with the Marquis of *Ormond*, and other Commanders, who bore their Commissions from the King? (287)

Along with emphasizing the point made by his creator on numerous other occasions, namely, that unlike the Dissenters, the Catholics have consistently shown their loyalty to the English monarchy, the speaker's words indirectly point up the fact that from the standpoint of future Protestant commentators the Catholics were damned no matter what they did during the decade of the 1640s; for whichever side they chose to fight on, they were necessarily fighting against a Protestant force, and given the politics of interpretation characterizing colonial Irish historiography they were fated to be subsequently condemned and punished for this fact, no matter which of the very different Protestant groups ultimately prevailed.

6

The *Reasons Humbly Offered* may be considered Swift's most direct contribution to eighteenth-century Irish historiography. As more than ironist he places himself here in the camp of those who struggled to present a convincing defense against the "chain of false witnesses" whose perjured testimony had become the official line—and the law—of the land. His endeavor in this instance may be understood in light of his general concern with the study of Irish history, as evidenced also in his request to the Duke of Chandos for the return of certain ancient records relating to Ireland, since "they are only valuable in the place of their birth, like the rest of our natives" (*C* 4:251). Swift's friendship with Anthony Raymond, Vicar of Trim, put him in contact with one whose deep interest in Irish culture and history resulted in a project to translate Keating's *History* into English and produced a pamphlet, *A Short Preliminary Discourse to the History of Ireland,* which Swift read and commented on.[44]

One can, of course, only speculate about the kind of full-length "History of Ireland" Swift might have written, but his tracts suggest that it would have diverged significantly from the standard Protestant ones both in perspective and in what one might call methodology. Swift's conviction that the Catholics had been "put out of all visible Possibility of hurting us" by their want of power (*PW* 9:172), his attack on those who insisted that all opposing positions "tendeth directly to Popery, Slavery, and Rebellion" (178), his scorn of those dedicated to "profanely idolizing the Memory" of William III (178), and his demystifying view of the commonly glorified Williamite Wars as an engagement far more destructive than the Rebellion of 1641, a bloody episode in "the contention of the British empire" accompanied with "such ravages and ruin . . . on both sides, as to leave [Ireland] a desert" (*PW* 12:132): these and related attitudes would surely have produced a history importantly at odds with the central shaping myths of contemporary Protestant histories, whether those defending the English interest in Ireland or those expressing the colonial nationalism of the Anglo-Irish gentry.

As for methodology, it seems clear that Swift, unlike other Protestant historians, would not have been content merely to cite the authority of some sacred text or to simply rely on earlier published accounts. Writing to the Earl of Oxford in 1727, for example, he noted that one Mr. Clayton "sent me one of his Books which contained a catalogue of Writings proper for one who would write a History of Ireland wherein I found he took many things very weakly upon trust, and referred the reader to papers which I found to contain nothing at all of the matter he mentions" (*C* 3:247). This critical bent, combined with a recognition of the need for scrupulous personal investigation of sources, is evident as well in his challenging of Clarendon's contention that "until the Year 1640 . . . [England] was in a State of perfect Peace and Happiness"; Swift counters that he has "found, by often rumaging for old Books in *Little Britain* and *Duck-Lane,* a great Number of Pamphlets printed from the Year 1630 to 1640" which testify to the contrary (*PW* 12:264).

What particularly interests me here is not only Swift's refusal to take on faith the judgment even of a historian he respected, but his sense of what constitutes historical evidence. As a popular writer and pamphleteer himself, Swift appreciated the extent to which pamphlets and other kinds of street literature (even those produced by his nemeses, the Puritans) can be important sources of historical testimony. We might recall that the Drapier associates his "Office as a Writer" with that of "my *Brethren,* the Makers of *Songs* and *Ballads*; who, perhaps, are the best qualified at present, to gather up the Gleanings of this Controversy" (*PW* 10:93). It is to these types of writings, even more than to

standard texts and authorities, that Swift was apt to look for
confirmation or refutation of points he had read. His comment
is interesting, moreover, in that it indicates his willingness to
take cognizance of unofficial voices from the margins rather
than merely accepting the pronouncements emanating from the
institutionalized center.

These attitudes help explain why, while many of his compatriots were busy composing smug tributes to the wonders of
Christian (or rather, Protestant) providence—exemplified by the
Bishop of Ferns and Leighlin's exhortation to "stick close to
the Foundation on which we now stand; the Foundation, on
which our *great Deliverer* King William, under the Direction of
God's good Providence, happily plac'd us"[45]—Swift was producing profoundly disturbing tracts exposing the hopeless situation
of "wretches . . . forced to pay for a filthy cabin and two ridges of
potatoes treble the worth, brought up to steal or beg, for want of
work, to whom death would be the best thing to be wished for,
on account both of themselves and the public" (*PW* 12:136),
and refuting those inclined to dismiss these circumstances as
"natural" misfortunes or part of God's plan. As he explained
at the conclusion of his *Letter to the Archbishop* concerning the
increasingly desperate plight of the weavers:

> My meaning is that a consumptive body must needs dye,
> which hath spent all its spirits and received no nourishment;
> Yet I am often tempted to pity when I hear the poor farmer
> and Cottager lamenting the hardness of the times, and im-
> puting them either to one or two ill Seasons, which better
> Clymats than ours are more exposed to, or to the scarcity of
> Silver which to a Nation of Liberty would be onely a sleight
> and temporary inconveniency, to be removed at a months
> warning. (*PW* 12:71).

Unlike Derek Mahon's modern-day Ecclesiastes—indeed, unlike
the vast majority of the Ascendancy class to which he putatively
belonged—Swift never turned a cold heart away from the heat of
the world, never closed one eye so that he could pretend to be
king of a shrunken universe drained of life.[46] His Irish writings
testify to a passion and a clear-sightedness that, given the circumstances of the time, were in and of themselves political acts.

From the height of his Enlightenment throne Hume delivered the grave verdict, "But the Irish have no philosophical historian."[47] Perhaps not. But it might be argued that eighteenth-century Ireland could lay claim to something far better: an astute historical commentator—in a sense, the "Witness in Behalf of the Publick" that Swift himself had held up as a model for his countrymen (*PW* 9:188)—whose body of morally and ideologically engaged writings set an enviable standard for succeeding generations of Irish intellectuals and activists, and whose unrelenting attacks against self-serving delusion, selective historical amnesia, and the myths men conquer and kill by are surely as much needed today as they were in his own time.

NOTES

1. J. C. Beckett, *The Study of Irish History*, New Lecture Series 13 (Belfast: Queen's University, 1963), 6.

2. Carlos Fuentes, *Myself with Others: Selected Essays* (New York: Farrar, Straus, & Giroux, 1988), 201.

3. Beckett, *The Study of Irish History*, 7.

4. Irvin Ehrenpreis, *Swift: The Man, His Works, and the Age*, 3 vols. (Cambridge: Harvard University Press, 1962–83), 2:59.

5. Obvious examples appear in his sermon, *Doing Good*, and in the *Fifth Drapier's Letter* ("To Lord Viscount Molesworth"). See *The Prose Works of Jonathan Swift*, ed. Herbert Davis, 14 vols. (Oxford: Basil Blackwell, 1939–1968), 9:239; 10:89. Hereafter designated as *PW* and cited in the text. While it is true that the characterization of Ireland as a woman has historically been used in reactionary and misogynistic ways—see, e.g., Richard Kearney, "Myth and Motherland," in Field Day Theatre Company, *Ireland's Field Day* (London: Hutchinson, 1985), esp. pp. 74–78; and Eavan Boland, *A Kind of Scar: The Woman Poet in a National Tradition*, LIP Pamphlet (Dublin: Attic Press, 1989), 11–14—I would argue that Swift uses the characterization for more progressive ends, eschewing the idealization and romantic mythology commonly associated with it. The film "Mother Ireland," produced by the Derry Video Workshop, presents a variety of perspectives on this matter.

6. Seamus Heaney, *Preoccupations: Selected Prose 1968–1978* (London: Faber & Faber, 1980), 56.

7. A particularly useful study in this connection is Ned Lebow, "British Historians and Irish History," *Eire-Ireland* 8 (1973): 3–38. Jacqueline R. Hill offers a more complicated and equivocal, less politically focused view in "Popery and Protestantism, Civil and Religious Liberty:

The Disputed Lessons of Irish History 1690–1812," *Past and Present* no. 118 (February 1988): 96–129. The work of Nicholas Canny offers some relevant perspectives on certain of the issues I deal with here. See especially "The Ideology of English Colonization: From Ireland to America," *William and Mary Quarterly* 30 (October 1973): 575–98; and "Identity Formation in Ireland: The Emergence of the Anglo-Irish," in Canny and Anthony Pagden, eds., *Kingdom and Colony: Ireland in the Atlantic World, 1560–1800* (Baltimore and London: Johns Hopkins University Press, 1987), 159–212.

8. See *Ireland and the Irish Question: A Collection of Writings by Karl Marx and Frederick Engels* (New York: International Publishers, 1972), *passim*; and James Connolly's writings on Ireland, especially *Labour in Irish History* (Dublin: New Books Publications, 1983) and *The Re-Conquest of Ireland* (Dublin and Belfast: New Books Publications, 1983).

Examples of cross-fertilization include Protestant involvement in the translation of Keating's *History* into English in 1723 and the Bishop of Down and Connor's *Defence of the Antient Historians* (Dublin, 1734), which attempts to counteract the scorn and neglect shown toward ancient Irish histories and evidences interest in an examination of historical manuscripts written in Irish (xiii–xiv).

9. M. Carey, *Vindiciae Hibernicae: or, Ireland Vindicated* (Philadelphia, 1819), xxix.

10. *The Historical Works of Giraldus Cambrensis*, ed. Thomas Wright and trans. Thomas Forester (London: G. Bohn, 1863), 134–35.

11. Edmund Spenser, *A View of the Present State of Ireland*, ed. W. L. Renwick (Oxford: Clarendon Press, 1970), 1.

12. Geoffrey Keating, *The General History of Ireland*, trans. Dermot O'Connor, 2nd ed. (London, 1732), "Preface," xix–xx.

13. Hugh Reily, "Preface" to *Ireland's Case Briefly Stated* (1695), n.p.

14. Sylvester O'Halloran, *An Introduction to the Study of the History and Antiquities of Ireland* (Dublin, 1772), xx.

15. Dennis Taaffe, *Vindication of the Irish Nation by Julius Vindex* (Dublin, 1801), 2.

16. Tom Paulin, *Liberty Tree* (London: Faber & Faber, 1983), 55.

17. Reily, "Preface" to *Ireland's Case Briefly Stated.*

18. Liz Curtis, *Ireland: The Propaganda War* (London and Sydney: Pluto Press, 1984), *passim.*

19. Connolly, *Labour in Irish History*, 1.

20. Cox, "To the Reader," in *Hibernia Anglicana: or, The History of Ireland from the Conquest to this Present Time*, Pt. I (London, 1689), n.p.

21. Jonathan Swift, *Journal to Stella*, ed. Harold Williams, 2 vols. (1948; Oxford: Basil Blackwell, 1974), 1:233.

22. *The Correspondence of Jonathan Swift*, ed. Harold Williams, 5 vols. (Oxford: Clarendon Press, 1963–1965), 2:173. Hereafter designated as *C* and cited in the text.

23. For a more extended consideration of *The History of the Four Last Years of the Queen* in the context of Swift's desire to be "a faithful historian" and to dispel misconceptions about the past see Fabricant, "Swift in His Own Time and Ours: Some Reflections on Theory and Practice in the Profession," in *The Profession of Eighteenth-Century Literature: Reflections on an Institution*, ed. Leo Damrosch (Madison: University of Wisconsin Press, 1992), 113–34.

24. Declan Kiberd, "Anglo-Irish Attitudes," in *Ireland's Field Day*, 83.

25. Cox, "An Apparatus: Or Introductory Discourse to the History of Ireland," in *Hibernia Anglicana*, n.p.

26. See Seamus Deane, "Civilians and Barbarians," in *Ireland's Field Day*, 33–42.

27. Cited in Canny, "The Ideology of English Colonization: From Ireland to America," 597.

28. *The Historical Works of Giraldus Cambrensis*, 137; and Spenser, *A View of the Present State of Ireland*, 104.

29. Keating, "Preface" to *General History of Ireland*, ii, v.

30. The Act is reproduced in an Appendix to Edmund Borlase, *The History of the Execrable Irish Rebellion* (London, 1680), 323–25.

31. For a useful discussion of the Rebellion see R. F. Foster, *Modern Ireland: 1600–1972* (London and New York: Penguin, 1989), 85–92. Countering W. E. H. Lecky's estimate of 4,000 Protestant casualties during the Ulster Uprising, Foster suggests 2,000 as a more credible figure (p. 85).

32. Joseph Story cites the estimates of 100,000 in *A Sermon Preach'd at St. Andrew's Church on the Anniversary of the Great Rebellion in 1641* (Dublin, 1733), 16. In his *History*, Clarendon claimed that 40,000–50,000 had been killed—a figure, interestingly, that Swift apparently considered a conservative estimate judging from his marginal comment, "at least" (*PW* 5:299). That Swift accepted these inflated casualty claims for the Ulster Rebellion makes his efforts to expose the myths surrounding it that much more remarkable and meaningful.

33. Sir John Temple, *The Irish Rebellion* (London, 1646), 90; 40.

34. David Hume, *The History of England; from the Invasion of Julius Caesar to the Revolution in 1688*, 8 vols. (London, 1822), 6:368.

35. Edmund Burke, "A Letter to Richard Burke, Esq., on Protestant Ascendency in Ireland," *The Works of Edmund Burke*, Bohn's British Classics, 8 vols. (London, 1854–1889), 6:78.

36. Carey, *Vindiciae Hibernicae*, x.

37. Borlase, "To the Reader," in *The History of the Execrable Irish Rebellion*, n.p.

38. Bishop of Clonfert, *A Sermon Preach'd at Christ-Church, Dublin on . . . the Anniversary of the Irish Rebellion* (Dublin, 1731), 18–19; 11.

39. Bishop of Rapho, *A Sermon Preached in Christ's-Church, Dublin on the Anniversary of Deliverance from the Gun-Powder Plot* (Dublin, 1721), 11; 20.

40. Bishop of Down and Connor, *A Sermon Preached at Christ-Church, Dublin on . . . the Anniversary Fast for the Martyrdom of King Charles the First* (Dublin, 1723), 12–14; 18.

41. For a brief overview which allows us to understand the Gulf War in a broader colonialist perspective see Ralph Schoenman, *Iraq and Kuwait: A History Suppressed* (Santa Barbara, Calif.: Veritas Press, 1990).

42. Edward W. Said, *Orientalism* (New York: Vintage, 1979), 16.

43. Borlase, *The History of the Execrable Irish Rebellion*, "To the Reader" (citation from letter by the Bishop of Meath, 1679), 18.

44. See Swift's letter to Raymond concerning the *Short Preliminary Discourse* (*C* 3:80–81). For a discussion of Raymond's involvement with Keating's *History* and his relationship with Swift, see Andrew Carpenter and Alan Harrison, "Swift, Raymond, and a Legacy," *Swift Studies* 1 (1986): 57–60.

45. Bishop of Ferns and Leighlin, *A Sermon Preach'd in Christ-Church, Dublin on . . . the Anniversary Day of Thanksgiving for the Discovery of the Gun-Powder Plot* (Dublin, 1737), 21.

46. For Derek Mahon's "Ecclesiastes" see *Contemporary Irish Poetry*, new and revised edition, ed. Anthony Bradley (Berkeley and Los Angeles: University of California Press, 1988), 336. The relevant lines are the following: "God, you could grow to love it, God-fearing, God- / chosen purist little puritan that, / for all your wiles and smiles, you are (the / dank churches, the empty streets, / the shipyard silence, the tied-up swings) and / shelter your cold heart from the heat / of the world. . . . / . . . Bury that red / bandana and stick, that banjo, this is your / country, close one eye and be king."

47. Cited in Walter D. Love, "Charles O'Conor of Belanagare and Thomas Leland's 'Philosophical' History of Ireland," *Irish Historical Studies*, 13.49 (March 1962): 1. After considering the endeavors of O'Conor and Leland to produce more scholarly and "objective" histories of Ireland, Love concludes that they failed and echoes Hume's verdict: "Ireland never found its 'philosophical' historian" (p. 25).

Swift, God, and Power

MICHAEL DePORTE

Swift was an Anglican priest for fifty years and a fierce defender of church doctrine and church prerogatives. He preached sermons on the superiority of Christianity to Greek philosophy and on the need to believe in the Trinity whether one understood it or not. He wrote that the biblical account of Creation seemed "most agreeable of all others to probability and reason."[1] He dismissed freethinkers as *"no Thinkers"* (9:78). He was uncompromising in his support of the Test Act and scornful of republican governments for "treating Christianity as a System of *Speculative Opinions*, which no Man should be bound to believe" (3:49).

Yet for all the militant orthodoxy of Swift's clerical views, questions about the true nature of his beliefs persisted throughout his career among members of his own church. According to the Whig journalist Abel Boyer, Swift failed to get an English deanship because the Archbishop of York thought it would be scandalous to bestow such preferment on a clergyman "who was hardly suspected of being a Christian."[2] According to tradition, Swift was greeted on the day of his installation as dean of St. Patrick's by an anonymous verse tacked to the front door of the cathedral:

> Look down, St. Patrick, look we pray
> On thine own church and steeple;
> Convert thy Dean on this great day;
> Or else, God help the People.[3]

And even after his death, Lady Mary Wortley Montagu could write her daughter that she regarded Swift's open contempt for

73

religion as "an object of Horror" which "could only be excus'd by Madness."[4]

Swift in turn saw himself as victimized by the conspiracy of envy, malice, and stupidity that inevitably organizes to confound men of genius, a conspiracy in this case of:

> . . . dull Divines, who look with envious Eyes,
> On ev'ry Genius that attempts to rise;
> And pausing o'er a Pipe, with doubtful Nod,
> Give hints, that poets ne'er believe in God.[5]

Lord Orrery suggests that Swift's "humourous disposition tempted him to actions inconsistent with the dignity of a clergyman," and that "such flights drew upon him the general character of an irreligious man." By way of illustration, Orrery repeats a story he heard about Swift betting another clergyman, Dr. Raymond, who could reach the church first to say evening prayers:

> RAYMOND, who was much the nimbler man of the two, arrived first at the door: and when he entered the church walked decently towards the reading desk. SWIFT never slackened his pace, but, running up the isle, left Dr. RAYMOND behind him in the middle of it, and stepping into the reading desk, without putting on a surplice, or opening the prayer-book, began the liturgy in an audible voice, and continued to repeat the service sufficiently long to win his wager.[6]

Letitia Pilkington tells a totally different story about Swift's demeanor in church:

> I was charmed to see with what a becoming piety the Dean performed that solemn service; which he had so much at heart that he wanted not the assistance of the Liturgy, but went quite through it without ever looking in the Prayer Book. Indeed, another part of his behaviour on this occasion was censured by some, as favouring of Popery; which was that he bowed to the Holy Table. However, this circumstance may vindicate him from the wicked aspersion of being deemed an unbeliever, since 'tis plain he had the utmost reverence for the Eucharist.[7]

Pilkington's account is the more plausible of the two. Everything we know about Swift suggests that he went out of his way to observe decorum in church. He complained to Stella once that Harley and Bolingbroke were trying to get him to preach before the Queen. He wished they would forget the idea, because should he do it, "all the puppies hereabouts will throng to hear me, and expect something wonderful, and be plaguily baulkt; for I shall preach plain honest stuff."[8] Pilkington's story may point to a strain of deep piety in Swift, but it may also indicate that Swift took seriously what he said in his *Letter to a Young Gentleman* about the importance of clergymen learning to memorize if they wished to make an impression on their congregations: "whatever is read, differs as much from what is repeated without Book, as a Copy doth from an Original" (9:71).

One of the most compelling stories of Swift's conduct as a clergyman is Patrick Delany's, another friend and early biographer. Delany reports that he lived some six months in Swift's house before realizing that the Dean was reading prayers to his servants every night in his bed chamber. So far was Swift from advertizing his piety, that he went out of his way to conceal it. Yet again, the story perhaps tells us less about Swift's spiritual life than about his sense of duty and desire to impose household order. He had long been concerned to inculcate good morals in his servants and often pointed out that the more deeply a person appears to be convinced himself, the more likely he will be to convince others.[9]

What, then, did Swift really believe? I think the place to begin is with his view of power, because the most pressing issues in his work are issues of power and contention: of king against parliament, established church against dissenters, Tory against Whig, Ireland against England, ancients against moderns, genius against dunce, believers against freethinkers, patriot against oppressor, false witnesses against honest citizens, lower clergy against bishops, Bickerstaff against Partridge, Drapier against Wood, body against mind, craziness against sanity, word play against logic, satirist against fool and knave, preacher against immorality and indifference.

Swift was infuriated by the way people like Wharton, Marlborough, and Walpole abused power; amused by the way others, like Dennis, exaggerated their power. He recalled that Dennis had once written a "three Penny Pamphlet against the Power of France," then gone into the country on a trip. When Dennis got within twenty miles of the channel, and he heard that a French ship had been sighted hovering off the coast, he returned to London in a panic, telling friends that Louis XIV had discovered where he was, and "sent a Privateer on Purpose to catch him" (4:250). Swift was as wary of power in others as he was eager to exercise power himself. "I detest abominate & abhor every Creature who hath a dram of Power in either Kingdom," he writes Pope in one letter. "I am absolute Lord of the greatest Cathedral in the Kingdom," he tells him in another.[10] And to the Duchess of Queensberry he says, not altogether in jest, "I now hate all people whom I cannot command, and consequently a Dutchess is at this time the hatefullest Lady in the World to me, one onley excepted" (i.e., the Queen, *Correspondence* 3:421).

Power is an obsessive theme in the *Journal to Stella*, beginning with the first news he writes of his arrival in London: "The Whigs were ravished to see me, and would lay hold on me as a twig while they are drowning" (*JS* 1:5), continuing through agitated accounts of how he secured remission of the First Fruits, how nearly everything he wrote was the talk of the town, how he acquired greater and greater influence in the Tory ministry, how he struggled mightily to reconcile Oxford and Bolingbroke, and almost as mightily to show his servant Patrick who was boss. He took pleasure in demonstrating his power by promoting the careers of younger men, particularly that of the poet William Harrison, for whom he secured a diplomatic post: "I long to see the little Brat; my own Creature," he wrote, on Harrison's return from Holland (*JS* 2:611). When Harrison became ill soon after, Swift told Stella that he was terribly upset because Harrison "is my own Creature" (*JS* 2:619). And when Harrison died, Swift wrote her: "no loss ever grieved me so much. poor Creature" (*JS* 2:620).

The energy of Swift's tracts and satires derives largely from ironic and not so ironic assertions of power. As author of the *Project for the Advancement of Religion and the Reformation of Manners*, Swift seeks to revolutionize the process of choosing people for public office. As author of *A Proposal for Correcting the English*

Tongue, he wants to fix the language "for ever" (4:14). As Simon Wagstaff, he wants to subdue the "Barbarism" of modern conversation and fix "for ever, the whole System of all true Politeness" (4:122). As M. B. Drapier, he tells the people of Ireland that what he has to say is more important than anything except their duty to God, and urges them to keep his letter by their side at all times (10:12). As Modest Proposer, he says he should have his statue erected as a "Preserver of the Nation" (12:109). And, as Jove in "The Day of Judgement"—most congenial role of all, perhaps—he announces the end of the world and the damnation of fools.

Swift delighted in what he once called the "Godlike" power of imagination ("To Congreve," l. 41). He wrote Gay that "the world is wider to a Poet than to any other Man," that "Poets in their Greek Name are called Creators" because "they resemble the great Creator by having an infinity of Space to work in" (*Correspondence* 3:360). In *Gulliver's Travels*, Swift invents new worlds and new creatures. In *A Tale of a Tub*, he resembles "the great Creator" by laying claim, however ironically, to the kind of importance and complexity we normally associate with sacred works:

> the Reader truly *Learned* . . . will here find sufficient Matter to employ his Speculations for the rest of his Life. It were much to be wisht, and I do here humbly propose for an Experiment, that every Prince in *Christendom* will take seven of the *deepest Scholars* in his Dominions, and shut them up close for *seven* Years, in *seven* Chambers, with a Command to write *seven* ample Commentaries on this comprehensive Discourse. I shall venture to affirm, that whatever Difference may be found in their several Conjectures, they will be all, without the least Distortion, manifestly deduceable from the Text.[11]

Concerns of power are obviously central to the *Travels:* Gulliver's enormous power in Lilliput; the power of everything and everyone except Gulliver in Brobdingnag, including infants, kittens, and insects; the power of technology on the flying island, of necromancy in Glubbdubdrib, and of reason in Houyhnhnmland; not to mention the power Gulliver hopes to exert as author of a book that will put "a full Stop . . . to all the Abuses and Corruptions" of England in six months time (11:xxxiv).

The *Tale*, for its part, is *entirely* about power: a father trying to control his sons through his will; sons banding together to subvert the will, then quarreling with one another as to who is truest to its spirit; Peter, calling himself *"Monarch of the Universe"*; the Grubstreet narrator calling himself "Secretary" of the universe and insisting on his "absolute Authority" as *"freshest Modern,"* to assert "Despotick Power over all Authors before [him]" (*Tale*, 115, 123, 130); at the heart of the text a digression proclaiming madness the ultimate source of power in the world; behind the text a young cleric as desperately ambitious, if not so crazy, as the *Tale*'s narrator. "All my endeavours from a boy to distinguish myself," Swift wrote Pope, "were only for want of a great Title and Fortune, that I might be used like a Lord by those who have an opinion of my parts; whether right or wrong, it is no great matter; and so the reputation of wit or great learning does the office of a blue riband, or of a coach and six horses" (*Correspondence* 3:330–31). After it became dangerous to acknowledge the *Tale*, Swift would defend it to Stella on the grounds that it gave him power to promote church interests: "They may talk of the *you know what*," he wrote her after his initial meeting with Harley to discuss remission of the First Fruits, "but, gad, if it had not been for that, I should never have been able to get the access I have had; and if that helps me to succeed, then that *same thing* will be serviceable to the church" (*JS* 1:47).

In serving the church Swift was equally preoccupied with questions of power. He saw the Church of England as besieged by secular and sectarian enemies; again and again he argues that its dominance is essential to the preservation of English society. "The Scheme established among us of Ecclesiastical Government," he writes in *The Sentiments of a Church of England Man*, is the "fittest of all others for preserving Order and Purity, and under its present Regulations, best calculated for our Civil State" (2:5). Any rational person who questions the importance of an established church should consult the experience of the seventeenth century. Toward the end of Elizabeth's reign, Swift explains in the *Contests and Dissentions in Athens & Rome*, a faction arose "which, under the Name of *Puritan*, began to grow popular, by molding up their new Schemes of Religion with *Republican* Principles in Government . . . [and] did at last overthrow the Constitution; and, according to the usual Course of such Revolutions, did introduce a Tyranny, first of the People, and then of a single Person" (1:230).

Swift was so passionate about the need for a national church that on one occasion he actually cites Cromwell as an authority on freedom of conscience:

> Cromwell's notion upon this article, was natural and right; when, upon the surrender of a town in Ireland, the Popish governor insisted upon an article for liberty of conscience, Cromwell said, he meddled with no man's conscience; but, if by liberty of conscience, the governor meant the liberty of the Mass, he had express orders from the parliament of England against admitting any such liberty at all. (9:262)

Swift's usual formulation of this position is more restrained but no less uncompromising. He advises his parishioners to take the view that freedom of conscience "ought to be fully allowed, as long as it is not abused, [and] never trusted with Power" (9:178). Still, he identified Christianity so strongly with the Church of England that toward the end of his life he wrote Ford that opposition to the church in both England and Ireland had made him give up "all hopes of Church or Christianity. A certain author (I forgot his name,) hath writ a book (I wish I could see it) that the Christian Religion will not last above 300 and odd years. He means, there will always be Christians, as there are Jews; but it will be no longer a Nationall Religion" (*Correspondence* 4:505).

Swift's hard line on dissent derives from his conviction that dissenters are not really motivated by doctrinal or liturgical concerns. That is why the final advantage proposed in abolishing Christianity—that it would "contribute to the uniting of *Protestants*, by enlarging the Terms of Communion, so as to take in all Sorts of *Dissenters*; who are now shut out of the Pale upon Account of a few Ceremonies"—won't work. What inspires dissenters to make so much fuss about "Ceremonies" is simply the "Spirit of opposition," which "lived long before Christianity, and can easily subsist without it" (2:34). Dissenters aspire not to purity, but to power. Swift's disdain of freethinkers derives from a similar view of their motives. They are not people engaged in honest inquiry, afflicted by honest doubts, seeking greater clarity and understanding; they just want freedom from moral restraint: "For, of what Use is Freedom of Thought, if it will not produce Freedom of Action; which is the sole End, how remote soever, in Appearance, of all Objections against Christianity? . . . This was happily expressed by him, who had heard of a Text brought for Proof of the Trinity, which in an antient Manuscript was differently read; he thereupon immediately took the Hint, and by a sudden Deduction of a long *Sorites*, most logically concluded: Why, if it be as you say, I may safely whore and drink on, and defy the Parson" (2:38).[12]

Christianity triumphed over Greek and Roman philosophy, Swift insisted, because it could draw on a source of power greater than intelligence and firmness of character. "The true Misery of the Heathen World" was "the Want of a Divine Sanction; without which, the Dictates of the Philosophers failed in the Point of Authority" (9:73). The ancient philosophers had no notion of "relying" on Providence; they would not have understood what it meant to place one's trust in God; they "trusted in themselves for all things," and therefore had no sure recourse in hard times: "upon every blow of adverse fortune, [they] either affected to be indifferent, or grew sullen and severe, or else yielded and sunk like other men" (9:245–46).

More importantly, the philosophers were never able to posit a compelling reward for virtue. "Human nature is so constituted," Swift argues, "that we can never pursue any thing heartily but upon hopes of a reward. If we run a race, it is in expectation of a prize, and the greater the prize the faster we run." Material rewards are inappropriate, first, because they do not appeal to man's higher nature, and second, because they are easier to acquire by vicious actions than by virtuous ones. The doctrine that virtue is its own reward, on the other hand, lacks imaginative power: "if there be any thing in this more than the sound of the words, it is at least too abstracted to become an universal influencing principle in the world, and therefore could not be of general use" (9:244).

But Heaven and Hell are concepts even the simplest person can understand; they are, Swift says, in his sermon *On the Testimony of Conscience*, "the great Principle for Conscience to work upon" (9:156), and essential to the welfare of society. "Great Abilities, without the Fear of God," Swift continues

> are most dangerous Instruments when they are trusted with Power. The Laws of Man have thought fit, that those who are called to any Office of Trust should be bound by an Oath to the faithful Discharge of it: But, an Oath is an Appeal to God, and therefore can have no Influence except upon those who believe that he is . . . a Rewarder of those that seek him, and a Punisher of those who disobey him: And therefore, we see, the Laws themselves are forced to have recourse to Conscience in these Cases, because their Penalties cannot reach the Arts of cunning Men, who can find Ways to be guilty of a thousand Injustices without being discovered, or at least without being punished. (9:156–57)

As a public spokesman for the church, Swift's views are straightforward. He sought to secure its position from attack, to discredit the motives of those who took part in such attacks, and to demonstrate that Christianity itself, particularly the doctrine of eternal rewards and punishments, is the only sure foundation of moral life. In the satires, though, we rub up against things that don't quite square with the religious tracts and sermons, and are hard to explain away. It is worth noting, for example, that the ridicule of freethinking in *Mr. Collins's Discourse* spectacularly ignores Swift's own advice that to preach against atheism is to risk perplexing "the Minds of well-disposed People with Doubts, which probably would never have otherwise come into their Heads" (9:78). Here are just a few of the things he gives "well-disposed people" to think about in the course of parodying Collins: first, that many other cultures in the world have scriptures they believe to be divinely inspired, and that some of those scriptures offer striking parallels to the New Testament; second, that the Bible itself is so difficult that a bishop said he thought it more "a Trial of our Industry than a Repository of our Faith" (4:33); third, that learned Christians cannot even agree about such central articles of faith as original sin and the resurrection of the dead.

It is the *Tale*, of course, that provoked the most serious questions about Swift's convictions. "*The religious author of A Tale of a Tub*," Warburton wrote in 1727, "will tell you, *Religion* is but a Reservoir of Fools and Madmen."[13] Wotton called the *Tale* "one of the Prophanest Banters upon the Religion of *Jesus Christ*. . . that ever yet appeared," and argued that in attacking Jack, Swift "wounds Christianity through his Sides as much as he had done before through *Peter's*."[14] Wotton's motives for finding blasphemy in the *Tale* were hardly disinterested. All the same, he had plenty to work with. The references to Peter's "Holy Pickle," his claim to have a cow that gave milk enough to fill three thousand churches, and an old signpost "with Nails and Timber enough on it, to build sixteen large Men of War," or those to Jack's practice of wrapping pieces of the will around sore toes, burning them under his nose to relieve fits, and swallowing them to cure stomach aches, were troubling to many who were neither Catholics or dissenters. Wotton went on to say that Swift's use of the word "Providence" in parodying the doctrine of predestination by having Jack walk about with his eyes shut was "a direct Profanation of the Majesty of God."[15]

Swift was sensitive enough on this latter score to substitute "Nature" and "Fortune" for "Providence" in the fifth edition. Wotton's other charges of impiety Swift shrugs off in a way that underscores the *Tale's* elusiveness and ambiguity, as when he says in his "Apology" that no reflection on the Trinity could have been intended by having three oratorical machines because in the original manuscript there were four, and that the fourth was "*blotted out*" by those who had possession of the manuscript "*as having something in it of Satyr . . . they thought was too particular*" (*Tale*, 8). In the *Tale* itself, though, other candidates for a fourth machine are explicitly considered and rejected, the narrator saying that if no other argument for exclusion had occurred to him "it were sufficient, that the Admission of them would overthrow a Number which I was resolved to establish, whatever Argument it might cost" (*Tale*, 57). What stirs even deeper suspicion is Swift's bland assertion that readers would find nothing objectionable in the *Tale* if they simply decode the irony which runs "*through the Thread of the whole Book*" (*Tale*, 8). Since no key to the irony is supplied, the impression left is less of a work which, though difficult, will yield its meaning to careful study, than of a work rich with possibilities for concealment and disguise.

Yet the most problematical implications of the *Tale* do not really stem from the exuberant ridicule of Peter and Jack. As Voltaire recognized, the allegory itself is subversive. Swift, he wrote, "tells us in his own vindication that he has not touched Christianity itself. He pretends to have respected the father while giving a hundred strokes of the birch to the three children. People of a difficult turn of mind believed that the stick was so long it reached to the father as well."[16] Comparison of Swift's allegory of the three coats with one of its likely sources—the tale of the three rings in *The Decameron*—is instructive. Boccaccio's story stresses the father's love for his sons: he is so anxious not to disappoint any of them that he has flawless copies made of his most precious possession, a gold ring. After his death each son thinks he has received the true ring for a legacy, just as Jews, Christians, and Mohammedans consider themselves inheritors of the true faith. The story of the coats, however, stresses not the father's love for his sons, but his desire to exercise power over them after he is gone. His will contains "*full Instructions in every particular concerning the Wearing and Management*" of the coats, menaces the sons with penalties for "*every Transgression or Neglect*," and warns them that their "*future Fortunes will entirely depend*" on following his wishes to the letter. (*Tale*, 73–74). The father never explains *why* such exacting care of the coats should matter.

In the "Apology" Swift said he could not understand why anybody should think the *Tale* dangerous when other books "*are kindly received, because they are levell'd to remove those Terrors that Religion tells Men will be the Consequence of immoral Lives. Nothing like which is to be met with in this Discourse*" (*Tale*, 5). His footnotes to the story of the coats, however, tell us straight out that the father represents "*the Divine Founder*," and the will, "*The New Testament*" (*Tale*, 73). Considering that the brothers never seem to suffer any of their father's threatened penalties, it is hard to see how the allegory really supports belief in those salutary "Terrors" Swift says are so essential to religion. One can argue that going mad is penalty enough. But one can argue with equal justice that Peter and Jack would never have lost their wits in the first place had their father left them the coats to wear as they saw fit, or had they simply forgotten the will and gone about their business. Looked at this way, one hard-headed moral of the story would be that

the father has no power except the power his sons accord him
in their minds.

Did Swift privately think that eternal rewards and punishments—that *"great Principle for Conscience to work upon"*—existed
only in the mind of the believer? There are hints that he well
may have. In his *Thoughts on Religion*, Swift describes love of life
as an extraordinarily irrational impulse. Were people guided by
"the dictates of reason, every man would despise [life], and wish
it at an end" (9:263). But if there truly are terrible punishments
for vice in the hereafter, and if the world is as full of knaves as
Swift continually assures us, why would it be rational for "every
man" to wish life at an end?

Swift's last, and most moving poem to Stella, written when
she was gravely ill, acknowledges the importance of future rewards, then side-steps the doctrine to offer consolation of a more
immediate sort:

> Were future Happiness and Pain,
> A mere Contrivance of the Brain,
> As Atheists argue, to entice,
> And Fit their Proselytes for Vice . . .
> Grant this the Case, yet sure 'tis hard,
> That Virtue, stil'd its own Reward . . .
> Should acting, die, nor leave behind
> Some lasting Pleasure in the Mind,
> Which by Remembrance will assuage,
> Grief, Sickness, Poverty, and Age
> And strongly shoot a radiant Dart,
> To shine through Life's declining Part.
>   Say, *Stella*, feel you no Content,
> Reflecting on a Life well spent?
>   (ll. 19–22, 25–26, 29–36)

It is in memory of the past, not expectation of the future, that
he urges her to take comfort.[17] Here, virtue *is* its own reward. In
commiserating with Pope on the death of the poet's mother Swift
says nothing of heaven: "I must condole with you for the loss of
Mrs. Pope. . . . But I could rather rejoyce with you because if any
circumstances can make the Death of a dear parent, and friend,
a subject for joy, you have them all, she dyed in an extream old

age, without pain, under the care of the most dutifull son that I have ever known or heard of, which is a felicity not happening to one in a Million" (*Correspondence* 4:169).

Nor does Swift ever speak of the hereafter when considering his own death, though he writes Bolingbroke that his reflections on death "begin when I wake in the Morning, and end when I am going to Sleep" (*Correspondence* 3:354). To the observation of William Howells that some think "the Desire of perpetuating . . . one's own Memory . . . a convincing Argument to prove the Immortality of the Soul," Swift replies with an unambiguous marginal comment: "Damned Dunce" (5:262). Nor is he more indulgent to himself when he confides to Pope that he has often wished "that God almighty would be so easy to the weakness of mankind, as to let old friends be acquainted in another state." Were he to write a "utopia for heaven," he continues, "that would be one of my Schemes. This wildness you must allow for, because I am giddy and deaf" (*Correspondence* 3:242).

When preaching Swift argues that the "excellency" of Christianity is that it enables ordinary people to achieve a nobility they would never otherwise attain by making virtue and self-interest one: "the primitive Christians . . . were altogether the product of their principles and doctrine," whereas "the great examples of wisdom and virtue, among the Grecian sages were produced by personal merit, and not influenced by the doctrine of any particular sect" (9:249). While it is true, he says, "that there hath been all along in the world a notion of rewards and punishments in another life . . . it seems to have rather served as an entertainment to poets, or as a terror of children, than a settled principle, by which men pretended to govern any of their actions. The last celebrated words of Socrates, a little before his death, do not seem to reckon or build much upon any such opinion" (9:245).

Yet it is precisely the individual merit of men like Socrates (fellow master of irony) that most attracted Swift. He owned a signet ring with the head of Socrates and chose to use this seal when signing a codicil to his will. Of that exalted "*Sextumvirate,* to which," Gulliver says, "all the ages of the World cannot add a Seventh," only one is a Christian (11:180). Swift preached that the doctrine of future rewards and punishments was important for ordinary people, but it is by no means clear how much real efficacy he thought the doctrine had. The most immoral people Gulliver encounters on his travels, the Lilliputians, are also the only people said to believe in Divine Providence, an afterlife, and a system of rewards and punishments. Their case for making belief in God a prerequisite for public office sounds exactly like the case Swift often made: "since Kings avow themselves to be the Deputies of Providence, the *Lilliputians* think nothing can be more absurd than for a Prince to employ such Men as disown the Authority under which he acteth" (11:44). No one else Gulliver visits even seems to have a religion, except for the Brobdingnagians, who, to judge from the description of their great temple, "adorned on all Sides with Statues of Gods and Emperors," are polytheists (11:98). As for the Houyhnhnms, they regard death just the way Swift said reasonable people should, without "the least Regret" (11:258).

If the allegory of the coats raises unsettling questions about the "Divine Founder's" arbitrariness and the nature of his power, the "Digression on Madness" raises potentially unsettling questions about the origin of Christianity: "if we take a Survey of the greatest Actions that have been performed in the World," one of which is *the contriving, as well as the propagating, of New Religions*: We shall find the Authors of them all" to be mad (*Tale*, 162). No sane person would dream of "subduing Multitudes to his . . . Visions" (*Tale*, 171). Indeed, the importance of preserving established religion is so persistent a theme in Swift's later writings, that he sees even a change to a "more pure and perfect" religion as a danger to public peace. Those not content to conform to the established church

> will compose a Body always in Reserve, prepared to follow any discontented Heads, upon the plausible Pretexts of advancing *true Religion*, and opposing Error, Superstition, or Idolatry. For this Reason, *Plato* lays it down as a Maxim, that *Men ought to worship the Gods, according to the Laws of the Country*; and he introduceth *Socrates*, in his last Discourse, utterly disowning the Crime laid to his Charge, of *teaching new Divinities*, or Methods of Worship. (2:11–12)

But what of the new divinity and method of worship taught by St. Paul? Claiming certain knowledge of "things agreed on all hands impossible to be known" (*Tale*, 166) is the sure sign of madness. How are we to distinguish Jesus from other propagators of new religions? The predictable answer, and the answer Swift gives in his sermons, is that Christianity is not the vision of a single man, but the direct revelation of divine will. It is no accident, he says, that Christianity should have been introduced into the world at a time when "all kinds of learning flourished," when philosophers were unable to agree about the most fundamental questions of life, and when impartial men of intellect were forced to acknowledge the "weakness of all human wisdom." The effect of reaching such an impasse, Swift continues, was to open a passage to let in "those beams of light, which the glorious sunshine of the gospel then brought into the world, by revealing those hidden truths, which they had so long before been labouring to discover, and fixing the general happiness of mankind beyond all controversy and dispute" (9:241). If we press further and ask how we can *know* the gospel to be the expression of God's will rather than the work of men, Swift's answers are more equivocal.

A common way of dealing with this question in the period was to argue that we can know the apostles were divinely inspired, rather than deluded enthusiasts, because their claims were supported by empirical proof: miracles. In his sermon *On the Trinity*, though, Swift reverses the argument, saying not that miracles prove the authenticity of scriptural revelation, but that miracles are so contrary to the "Rules of Nature and Reason" we would never believe them unless they were affirmed by Scripture:

> There is no Miracle mentioned in Holy Writ, which, if it were strictly examined, is not . . . contrary to common Reason . . . and therefore we may with equal Justice deny the Truth of them all. For Instance: It is against the Laws of Nature, that a Human Body should be able to walk upon the Water . . . or that a dead Carcase should be raised from the Grave after three Days, when it began to be corrupted which those who understand Anatomy will pronounce to be impossible by the common Rules of Nature and Reason. Yet

these Miracles, and many others, are positively affirmed in
the Gospel; and these we must believe, or give up our Holy
Religion to Atheists and Infidels. (9:165–66)

In other words, we should believe because the consequences
of disbelief are unthinkable; because nothing is gained by ques-
tioning Scripture: "Men should consider, that raising Difficulties
concerning the Mysteries in Religion, cannot make them more
wise, learned, or virtuous; better Neighbours, or Friends, or more
serviceable to their Country; but, whatever they pretend, will
destroy their inward Peace of Mind, by perpetual Doubts and
Fears arising in their Breasts" (9:166–67). This is as close as Swift
gets to talking about the need for religion from the inside. His
most frequent concern is for the public ramifications of shared
belief: "All government is from God, who is the God of order,"
he declares in his sermon on *Doing Good*, "and therefore whoever
attempts to breed confusion or disturbance among a people,
doth his utmost to take the government of the world out of God's
hands, and to put it into the hands of the Devil . . . no crime . . .
can equal the guilt of him who doth injury to the public" (9:238).

Swift talks about God as the ultimate authority for doctrines
of imperative social importance, about crimes against social order
being crimes against God, but about individual relationship to
God he says remarkably little. Indeed, there is a great deal in
Swift's writing to suggest that he found the whole matter of
a personal relationship with God disquieting. Certainly he distrusted those who claimed to derive their authority from private
communion with the Lord. Society must be protected against
self-serving appeals to the Almighty. This is why virtually every
society has an established church; the precaution

> is founded upon the strongest Reasons; the mistaken, or af-
> fected Zeal of Obstinacy, and Enthusiasm, having produced
> such a Number of horrible destructive Events, throughout
> all *Christendom*. For, whoever begins to think the National
> Worship is wrong, in any important Article of Practice or
> Belief; will, if he be serious, naturally have a Zeal to make as
> many Proselytes as he can: And a Nation may possibly have
> an Hundred different Sects with their Leaders: every one
> of which, hath an equal Right to plead, that they must *obey*

God rather than Man, must *cry aloud and spare not*; must *lift up their Voice like a Trumpet.* (12:243–44)

Swift had no patience with qualms of conscience about conforming to established religious practice. He dismissed the Quakers' request for permission from parliament to give their "Solemn Affirmation and Declaration" before magistrates, rather than having to swear an oath, as a "foolish Scruple" expressive not of spiritual conviction but of obstinacy (7:106). Nor could he stomach the theory that kings, as God's anointed, are responsible only to God. What such theory actually meant was that kings should be allowed to do whatever they want.[18] Henry VIII, for Swift the most "infernal beast . . . who ever reigned in the world" (13:123), probably thought he was doing God's will when, under cover of reformation, he despoiled the church of its lands.

In attacking the argument that since Heaven is governed by an absolute monarch, earthly nations should be too, Swift remarks that "no Reason can possibly be assigned, why it is best for the World that God Almighty hath such a Power, which doth not directly prove that no Mortal Man should ever have the like" (2:17).[19] Unstated, but implicit here, is that God does not exercise the kind of direct power over individual lives kings do. His controlling hand may be seen in the cosmos at large. "The Motions of the Sun and Moon; in short, the whole System of the Universe," Swift writes, "are in the utmost Degree of Regularity and Perfection . . . as far as Philosophers have been able to discover and observe." But sublunary things God has left to themselves, in "a State of Imperfection, on purpose to stir up human Industry; without which Life would stagnate, or indeed, could not subsist at all" (4:245).

What comes across most strongly in Swift's references to God is a sense of His remoteness and unknowability. "Miserable mortals!" he noted privately, "can we contribute to the *honour and Glory of God?* I wish that expression were struck out of our Prayer-books" (9:263). The concept of divine authority might be necessary to enforce morality, but in practice, Swift liked to observe, you could offend God "with more Security than the Memory of a dead Prince" (9:151).[20] His ode to Sancroft opens with an affirmation of the divine—"Truth is eternal." But the second stanza almost qualifies it out of existence: "where is ev'n thy Image on our earth?/ . . . God himself has said, He shall not find it here" (ll. 1, 17, 20). Those who pretend to the most certain knowledge of the Divine Will in fact know nothing of God:

> "You who in different Sects have shamm'd,
> And come to see each other damn'd;
> (So some Folks told you, but they knew
> No more of Jove's Designs than you) . . ."
> ("The Day of Judgement," ll. 13–16)

As for people's claims to have had direct experience of spiritual forces—good or evil—Swift dismisses them as the intoxications of pride: "I laugh aloud," he writes in *The Mechanical Operation of the Spirit*,

> to see these Reasoners . . . engaged in wise Dispute . . . whether they are in the Verge of God or the Devil, seriously debating, whether such and such Influences come into Mens Minds, from above or below, or whether certain Passions and Affections are guided by the Evil Spirit or the Good. . . . Thus do Men establish a Fellowship of *Christ* with *Belial*, and such is the Analogy between *cloven Tongues*, and *cloven Feet*. . . . it is a Sketch of Human Vanity, for every Individual, to imagine the whole Universe is interess'd in his meanest Concern. Who, that sees a little paultry Mortal, droning, and dreaming, and drivelling to a Multitude, can think it agreeable to common good Sense, that either Heaven or Hell should be put to the Trouble of Influence or Inspection upon what he is about. (*Tale*, 275–76)[21]

When St. Paul defined faith as "*the Evidence of Things not seen*," Swift says, he meant simply "that Faith is a Virtue by which any Thing commanded us by God to believe, appears evident and certain to us, although we do not see, nor can conceive it" (9:164). It is fanatics who think they can conceive the inconceivable, see "things Invisible,"[22] and who, by projecting their hopes and fears upon the largest possible canvas, bring Christ and Belial into fellowship.

Swift had none of Johnson's interest in sightings of ghosts as possible evidence of life beyond the grave: "Spirits are never seen by more than one Person at a Time: That is to say, it seldom happens that above one Person in a Company is possest with any high Degree of Spleen or Melancholy" (1:242). Nor was he tempted to believe that dreams might be evidence of supernatural communication:

> Those Dreams that on the silent Night intrude,
> And with false flitting Shades our Minds delude,
> *Jove* never sends us downward from the Skies,
> Nor can they from infernal Mansions rise
> But all are meer Productions of the Brain. . . .
>   ("On Dreams," ll. 1–5)

Dreams tell us nothing of otherworldly realms, however much they may reveal about the dreamer himself. In the disgruntled journal Swift kept at Holyhead while waiting for the weather to clear so he could get a ship to Ireland, he records a strange dream of his own:

> Last night I dreamt that Ld Bolingbroke and Mr Pope were at my Cathedrall in the Gallery, and that my Ld was to preach. I could not find my Surplice, the Church Servants were all out of the way; the Doors were shut. I sent to my Ld to come into my Stall for more conveniency to get into the Pulpit. The Stall was all broken; the[y] sd the Collegians had done it. I squeezed among the Rabble, saw my Ld in the Pulpit. I thought his prayer was good, but I forget it. In his Sermon, I did not like his quoting Mr. Wycherly by name, and his Plays. (5:205–6)[23]

Looked at in one way, this is a nightmare of impropriety, violation and loss. Swift's pulpit is usurped by a deist who quotes Wycherly. He loses his surplice; the Church servants vanish just when he needs them; undergraduates from his old college advertise their disrespect by wrecking his stall, leaving him to hear the offensive sermon "squeezed among the Rabble."

But we should not forget that while Swift is the authority mocked in this dream, he is also the one who conjures up the mockery. In dreams, Addison observes, the soul "converses with numberless Beings of her own Creation . . . is transported into ten thousand Scenes of her own raising . . . is herself the Theatre, the Actors, and the Beholder."[24] Johnson once dreamt that someone got the better of him in an argument. He brooded about the defeat till it dawned on him that the dream was, after all, *his* dream. "I should have seen," he told Bennet Langton, "that the wit of this supposed antagonist, by whose superiority I felt myself depressed, was as much furnished by me, as that which I thought I had been uttering in my own character."[25] By the same token we might say that Swift is not only the insulted dean, he is also those agencies of anarchy and irreverence: Bolingbroke, the neglectful servants, the rowdy students.

Swift made a point of scrupulous public behavior and militant service to the church. In the dream, though, he goes on holiday, makes mischief in the pulpit, "loses" his surplice and refuses to look for it, creates havoc in the stalls,[26] then squeezes in among the anonymous rabble where he is safe from detection. This final touch is a wonderfully literalized metaphor for the way Swift's irony often dissociates him from unseemly assertions. When Swift says that he relishes his position as *"freshest Modern"* because it gives him "a Despotick Power" over earlier authors (*Tale*, 330), or that life without delusion would be insipid (*Tale*, 351), or that no rational person would advocate restoring Christianity in the form practiced by the apostles (2:27), or that seven months would be plenty of time for people to correct their vices and follies were they "capable of the least Disposition to Virtue or Wisdom" (11:xxxv), he does so in a way that lets him hide behind others, much as he does in this dream of cathedral pranks. It is the crazed narrator of the *Tale*, the temporizing churchman of the *Argument*, and the misanthropic Gulliver who say these things, not he. But it is Swift who thinks them up.

This dream of cathedral misdeeds epitomizes the problem of assessing Swift's private religious convictions. One of the few truly personal religious rituals we know Swift observed was to read the third chapter of Job every year on his birthday. That he should read the third chapter, rather than the explanatory prologue or the celebratory epilogue, is telling. For it is in the third chapter that Job curses the day he was born and asks "Why is light given to a man whose way is hid,/ And whom God hath hedged in?"[27]

In a sermon, Swift might hold up Abraham as exemplifying the power of faith, extol his willingness to believe "that God would raise from him a great Nation, at the very same time that he was commanded to sacrifice his only Son, and despaired of any other Issue" (9:163). But Job is a figure to touch his heart. More even than the falsely accused Naboth, whom Swift memorialized in Naboth's Vineyard—that three-acre plot he enclosed for his horses—Job epitomized the kind of undeserved suffering with which Swift so readily identified. His letters and private writings are filled with complaints of unearned misfortune—from the great fish that dropped off his line when he was a little boy to the preferment he never received in England. The weaknesses he confesses to friends are less moral failures than failures of power visited on him by sickness or age: loss of memory, of stamina, of invention, of the ability to do serious work. It is impossible to imagine Swift standing four hours in the rain, like Johnson, to atone for some long-ago act of thoughtlessness. It is easy to imagine him asking Job's question—"Wherefore do the wicked live,/ Become old, yea, wax mighty in power?"—and hearing in return something like the voice of inscrutable power that comes out of the whirlwind: "Where wast thou when I laid the foundations of the earth?" "Presume not God to scan," Pope admonishes readers in the *Essay on Man*, with an assurance that suggests he pretty much knows what God had in mind for the world:

> Why has not Man a microscopic eye?
> For this plain reason, Man is not a Fly.[28]

The God of Swift's *Day of Judgment*, like the God of Job, is aloof, implacable, something of a trickster.

Of all the stories that bear on Swift's religious outlook, I think the most mysterious and haunting is Deane Swift's account of a Sunday visit to Swift two years after he had been declared of unsound mind. Swift was sitting in a chair, and when he reached for a knife that lay on the table, his housekeeper moved it away. Deane Swift recalls that "he shrugged his shoulders, and, rocking himself, said *I am what I am, I am what I am*: and, about six minutes afterwards, repeated the same words two or three times over" (*Correspondence* 5:214).[29] The words may mean nothing. They may mean only that despite loss of powers Swift still knows who and what he is—more than can be said of Gulliver, who studies himself in a mirror yet continues to think himself what he is not: a Houyhnhnm. But inasmuch as the words are St. Paul's, whom Swift cited more perhaps than any other figure in the Old or New Testament, they invite a larger reading. Paul has been speaking of the promise of eternal life offered all people through Christ's Resurrection, and of his own place among those who witnessed it:

> And last of all he was seen of me also, as one born out of due time. For I am the least of the apostles, that am not meet to be called an apostle, because I persecuted the church of God. But by the grace of God I am what I am: and his grace which was bestowed upon me was not in vain; but I laboured more abundantly than they all . . . (1 Corinthians 15:8–11)

It is tempting to see flitting across Swift's mind some deeply personal and darkly ironic sense of kinship with Paul. Like Paul, he had been "born out of due time." Like Paul he had not come early or easily to the Church. Like Paul, his writings had been misunderstood: "I have often been offended to find St. Paul's allegories, and other figures of Grecian eloquence, converted by divines into articles of faith" (9:262). And he, too, had tried to make up for his lateness by laboring "more abundantly than they all," fighting, as he told Lady Worsley, "with Beasts like St. Paul, not at Ephesus, but in Ireland" (*Correspondence* 4:79). This labor might well have seemed abundant to Swift because he appears to have performed it without Paul's experience of personal revelation, without Abraham's faith, which embraced impossibility and contradiction, and without clear expectation of that personal reward he assured his parishioners was the very basis of Christianity.

NOTES

An earlier, shorter version of this essay appeared in *Swift Studies* 8 (1993) as *The Road to St. Patrick's: Swift and the Problem of Belief.*

1. *The Prose Works of Jonathan Swift*, ed. Herbert Davis, 14 vols. (Oxford: Basil Blackwell, 1939–68), 9:264. Subsequent parenthetical references are to this edition.

2. Irvin Ehrenpreis, *Swift: The Man, His Works, and the Age*, 3 vols. (Cambridge, Mass: Harvard University Press, 1962–83), 3:633.

3. Jonathan Smedley, *Gulliveriana: or a Fourth Volume of Miscellanies* (London, 1728), 78. Similar charges are voiced in "A Panegyric on Dean Swift" (ll. 75–96), which Swift may actually have written himself.

4. *Complete Letters of Lady Mary Wortley Montagu*, ed. Robert Halsband, 3 vols. (Oxford: Clarendon Press, 1965–67), 3:57.

5. "The Author upon Himself" ll. 1–6. All passages of Swift's poetry are quoted from *Poetical Works*, ed. Herbert Davis (London: Oxford University Press, 1967). Subsequent line references appear in the text.

6. John Earl of Orrery, *Remarks on the Life and Writings of Dr. Jonathan Swift* (London, 1772), 193.

7. Letitia Pilkington, *Memoirs*, ed. Iris Barry (London: Routledge, 1928), 50.

8. *Journal to Stella*, ed. Harold Williams, 2 vols (Oxford: Clarendon Press, 1974), 1:126. Cited hereafter as *JS*.

9. Swift speaks of the importance of servants understanding the "Principles of Religion" in his sermon on the *Causes of the Wretched Condition of Ireland* (9:205). In *Thoughts on Various Subjects*, he notes that "Positiveness is a good Quality for Preachers and Orators; because whoever would obtrude his Thoughts and Reasons upon a multitude, will convince others the more, as he appears convinced himself" (1:241). He speaks most memorably about the persuasive power of conviction in the "Digression on Madness": when one has made a "Proselyte" of oneself, it is not hard to bring over others.

10. *The Correspondence of Jonathan Swift*, ed. Harold Williams, 2nd ed., 5 vols (Oxford: Clarendon Press 1963–65), 4:383 and 171. Cited hereafter as *Correspondence*. Swift told Mrs. Pilkington he was "an absolute monarch in the *Liberties*, and King of the Mob" (Pilkington, *Memoirs*, 62). Orrery describes Swift as sitting in the chapter house "like JUPITER in the Synod of the Gods" (*Remarks*, 51).

11. *Tale of a Tub, To which is added The Battle of the Books and the Mechanical Operation of the Spirit*, ed. A. C. Guthkelch and D. Nichol Smith, 2nd ed. (Oxford: Clarendon Press, 1958), 185. Cited hereafter as *Tale*.

12. Swift makes this point again in his sermon *On the Trinity:* "Men of wicked Lives would be very glad there were no Truth to Christianity at all . . . If they can pick out any one single Article in the Christian Religion which appears not agreeable to their own corrupted Reason, or to the Arguments of those bad People, who follow the Trade of seducing others, they presently conclude, that the Truth of the whole Gospel must sink along with that one Article" (9:159).

13. Warburton's remarks on the *Tale* in *A Critical and Philosophic Enquiry into the Causes of Prodigies and Miracles, as related by Histories*

(1727) are reprinted in *Swift: The Critical Heritage*, ed. Kathleen Williams (New York: Barnes & Noble, 1970), 71.

14. *Tale*, 324, 323.

15. *Tale*, 324.

16. Letter 22 (1734), *Melanges*, in *Swift: The Critical Heritage*, 74.

17. In the three moving prayers Swift wrote for Stella during this last illness he mentions the hereafter only in the first, and then briefly: "Accept the good Deeds she hath done, in such a Manner, that at whatever Time Thou shalt please to call her, she may be received into Everlasting Habitations" (9:253). David Nokes calls attention to the odd note of qualification in Swift's account of his mother's death: "If the way to heaven be through piety, truth, justice and charity, she is there." The "if," he observes, "hints at those dark shadows of doubt that lurk beneath all Swift's attempts at assertions of faith." See *Jonathan Swift, A Hypocrite Reversed* (London and New York: Oxford University Press, 1985), 114.

18. "The Folly of this Reasoning will best appear," Swift says, "by applying it in a parallel Case: Should any Man argue, that a Physician is supposed to understand his own Art best; that the Law protects and encourages his Profession: And therefore, although he should manifestly prescribe *Poison* to all his Patients, whereof they must immediately die; he cannot be justly punished, but is answerable only to God" (2:19).

19. "No imaginable things/ Can differ more than *GOD* and *KINGS*," Swift wrote in "A Libel on Doctor Delany" (ll. 195–96).

20. Swift makes the same point in the *Argument against Abolishing Christianity*: "Great Wits love to be free with the highest Objects; and if they cannot be allowed a *God* to revile or renounce; they will *speak Evil of Dignities*, abuse the Government, and reflect upon the Ministry; which I am sure, few will deny to be of much more pernicious Consequence; according to the Saying of *Tiberius; Deorum offensa Diis curae*" (2:29).

21. There is no very obvious irony to dissociate Swift from the narrator in this passage, which gave great offense. In the 5th edition he sought to make the language less objectionable by changing "such is the Analogy between" to "such is the Analogy they make between."

22. "Vision is the Art of seeing Things Invisible" (4:252).

23. I have discussed this dream to somewhat different ends in "Night Thoughts in Swift," *Sewanee Review* 98 (1990), 646–63, and in "'Mere Productions of the Brain': Interpreting Dreams in Swift," *Literature and Medicine during the Eighteenth Century*, ed. Roy Porter and Marie Roberts (London: Routledge, 1993), 118–35.

24. *The Spectator*, ed. Donald F. Bond, 5 vols. (Oxford: Clarendon Press, 1965), 4:229.

25. Langton passed this story along to Boswell, who wrote it up. See *The Life of Johnson*, ed. R. W. Chapman (London: Oxford University Press, 1953), 1069.

26. Ehrenpreis notes that as an undergraduate Swift was cited for an unusually large number of disciplinary violations, once for starting "tumults" in the college and insulting the junior dean, whose pardon he was later forced to beg on bended knee *(Swift: The Man, His Works, and the Age*, 1:69).

27. He wrote Mrs. Whiteway three days before his seventy-first birthday: "I hope at least things will be better on *Thursday*, else I shall be full of the spleen, because it is a day you seem to regard, although I detest it, and I read the third chapter of *Job* that morning" (5:128).

28. *An Essay on Man*, ed. Maynard Mack, vol. 3,i of *The Poems of Alexander Pope* (New Haven: Yale University Press, 1950), 38–39 (1:ll. 193–94).

29. Though a series of small strokes had left Swift largely unable to speak, the degree to which his mind was affected is by no means clear. He could not speak coherently, but as Ehrenpreis has said, the final indignity was to have people think "him imbecilic at just the moment when intelligence drove him to reach them with words" (3:918).

Swift and Romance

MARGARET ANNE DOODY

My topic may seem perverse. After all, in *Gulliver's Travels*, as we remember, the palace at Lilliput is set on fire "by the Carelessness of a Maid of Honour, who fell asleep while she was reading a Romance."[1] We may take this, if we will, as a symptom of Swift's own distrust of novelistic narrative of all kinds; the romance here is associated not only with female waste of time but also with incendiarism.[2] Moreover, this particular romance evidently committed the crowning sin of being boring. It is certainly but a poor compliment to the romance in question, which is not named. Yet perhaps it was too interesting, so the Maid sat up past her bedtime, trying to have some private time. Richardson improves upon Swift's hint in *Clarissa*, where Lovelace, in his elaborately plotted arrangement of the "fire" at Mrs. Sinclair's weaves into his tale the impressively detailed pseudo-fact that the accident was owing "to the carelessness of Mrs. Sinclair's cook-maid, who, having sat up to read the simple *History of Dorastus and Faunia* when she should have been in bed, had set fire to an old pair of callico window-curtains" (4:365).[3] Yet within both of these eighteenth-century works of fiction, the reference to "Romance" may serve not as a means of disposing of an unwanted form but rather as a (comic) admission of the presence of Romance within this romance, and the presence of awkward readers and the insistent absorption of the act of reading—an absorption that makes people careless.

My own project here must inevitably seem perverse, for I want to ignore some or most of the elements in *Gulliver's Travels* which we usually focus upon—and even to ignore temporarily its primary nature as a satire and the questions regarding the historical author's historically satiric intentions. I am going to look at what is often called "background." But we are getting less satisfied with that term. Individual works don't rise like clear blue vases against a background of wallpaper—the "background" proves to be an aspect of the fabric of a work. I believe that all novels are interconnected—at least, I mean in the Western tradition, a tradition which includes influences from Asia and Africa. All novels are connected, and every Western novel is related—in some way, at more or less distance—to every other. Swift's *Gulliver's Travels* is related to the context of Western fiction which is far larger than the developing eighteenth-century English novel. In that full context it looks a little less singular, for the major trends of Western fiction have never been entirely realistic. It is a satiric romance deriving from a host of romances. Let us not forget that the word "Novel" was not the dominant word for the longer prose fiction, and that the word "Romance" could still be used in a positive sense, at least in the first part of the century. In 1715 an English translator of Huet hopes that England will be able to produce romances.[4] Western literature included, as Huet shows, the whole tradition of prose fiction in the West from antiquity. Prose fiction in Greek and Latin had enjoyed a terrific boom in the Renaissance. Works by Heliodorus, Achilles Tatius, Longus, and others were translated and retranslated, as well as the almost omnipresent Latin novel *Asinus Aureus* or *Metamorphoses* by Apuleius. Boccaccio's early novel *Filocolo* shows the influence of Greek romance, well before the age of print, but once the age of print arrived the older fictions as well as new ones had an immensely expanded readership. If you liked reading novels—however much you kept this pastime to appropriately infrequent idle moments—in the seventeenth or eighteenth century, the literature you read included a number of highly popular works, like Heliodorus' *Aithiopika*, which have been occluded in the last two centuries. The anonymous editor of *The Adventures of Theagenes and Chariclia, A Romance* (2 vols., 1717), reproducing yet another English edition of this popular story, says "this book may be styled the *Mother Romance* of the World."[5] The association of Romance with the feminine indicates that prose fiction is considered suspiciously "feminine" as novelists have found, no matter how we change the name of the genre. Novels of all kinds were going to be treated more and more negatively at the mid-eighteenth century. The seventeenth century (in which Swift was born) was in many ways the heyday of free writing of fiction, not yet policed by copious reviews and culturally heightened self-consciousness.

The simplest, most direct relation of Swift's *Gulliver's Travels* to older prose fiction is to be found in its relation to Lucian. Marjorie Hope Nicolson's book, still indispensable and never superseded, on Voyages to the Moon in the seventeenth century, traces the history of certain elements of science fiction and science fantasy, a history in which Lucian figures largely as a point of origin and a useful model for many writers.[6] Swift's book is undoubtedly closely related to this strain of science-fantasy and belongs in some respects in the category "science-fiction." In saying as much I am merely following the useful work of W. A. Eddy in *Gulliver's Travels: A Critical Study* (Princeton, 1923). Eddy was the first to study the sources of *Gulliver's Travels* and in some ways still the best; his suggestions have still not been followed up, as we went chasing other hares. I am merely repeating Eddy when I insist on the very strong relation of Lucian to Swift's satire, but it may be worth repeating, as Lucian is an author often left out of account in the nineteenth and twentieth centuries.

In the work known for centuries in Europe as *Vera Historia* (*A True History*), Lucian writes a satiric and parodic travel narrative, pointing out at the outset that his is the only true narrative, for he is the only such writer who professes that he is lying, whereas other writers expect us to swallow their fables for truth. In his impish story, Lucian has his hero (the "I") carried away to other lands, including the moon, which appears to his airborne ship as "a large land mass like an island in the sky"[7]—very like the Flying Island of Laputa, in short. Once he is there, the hero and his friends become caught up in an ongoing war and are pressed into service by Endymion, king of the moon people. " 'Once I win this war I'm involved in against the people living on the sun,' he added, 'you can stay here with me and live happily ever after' " (18). The war does not go too well for the Moon; the Sun people capture the humans and carry them off, "our hands tied behind our backs with a strip of cobweb" (22). Peace is eventually made, and the humans are asked to remain: "Endymion asked us to stay on and take part in founding the colony, promising to give me his own son in marriage (there are no women on the moon)" (23). Lucian invents an entire alternative biology, something which Swift refrains from doing; the only touch of it is in the description of the wry-necked Laputans. In the Lucianic story of arriving in a strange country and taking part in a current (and ridiculous) war, however, we can recognize the outline of Gulliver's life in Lilliput. But I want to deal with other aspects than the satiric—with the "romantic" or "novelistic" elements in *Gulliver's Travels*. This gives me an interest in a text attributed to Lucian (in Swift's time as earlier) though not nowadays allotted to him—the Greek novel *The Ass*. *The Ass* is a transformation story, closely related to Apuleius's story; for centuries it has been suggested either that Pseudo-Lucian was a source for Apuleius, or (more likely) Apuleius and the author of *Onos* were drawing on a common source.

Both of these novels deal with the helpless (male) self transformed. And here is the first point where I wish to engage in a comparison of Swift's romance with other and earlier romances. *The Ass, The Golden Ass, Gulliver's Travels*—all three deal in very physical terms with the changes and violence wrought upon a shrinking self which has to try to cope with an entirely new set of circumstances. The hero (named *Lucius* in Pseudo-Lucian and in Apuleius) is bewildered by the paradoxical condition of feeling the same—feeling an identity with his "normal" human self— while being viewed as entirely different, and being treated (mistreated) as is appropriate to another condition. Always defined against his own self-image, the man-as-ass is perpetually in a condition of inordinate psychic strain. In *Gulliver's Travels*, Swift picks up that kind of psychic stress, although he plays with variations upon the cause. It is not the hero who is transformed, but the worlds he is in—places which, like Lucian's satiric alternative societies, exhibit, though less outrageously, alternative biologies which make Gulliver's own biological self "abnormal." In all of these works the physical facts of biological existence are insisted upon—including the excremental activity.

At illi . . . quandam destinatum rursum caedendo confecissent profecto, nisi dolore plagarum alvus artata, crudisque illis oleribus abundans et lubrico fluxu saucia, fimo fistulatim

excusso, quosdam extremi liquoris aspergine, alios putore
nidoris faetidi a meis iam quassis scapulis abegisset.

[But the men . . . began to beat me again and would have
killed me if my belly, compressed with the pain of the blows
and full of an abundance of raw vegetables and weakened by
a slimy flux, had not thrown out excrement like water from a
pipe, forcing them away from my shattered back, some with
the spray of the liquid, others by the putrid stink.] (1:Bk. X,
188)[8]

Much more decorously, it is true, Gulliver forces the Lilliputians
away from him, first when he wishes to make water and later
too one imagines when he disburthens himself. One pities the
unfortunate two servants who must work with wheelbarrows to
remove this daily product.

The violence of the ass's pain is picked up again in the
description of the suffering dog in Book III of *Gulliver's Travels*.
The dog is blown up by the operation of the bellows by the
brutal physician—an operation which calls to mind Cervantes'
"Prologo" of Part II of *Don Ouixote* with its odd anecdote. In
Seville, according to Cervantes, there once was a man who was
in the habit of seizing any stray dog, thrusting a straw into its
fundament and blowing it up as round as a ball. This man would
then say to bystanders "and there always were many," " 'Perhaps
now your worships think that it is little labor to blow up a dog?' "[9]
In Swift's scene we see that a good deal of work goes into blowing
up a dog (*hinchar un perro*) and that the animal suffers in the
infliction of inflation, like Lucius being beaten: "the Animal was
ready to burst, and made so violent a Discharge, as was very
offensive to me and my Companions" (155). The noxiousness of
its discharge does not save this animal as it once saved Apuleius'
Lucius, "The Dog died on the Spot. . . ."

Lucius the ass is always greedy (he was saved because of
having eaten too many vegetables). Later he is able to indulge
his taste for large quantities of food cooked for human beings
when he serves the slaves of a pastry-cook and chef:

In the evenings after luxurious dinners . . . my masters used
to bring back to their little lodging numerous leftovers:

one brought pork, pullets, fish and generous remnants of every kind of meat; the other, breads, crisp biscuits, fritters, hook-shaped pastries, small biscuits and many other honeyed tidbits. When they had locked up and gone to the baths for refreshment, I would stuff myself full with these divine dainties. (2: Bk. X, 240)

Once he is discovered, the slaves and their masters realize there is money to be made out of Lucius' prowess in eating, especially once the master has tested this ass by offering him a feast of spicy food and good wine. "And I, although I was beautifully stuffed, wishing to be agreeable and win his commendation, hungrily fell to on the delicacies exhibited." He proves that he is fit to be instructed, tamed, and shown as a spectacle. "I had made my master famous with my wonderful arts. . . . 'Here' [people] said, 'is the man who possesses as friend and dinner-companion an ass—a wrestling ass, a dancing ass, an ass who understands human voices and can express his own meaning by nods' " (2: Bk. X, 249).

Swift's Gulliver has many of the same propensities—including the ability to save himself (temporarily at least) from extinction or banishment by becoming a spectacle and show. In Lilliput he shows off his eating prowess—very like the Golden Ass:

One day his imperial Majesty being informed of my Way of living, desired that himself, and his Royal Consort, with the young Princes of the Blood of both Sexes, might have the Happiness . . . of dining with me. They came accordingly. . . . *Flimnap* the Lord High Treasurer attended there likewise, with his white Staff; and I observed he often looked on me with a sour Countenance, which I would not seem to regard, but eat more than usual, in Honour to my dear Country, as well as to fill the Court with Admiration. (45)

It is an asinine thing to do, to eat more than usual. Once the pleasure in the wonder at the show has abated, the expense will become more and more noticeable.

Gulliver's odd mixture of pride and greed, like that seen in Lucius, exhibits and emblematizes his asininity. The ass in an older mythology, as Jack Winkler remarks in his commentary on Apuleius, is an emblem or symbol of Seth/Typhon, the enemy of Isis. In *The Golden Ass,* Lucius-as-ass has set himself in opposition to Isis and can be saved only by her.[10] Gulliver, I'd like to suggest—though this speculation isn't necessary to my main argument—likewise sets himself up against the Goddess (comically), illustrated in his urination on the Queen's palace. The Goddess figure reappears in the figure of Glumdalclitch (who treats him like a baby in Book II) in a land which fully illustrates the power of Ceres. In Book IV Gulliver rejects the power of Aphrodite in his rejection of the woman who makes advances to him—yet at the same time, he is comically yoked within a parody of marriage. The "Sorrel Nag" is Gulliver's companion and mate in Houyhnhnmland. Fortuna (Fortune) we may remember in Apuleius' story turns Lucius the ass into the partner of the white horse that he himself owns (or owned):

> Sed quid ego pluribus de Fortunae scaevitate conqueror, quam nec istud puduit me cum meo famulo meoque vectore illo equo factum conservum atque coniugem?

> [But what can I say more in complaint against the savagery of Fortune, than that she was not even ashamed of making me the fellow-slave and yoke-mate of my own servant and carrier, my own horse?] (2: Bk. VII, 8)

Gulliver boasts that the "Sorrel Nag" is "my Fellow-Servant (for so at this Distance I may presume to call him)" (245), when that horse is ordered by Gulliver's master to follow the talking Yahoo's "instructions." Gulliver asked for this particular helper: "I knew he had a Tenderness for me," Gulliver adds (246). This English traveler is ridiculously proud of what causes shame to Apuleius' hero. Gulliver is a horse's "Fellow-Servant"—an almost literal translation of "*conservum.*" As several commentators have noted, Apuleius' word "*coniugem*" normally means "spouse" or "marriage partner," and Lucius is involved in a parodic marriage with his own (male) white horse. In Houyhnhnmland, of course, white is an inferior color, and Gulliver is partnered with a *sorrel* horse. In Gulliver's eyes, at least, this partnership exists—he calls himself a "Fellow Servant" with the Nag because that moves him up in the world. But in the Houyhnhnm's eyes, he cannot be even a servant, or a slave—he is classed with the beasts, the Yahoos. So is Lucius also, like Gulliver—Lucius reclassifies himself and the horse in terms of human beings: *famulus, servus.* As a Yahoo, Gulliver is inferior *even* to the asses. The ass-theme emerges directly in *Gulliver's Travels* towards the end of Book IV, when the Houyhnhnms discuss the matter at their assembly, and decide

> That, the Inhabitants taking a Fancy to use the Service of the *Yahoos,* had very imprudently neglected to cultivate the Breed of *Asses,* which were a comely Animal, easily kept, more tame and orderly, without any offensive Smell, strong enough for Labour, although they yield to the other in Agility of Body; and if their Braying be no agreeable Sound, it is far preferable to the horrible Howlings of the *Yahoos.* (237)

The disagreeable sound of the ass's bray was not only proverbial, but enshrined in religious custom, according, for instance, to Plutarch, who tells us "The people of Busiris and Lykopolis do not use trumpets at all because they make a noise like an ass; and they believe the ass to be in general not a pure but a daemonic beast. . . . In the sacrifice to Helios they instruct those who venerate the god not to wear golden objects . . . nor to give food to an ass."[11] We may note that the last taboo is broken by the cook and baker and their master in Apuleius and, metaphorically, by all who give food to Gulliver—as well as literally by Tristram Shandy when he gives the ass a macaroon.[12] Gulliver shouts and hollers and brays—see the account of his rescue from the rocky island at the beginning of Book III, when he sees the flying island: "I called and shouted with the utmost Strength of my Voice" (131). The noises Gulliver makes confirm his Houyhnhnm acquaintance in the opinion that he is a Yahoo, inferior even to an ass in all respects including voice. If Lucius is embarrassed by being able to make only assy noises, Gulliver cannot even rise to that.

Apuleius' novel is only one version of a story perpetually told in novels of all kinds—the story of the hapless self injured, mutilated, transformed, displaced. One of the most common devices used in ancient and early modern fiction to image change and to effect it at the plot level is the shipwreck. Defoe's *Robinson Crusoe,* to which *Gulliver's Travels* is a direct response, is only one strong example of the use of a well-known device or trope of fiction—and *Robinson Crusoe* should itself be seen against the rich background of the fiction of "romance"—or of the story of the Novel of which it is a part. The ancient novelists use the shipwreck with a considerable degree of sophistication and variety. Heliodorus in his *Aithiopika* has caused his characters to encounter the vision of an annoyed Odysseus, condemning them to some accident and delay in requital for the lack of honor they have paid to him—a comic emblem of the Novel's usurping disrespect of the Epic. Achilles Tatius, through incremental repetition of accidents at sea and ghastly events on shipboard, plays with the shipwreck theme, as does Boccaccio in his fourteenth-century adaptation of the Greek novel motifs. The hero of his *Filocolo*, shipwrecked near Parthenope, (Napoli) complains to the gods, asking why they are persecuting him, "I am not Aeneas!"[13] In the Preface to *Ibrahim, ou L'illustre Bassa*, Madeleine de Scudéry (or her brother Georges) comments upon the frequent use of shipwrecks in fiction:

> As for me, I hold, that the more natural adventures are, the more satisfaction they give; and the ordinary Course of the Sun seemes more mervailous to me, than the strange and deadly rayes of Comets; for which reason it is also that I have not caused so many Shipwracks, as there are in some antient Romanzes . . . one might think that *Aeolus* hath given them the Winds inclosed in a bagg, as he gave them to *Vlysses*, soe patly doe they unchain them; they make tempests and shipwrack when they please, they raise them in the Pacifique Sea, they find rocks and shelves where the most expert Pilots have never observed any. . . . Howbeit I pretend not hereby to banish Shipwracks from *Romanzes*, I approve of them in the workes of others, and make use of them in mine; I know likewise that the Sea is the Scene most proper to make great changes in, and that some have named it the Theater of inconstancie. . . .[14]

Swift of course does raise storms (and other accidents) in the literal Pacific Sea (see the beginning of Book II). His well-thought-out pattern of sea-incidents is based on true accounts like that of Dampier, as others have noted, but it also goes back to the novel tradition that stretches from antiquity. As Scudéry admits, one has to approve of shipwrecks in fiction; "the Sea is the Scene most proper to make great changes in." One catches here something of the late Renaissance sophistication about the emblems and tropes of fiction, and their sense of the depth of metaphorical meaning in fictional incident—a sense that Swift inherited and which enabled him to write fiction (and nonrealistic fiction, "romance," at that).

Both Defoe and Swift could draw on a great body of fiction dealing with transformed states, interracial and intercultural encounters, and sea-changes. Shipwrecked or marooned characters pop up in the pages of fiction. Of course, they still continue to do so—think of George Eliot's *Daniel Deronda* (1876) or Fay Weldon's *The Hearts and Lives of Men* (1987). In Cervantes' last novel, *Persiles y Sigismunda*, there are many surprising characters who have suffered shipwrecks along with other complex accidents. "Whether thou chuse Cervantes' serious air" is a line which can certainly bear reference to *Persiles* as well as to *Don Quixote.*[15] Early in Cervantes' last novel—which was, I believe, a major influence on both Defoe and Swift—we encounter Antonio, a man who has suffered misfortunes. A Spaniard, he was on an English ship leaving Lisbon for England. On the voyage he got into a quarrel with an English sailor and slapped him in the face. This led to a riot—one of the English gentlemen saved Antonio from being killed, but he was cast adrift in the ship's boat, a little dinghy, with some salt fat and hardtack and two barrels of water. He drifts and rows, is nearly swamped by water, arrives on a rocky shore of a wolf-haunted island and has to flee. Eventually he is tossed upon a wild shore, and laments it, seeing here only the theater of his misfortunes. He sees no people, only mountain goats and small animals. Antonio is soon, however, comforted by the appearance of "a young Barbarian maide, about fifteene yeares of age."[16] He first sees her on the beach, gathering shellfish from the rocks. He takes her in his arms, takes her to his cave and kisses her (but does not rape her). She responds with interest and curiosity, and feeds him with bread not made from wheat; next day she comes to him with more supplies.

Antonio, referred to perpetually as "Spanish barbarian" finds in his "Barbarian maide" Ricla a perfect and providential helpmate. The two marry. His response to her is very visibly the opposite of the response of the terrified Gulliver to the Houyhnhnm girl in Book IV of *Gulliver's Travels.* (Ricla also represents what is so notably missing on Crusoe's island, a lack which Crusoe himself doesn't seem to notice.) The sensations and experiences of Antonio during his marooning-*cum*-shipwreck are very similar to those of Gulliver at the beginning of Book III and to his confused and chaotic travels after leaving Houyhnhnmland, before he is picked up by the Portuguese crew captained by Pedro de Mendez. Some symmetry of reference seems to be involved here. Cervantes' barbarian Antonio is an inhabitant of the Iberian peninsula who embarks *in* Lisbon on an English ship going to England—he is cast adrift by the *English*. In Swift's story (if we keep Cervantes' story in mind) the Portuguese crew are returning good for evil; this crew bound *for* Lisbon rescues an Englishman who is, in their eyes, marooned and adrift—as indeed Gulliver certainly was set adrift by an English crew before he settled among the Houyhnhnms as a Yahoo. In his ill-humor with the crew, Gulliver resembles the young Spanish barbarian who hit a foreign sailor—but Gulliver of course would not wish to touch a human.

In Cervantes' novel we encounter another victim of the sea, another actor in that "Theatre of inconstancie" in Rutilio, the former dancing master of Siena. After some vicissitudes, including his being condemned to death for a seduction and rescued by a witch, and then eluding the power of werewolves, he settled in Norway. He settles with his master and teacher, who is a goldsmith, and on a voyage with that master is wrecked and cast up on a barbarian shore where the first thing he sees is "a Barbarian hanged on a tree":

> having put off my clothes, and buried him in the sand, I put on his attire, which could not chuse but fit mee well, being none other but skinnes unsewed and never cut out by measure but bound onely on the body, as you have seene. The better to dissemble their language, and not bee knowne for a stranger, I fained my selfe dumbe and deafe: and with this industrie I passed farther into the Isle, skipping & capering in the aire. . . .
>
> . . . with this policie I passed for a Barbarian, and dumbe; and the children to see me leape, fed mee with such victualls as they had. (Bk. I, chap. 9, p. 43)

Rutilio the shipwrecked barbarian represents we might say the state of being shipwrecked in itself—strandedness. In all of these novels, and I am inclined to say in the Novel in general as a genre, coming to a shore is very important. Traversing, changing— coming to a new experience, a new phase of life—all of these are represented by the arrival on a shore. To arrive on a shore is to arrive at an Other Place, to begin to accept becoming Another Self. The traveler to another shore is symbolically naked, unclothed, or inadequately clothed and accoutered—even if like Charlotte Bronte's Lucy Snowe, crossing the Channel in Villette, he/she has brought a small trunk along (or has tried to do so). The Novel tends, in its stories and in its metaphors, to dwell on shores, on marshy or sandy margins where earth and water mingle and are not yet separated. Novel characters must always live on an edge, for a while. Gulliver, of course, lives very visibly on an edge several times—ranging from the shallow waters and soft shore of Lilliput to the current-driven edge and hard rocks of the shore of the uncomfortable island to which the castaway takes his canoe in the first chapter of Book III. "I found the Island to be all rocky, only a little intermingled with Tufts of Grass" (129). He lives hard, like Cervantes' Antonio and the "Barbarian maide": "I gathered Plenty of Eggs upon the Rocks, and got a quantity of dry Sea-weed, and parched Grass, which I designed to kindle the next Day, and roast my Eggs as well as I could. . . . My bed was the same dry Grass and Sea-weed which I intended for Fewel [sic]. . . . I considered how impossible it was to preserve my Life, in so desolate a Place" (130).

In another canoe, made of Yahoo skins, Gulliver hides on another shore, hoping to escape the observation of European human beings:

> I . . . got into the same Creek from whence I set out in the Morning; choosing rather to trust my self among these *Barbarians* than live with *European Yahoos.* I drew up my Canoo [*sic*] as close as I could to the Shore, and hid my self behind a Stone by the Little Brook. . . .

Cowering behind a stone at the edge of an island, Gulliver is discovered by the Portuguese seamen:

at last they found me flat on my Face behind the Stone. They gazed a while in Admiration at my strange uncouth Dress; my Coat made of Skins, my wooden-soled Shoes, and my furred Stockings; from whence, however, they concluded I was not a Native of the Place, who all go naked. (249–250)

Gulliver is not one of the local tribes, those he termed "Barbarians"—because he is clothed. But his dress proclaims him a Barbarian. Cervantes' Rutilio dressed in skins attracts our attention with a kind of horror—not just because he is wearing uncouth clothing, but because he stole the rough skin garments from a dead man. He is like an executioner, taking the clothes of a hanged man. Rutilio, once a dancing-master (that is, someone who represents and teaches an excess of "civilization") and also formerly a goldsmith (that is, one who dresses people in layers of wealth) undergoes a devolution of civilization. A process of regression seems visibly at work in his fate—interestingly, layers are peeling off, like Peer Gynt's onion. He seems to be unselving in stages. Gulliver's unselving in stages takes longer. We watched him accustom himself to the simplicity demanded by his life in Houyhnhnmland:

When my Cloaths were worn to Rags, I made my self others with the Skins of Rabbets, and of a certain beautiful Animal about the same size, called *Nnuhnoh*, the Skin of which is covered with a fine Down. Of these I likewise made very tolerable Stockings. I soaled [*sic*] my Shoes with Wood which I cut from a Tree, and fitted to the upper Leather, and when this was worn out, I supplied it with the Skins of *Yahoos*, dried in the Sun. (241)

The Portuguese sailors wonder at Gulliver's clothes, including the wooden-soled shoes; they don't know what the uppers of these shoes are made of—fortunately for them. Rutilio attracts our wonder and horror because he is wearing a dead man's skins: Gulliver, because he is literally dressed in dead men's skins.

The figure of the Man in Skins turns up at odd moments in fiction, throughout the history of fiction. The most benevolent example of the figure is old Philetas in Longus' *Daphnis and Chloe*. He is described when he comes to see the two pubescent lovers; he is

*presbytēs sisyran endedymenos, karbatinas hypodedemenos, pēran
exērtēmenos kai tēn pēran palaian.*[17]

(an old man wearing a rough outer garment of goatskin,
with brogues of undressed leather upon his feet, and his
leather wallet–an extremely antiquated leather wallet—
hanging down.)

It is this old man who tells Daphnis and Chloe about the appearance of Eros in his garden—thus giving the youths the name
of the god they serve and the name of the passion they feel
(Love). Philetas can have the vision of Eros, and pass on the
identification of Love, because he himself is past it—as indeed
we may gather from the description, with the comic emphasis
upon the antiquity or obsolence of his bag. The Man in Skins,
whenever he appears in fiction, is an outsider, someone outside
the central emotions, conduct, and structures known in society. It
was the genius of Defoe to take this marginalized supernumery
and make him into the central character or consciousness of
the novel. But Defoe neither exhausts all the potential meanings
nor subsumes all the representations of this figure (that is, men
in skins in eighteenth-century fiction do not have to be merely
allusions to Robinson in his goatskin garment and moccasins,
his *sisyra* and *karbatinai*). Fielding's old Man of the Hill belongs
to the whole tradition out of which he arises. He is aged, like
Philetas—but unlike Philetas he cannot offer a vision of Eros.
His story of his own life and desires is a sour story which has
left him soured. Unlike Robinson, but very like Gulliver, he has
chosen an antisocial solitude. He is frightening to look at:

> This Person was of the tallest Size, with a long Beard as
> white as Snow. His Body was cloathed with the Skin of an
> Ass, made something into the Form of a Coat. He wore
> likewise Boots on his Legs, and a Cap on his Head, both
> composed of the Skin of some other Animals. (*Tom Jones*,
> Bk. VIII, chap. x)[18]

It is because of what we know about Gulliver that Fielding can
make us shudder at the phrase "Skin of some other Animals,"
and because of Gulliver's Yahoos and Apuleius' Lucius, we are
not likely to be happy about the "Skin of an Ass."

What Gulliver has in common with all of these—Philetas, Robinson, the Man of the Hill—is a tendency to be both judgmental and prophetic—prophetic in the sense of "telling it like it is" rather than in the sense of foretelling the future. The figure of the Man in Skins, whenever and wherever we encounter him, is always oracular. What a Man in Skins has to say is never the whole truth, for this marginal personage cannot know the whole truth, just as he cannot be integrated into a careless society while remaining poised aside from it. But what the oracular Man in Skins has to say is always *some* truth. One of the later avatars of this figure is James Fenimore Cooper's Natty Bumppo, the deerslayer, Leatherstocking, who appears in all of Cooper's novels as an important figure but not the conventional hero of each story—a role borne by another. Natty, always the Man in Skins, comes to be a Philetas, an old man in skins, when we see him in *The Pioneers* (1823). Tall, thin, sun-tanned, wearing a foxskin cap and a "kind of coat, made of dressed deer-skin," he also wears "deer-skin moccasins" and "long leggings of the same material as the moccasins, which, gartering over the knees of his tarnished buck-skin breeches, had obtained for him . . . the nick name of Leatherstocking" (*The Pioneers*, chap. 1).[19] As usual, the figure of the Man in Skins arouses in the reader fascination combined with a certain unease or aversion. The Man in Skins represents some sort of primary state which is a "pre" state, something precedent to a number of other things (such as civilization). Yet that pre-state may also be the post-state to which we tend (after love, marriage, or civilization are done for, or when life itself tends to its end). We fear the advent of the Man in Skins, for he is always a reminder of loss. For Cooper, of course, Bumppo is a reminder of historical loss—the loss of that first phase of individualistic pioneering without need of settlement, the absolute freedom without need of law which it must be the purpose of the other project, the founding of colonies and of the nation of America, to make men relinquish. But the Man in Skins always announces a number of losses, of deprivations. Like John the Baptist, another famous Man in Skins, this figure tells us we must give something up. Daphnis and Chloe, instructed by the mildest and most benign of these figures, must relinquish their childhood state and enter into an adult awareness of heterosexual love. Even such a gain as this means an advent of loss as well as of suffering—closing in the prospect of arriving at old age, and a new deprivation when love becomes impossible once more.

Gulliver is a Man in Skins, external to society, outside the world of marriage and civility. The Portuguese try forcibly to reintroduce him to these things—they strip him of the skins and put European clothing on him. But the captain's shirt smells too human, and inwardly Gulliver remains the Man in Skins comically clinging to his own "barbarism" as a means of informing us about our own. For the truth is that we're all Yahoos—this is the other side of Swift's coin. I am not using the novel's relation to other novels to try to push a view of Swift's story as "soft-boiled" in its moral. Gulliver is bizarre and stupid, with an un-Christian love of barbarism and an un-Platonic love of lurking in caves. These are unworthy and unreasonable tastes which the Portuguese sailors cannot but reprehend—and the more so, perhaps, if they have read Cervantes' *Persiles y Sigismunda*. From their point of view, Gulliver fits in very nicely with the pattern of barbarism in need of further development—the type encountered by the central characters of Cervantes' last novel in their journey towards holiness and fulfillment. But at the very same time, Gulliver's view of human beings holds true—except that he will not recognize that he is to be identified as human and thus must share in the condemnation.

Gulliver in his own progress is both civilized and civilizing hero and crude barbarian. The mixture of elements can be better understood if we consider Swift's story in the light of a work perennially popular from the eighth century A.D. through the Enlightenment, a work (or works) forgotten until very recently. This is the strange book best known as the *Alexander Romance*, though it has many other titles, such as *The Life of Alexander*, *History of Alexander*, *The Story of the Battles of Alexander* and so on. In the Middle Ages it existed in several distinct versions, a matter succinctly explained by Richard Stoneman in his preface to *The Greek Alexander Romance* published by Penguin Books (1991). This is a story (in its various versions) which has had an astonishingly wide influence over Western fiction; it can be felt in Dante and Chaucer, we can suspect it in Scudéry and Bunyan. There is a direct reference to it in Behn's *Oroonoko* (1688), or at least to material coming directly from that narrative.[20] It lies, I am convinced, in the background of *Gulliver's Travels.*

The Story of Alexander might well be entitled "Alexander's Travels," for of course Alexander, conqueror of many lands, travels to many lands, some merely remote and some altogether fabulous. It does not seem to have been appreciated by the classical scholars who have worked on this text that the representation of the Alexander story in this fictional form offers a very sophisticated critique of Alexander's project. The story is told with an apparent simplicity of narrative which hides a deal of cunning in the strategies. Alexander, dauntless, heroic, godlike, is yet psychologically weakened by a dubious parentage which both confirms his claim to be a descendant of the god Ammon and denies him the right of inheritance to Philip's kingdom. Son of a secret liaison between Queen Olympias and an Egyptian priest, Alexander, quasi-Egyptian, is never quite sure what culture he serves, what heritage he has. That which makes him godlike makes him ambiguous. He kills his biological father, but remains in thrall to his mother, Olympias, and throughout his story he has complex relations with women and with the feminine. It is the voices of birds with women's faces (harpies in short) that warn him he can go no further; it is a woman, a black woman, Queen Candace of Ethiopia, who gets the better of him. Part of his response to the strange kingdoms he enters is always terror, which makes him furious. His project is justified in that he encounters both foes and barbarians—barbarians who prove to the Greek forces that they are in the civilizing right of it to come and conquer.

Alexander, like Gulliver, is consumed with curiosity to see new wonders and to make experiments. As he writes to his mother, Olympias, he conducted an experiment in "the country of the Apple-eaters":

> There we saw a huge man with hair all over his body, and we were frightened. I gave orders to capture him. When he was taken, he gazed at us ferociously. I ordered a naked woman to be brought to him; but he grabbed her and ate her. (*The Greek Alexander Romance*, 116)[21]

Not "Apple-eaters," evidently, but raw-flesh-eaters. Alexander's experiment is here carried out at the cost of the female's life, but the hairy man's cannibalism triumphantly proves his inhumanity. (I think this episode is recollected in *Candide*, in the adventure of the Oreillons in South America.)[22] Alexander is Gulliver's prototype not only in his curiosity, but in his activities as a sort of super-projector. He and his men come upon a troop of "animals resembling men": "from their heads to their navels they were like men, but below they were horses" (124). Using trickery, Alexander is able to trap and kill a lot of them with great bloodshed. He doesn't wish to kill them all:

> Alexander wanted to capture some of them and bring them back to our world. He brought about fifty out of the ditch. They survived for twenty-two days, but as he did not know what they fed on, they all died. (125)

The *Alexander Romance* seems satiric and ironic in itself—before Swift, as it were, gets there. Alexander is a careless collector who wants to exhibit the centaurs but forgets to find out what to feed them.

Alexander is, in some of the lights offered by this book, a mad exploiter, forcing upon the world the horrible benefit of his conquest, a hero of what Swift calls "conquests and systems." At one point in the *Alexander Romance* the hero is directly rebuked by a group who set themselves over against him, absolutely. Having conquered India he encounters the "naked philosophers," the gymnosophists, who are not afraid of him, as they have no wealth he can steal, and want nothing from him. Rather, they let him see that they judge him. Their creed is explained in an exchange of questions and answers:

> Alexander asked them some questions. "Do you have no graves?" was the first.
> "The ground where we dwell is also our grave," came the reply. "Here we lie down and, as it were, bury ourselves when we sleep. The earth gives us birth, the earth feeds us, and under the earth when we die we spend our eternal sleep."
>
> . . .
>
> "Which is the wickedest of all creatures?"
> "Man," they replied.

And he, "Why?"

"Learn from yourself the answer to that. You are a wild beast, and see how many other wild beasts you have with you, to help you tear away the lives of other beasts."

Alexander was not angry, but smiled. Then he asked, "What is kingship?"

"Unjust power used to the disadvantage of others; insolence supported by opportunity; a golden burden." (132)

The gymnosophists' answer, that is, is that humans are Yahoo, and Alexander a chief Yahoo. In a way, little needs to be added in Swift's book, save his satire on the idea of the naked philosophers themselves. The Houyhnhnms are the only true naked philosophers, our humanity not being capable of furnishing true gymnosophists. These horse-people truly accept death and dying.

> [H]er Husband . . . she said happened that very Morning to *Lhnuwnh*. The Word is strongly expressive in their Language, but not easily rendered into *English*; it signifies, *to retire to his first Mother*. (*Gulliver's Travels*, 240)

The Houyhnhnms do not have tombstones, anymore than the gymnosophists.

The *Alexander Romance* itself could also have been instrumental in suggesting to Swift the employment of horses as the wise race. As we have seen, there are men-horses in the narrative, but the most important horse is Alexander's steed Bucephalus, who has some rational characteristics. Bucephalus, visiting Alexander on the king's deathbed, sheds tears. The Sorrel Nag doesn't go quite that far on bidding farewell to Gulliver, though the last word from Houyhnhnmland is the sound of "the Sorrel Nag (who always loved me) crying out . . . Take care of thy self, gentle *Yahoo*" (248). Bucephalus also possesses the violence that Gulliver himself at length wishes to attribute to the gentle Houyhnhnms. When Bucephalus comes into the presence of the man who has poisoned Alexander, the horse takes revenge for his dying master:

> When Bucephalus saw him, he cast off his morose and dejected look, and, just as if he were a rational, even a clever man—I suppose it was done through Providence above—he

avenged his master. He ran into the midst of the crowd,
seized the slave in his teeth and dragged him to Alexander;
he shook him violently and gave a loud whinny to show that
he was going to have his revenge. Then he took a great
leap into the air, dragging the treacherous and deceitful
slave with him, and smashed him against the ground. The
slave was torn apart; bits of him flew all over everyone like
snow falling off a roof in the wind. (*The Greek Alexander
Romance*, 157)

(This event is the less surprising if we remember that Bucephalus
was a man-eating and untameable horse until young Alexander
tamed him.)

The description of Bucephalus' revenge may remind us of
Gulliver's fantasy of the Houyhnhnms' violent resistance to a
European conquest:

Their Prudence, Unanimity, Unacquaintedness with Fear,
and their Love of their Country would amply supply all
Defects in the military Art. Imagine twenty Thousand of
them breaking into the Midst of an *European* Army, con-
founding the Ranks, overturning the Carriages, battering
the Warriors faces into Mummy, by terrible Yerks from their
hinder Hoofs; For they would well deserve the Character
given to *Augustus: Recalcitrat undique tutus.* (257–58)

We may reflect, however, that Gulliver's fantasy may be pious
wish, implicitly denied in the *Alexander Romance* where the
centaurs, who were unanimous, brave, and patriotic were still
miserably defeated because "as beasts they were incapable of
understanding the devilment of men" (124). They decide to
charge into the Macedonians, despising them for their cowardice,
but they tumble into the treacherous grass-covered ditch that has
been dug to receive them. Unused to lying, the Houyhnhnms
would be outdone by the treacherous Europeans, who, like Alexander's Greeks and Macedonians, do not mind looking cowardly
for a time if they can obtain their ends by any means.

Gulliver, then as we have seen thus far, is an Ass, a Victim of
Shipwreck, a Man in Skins, and a parodic Alexander. But there
are two other aspects of Gulliver which strongly relate him to

character types and characteristic events in other fiction. Gulliver is both the Enslaved Person and the Foundling Child—the latter in a special category as Floating Child.

In many novels, central characters undergo a period of enslavement, or at least of imprisonment accompanied by destitution. I believe this experience underlies the plot of the Novel and that metaphorically it can be found in all novels, but novel characters at the most literal level of plot often are forced to enter prisons, vicious schools, insane asylums, etc., in order to fulfill this novelistic fate. In the Greek novels of antiquity the central characters are customarily enslaved for a certain length of time. The slavery involves captivity and customarily bondage. Gulliver is in bondage when tied with strings by the Lilliputians, as Lucian's hero was seized by the sun-people and bound with cobwebs. Even when the slavery is in the most luxurious circumstances, it is nonetheless painful for the person(s) undergoing it. Joseph is the biblical archetype of the wrongfully enslaved free person who becomes servant in a palace. He is the Imprisoned Courtier, whose very virtue in refusing Potiphar's wife lands him in renewed captivity.

In Heliodorus' *Aithiopika*, both hero and heroine become the captive of the Persians, nominal slaves of Oroondates, the satrap of the Great King, but really the possession of Arsake, his wife, who reigns as queen in her palace at Memphis in Persian splendor. She is much attracted to the hero, Theagenes, who decides to humor her and use his enslaved position with good grace in order to preserve both himself and his beloved Charikleia. Theagenes becomes a special type of the Enslaved Person of fiction—he becomes the Imprisoned Courtier, entering the world of court life with its petty jealousies and jockeyings. In Theagenes' case, he must watch out for his fellow-slave Achaimenes, son of the Queen's nurse Kybele, who wants Charikelia for himself.

> The next day Achiamenes took him to wait at table, as Arsake had commanded. He changed into the sumptuous Persian apparel she had sent him and, with a mixture of delight and disgust, bedecked himself with bangles of gold and collars studded with precious gems. Achaimenes then

tried to demonstrate and explain to him something of the art of cup bearing, but Theagenes ran to one of the tripods on which the cups stood, picked up one of the precious vessels, and exclaimed: "I have no need of teachers! I shall use my instinct in serving my mistress. . . ."

He mixes a delicious drink and serves the cup with "exquisite grace" to the charmed Arsake.

> The rage and envy that filled his [Achaimenes'] heart were so obvious that even Arsake noticed him scowling and muttering something under his breath to his companions. (Bk. VII)[23]

Gulliver, we may remember, begins his life in Brobdingnag as a slave—as he tells the Queen:

> She asked, whether I would be content to live at Court. I bowed down to the Board of the Table, and humbly answered, that I was my Master's Slave, but if I were at my own Disposal, I should be proud to devote my Life to her Majesty's Service. (*Gulliver's Travels*, 80)

When the Queen graciously makes the purchase, Gulliver is not slow to pick up the manner of court flattery which the necessity of surviving has evidently taught him. He tells her

> I was out of all fear of being ill treated under the Protection of so great and good an Empress, the Ornament of Nature, the Darling of the World, the Delight of her Subjects, the Phoenix of the Creation. . . . (80–81)

Like Theagenes, he arouses the jealousy of a rival—in his case, the palace Dwarf. Gulliver becomes the pet courtier. Like Theagenes he wears silken garments:

> The Queen likewise ordered the thinnest Silks that could be gotten, to make me Cloaths; not much thicker than an *English* Blanket. . . . They were after the Fashion of the Kingdom, partly resembling the *Persian*, and partly the *Chinese*; and are a very grave decent Habit. (83)

Gulliver does not have to wait at table as a cup-bearer, like those Ganymede figures Theagenes and Joseph—indeed, he could not physically do so. But his life at the Brobdingnagian court is very strongly associated with the table.

> The Queen became so fond of my Company, that she could not dine without me. I had a Table placed upon the same at which her Majesty eat, just at her left Elbow . . . I had an entire set of Silver Dishes and Plates, and other Necessaries. . . . She [the Queen] drank out of a Golden Cup, above a Hogshead at a Draught. (83–84)

Arsake sent her prisoners some food in her own golden dishes (chap. 18); this is "Persian" style. Swift's comedy parodies the oriental splendor.

Of course the palace of Brobdingnag does not have the secret and unwholesome eroticism of the palace of Memphis. Yet there *is* an Oedipal eroticism diffused through the second book of *Gulliver's Travels* which can seem reminiscent of certain elements in the *Aithiopika*. In both cases, imprisoned visitors are subjected perforce to a smothering maternal rule. Kybele, the old nurse, speaks to Arsake as her baby and also treats the imprisoned pair as infants, addressing them as "My children," "*O tekna.*" Taking the hint, Theagenes repeatedly addresses her as "Mother" (*O mēter*).[24] Gulliver is perpetually mothered in Brobdingnag, by Glumdalclitch chiefly but also by the Queen. A good case could be made out for Brobdingnag as the land of the Feminine, the abode of Ceres. Ceres is properly worshipped by the King, who forswears fighting and violence, armies and the gift of gunpowder, and celebrates the virtue of making "two Ears of Corn, or two Blades of Grass to grow upon a Spot of Ground where only one grew before" (111). Unlike the realm of the Persian in Heliodorus' story, this feminine place is a good place—the Great Good Place indeed! But Gulliver can partake of its goodness only by becoming like a little child.

This leads me to the last comparison. Gulliver has, as we have seen, in his time played many parts in Romance's repertoire: Curious Traveler, Metamorphosized Man (or Ass), Man in Skins, Enslaved Person, Imprisoned Courtier. The last role I wish to look at may be described as the Foundling, or Rescued Child. More particularly, Gulliver belongs to what may be called a subset of that category, the Precious-Child-in-a-Floating-Box. Moses may be called the most famous as well as the most important representative of that type. But the literary tradition offers numerous other examples in prose fiction.

The most famous case is that of the celebrated Amadis of Gaul. Amadis is illicitly conceived and born illegitimate. His mother, Elisena, long virtuous and known for her great discretion, falls in love with an attractive visitor, King Perion, invited by her father to his castle. The two lovers have ten nights of passion—and Amadis is the result. The Princess bears him secretly, with the help of her maidservant, who also devises the "ark" in which the baby is to be cradled:

> she obtained four boards large enough so that a baby with its swaddling clothes could be contained therein as in an ark, and as long as a sword, and she caused certain materials to be brought for making a pitch with which she might join them together so that water would not enter.[25]

After the birth, the Princess and her faithful Darioleta place the handsome child in the box, along with the sword of King Perion his father, and a letter saying the infant is "Amadis, the Ill-Timed" (*"Amadis sin Tiempo"*).

> This done, she [Darioleta] put the plank on top so well joined and calked that neither water nor anything else could enter there. And taking it in her arms and opening the door, she put it in the river and let it go. And as the water was high and strong it soon passed out to sea, which was not more than half a league away. (Bk. I, 36)

The strange floating object is miraculously saved: a passing ship contains a Scottish knight, Gandales, and his wife, who have just become parents:

> And going at full speed on their way to Scotland, the morning being already clear, they saw the ark floating on the water; and summoning four sailors, he ordered them quickly to cast off a small boat and bring the ark to him, which was speedily done, although the ark had already floated a long distance from the ship. (36)

The Scottish knight and his wife discover the infant; the knight picks the child up, saying "This is from some good place." The wife "put it to the breast of that nurse who was rearing Gandalin, her own son." The baby thus delivered unharmed to its foster parents is called "Child of the Sea" (*el Donzel del Mar*).

Gulliver in Book II is always living in boxes. When Glumdalclitch attends the royal party on a tour of the coast, an accident happens at the seaside; a huge Brobdingnagian bird picks up Gulliver's box and drops it into the sea. Gulliver describes, as baby Amadis could not, the horror of being in the sea and in danger of the waves, as the tight box begins to leak a bit. It is less surprising that Gulliver's box is discovered by a passing ship than that Amadis' container is so discovered, as Gulliver's ark is so huge (a "Swimming House") in the eyes of the English sailors. But, like a baby, Gulliver is "taken into the Ship in a very weak Condition." The Captain is puzzled and "desired I would give him a Relation of my Travels, and by what Accident I came to be set adrift in that monstrous wooden Chest" (II, 118–19).

The Captain thinks of the other alternative, that Gulliver was in that box as a punishment for his crimes. But Gulliver was in the box because of his toylike innocence, the entertaining charm and helpless passivity that he had displayed, babylike in the land of the Big People (which is what children call adults). As a precious child, he has been preserved in his floating box in the sea, according to the best romantic tradition. He does come "from a good place." Unlike Amadis, he loses rather than regains the breast when he is taken aboard. He is a "Child of the Sea"—but once his box is destroyed and he has displayed all the tokens he has with him, he must consent to be adopted into normal English adult life. Unlike the hero of fiction, he will not recover the lost heritage—he can never get back to the feminine comforts and discomforts of Brobdingnag, the babyish pleasure of the company of "my dear little Nurse" (II, 99). Perhaps he is never again as close to the female sexual organs as he was then, in an infancy which placed him perilously close to the holy organs and the monstrous breast. He has lost his Motherland. Unlike Amadis (or Tom Jones, the Foundling) he cannot reclaim anything, or assert a title to something. He tries, at the end of the story, to assert his title to be considered a Horse, but this is not a title he can win by any feats. We can, however, if we wish, call him an Ass—and ourselves too.

Swift had, I believe, a very deep and long-standing knowledge of all kinds of fiction, including long works of prose fiction, or "Romances." One of the reasons *Gulliver's Travels* lasts so very well is that it draws upon the deep traditions of prose fiction in the West and is itself a virtuoso performance within that tradition.

NOTES

1. Jonathan Swift, *Gulliver's Travels*, ed. Robert A. Greenberg (New York and London: W. W. Norton, 1970), 37. All citations refer to this edition.

2. "Women in (religious or moral) Guides are often advised that their imaginations can become overheated if they read romances (the source of Swift's joke about maids of honor in Lilliput). . . ." J. Paul Hunter, *Before Novels: The Cultural Contexts of Eighteenth-Century Fiction* (New York and London: W. W. Norton, 1990), 265.

3. Samuel Richardson, *Clarissa: Or the History of a Young Lady*, rpt. of 3rd edition (1751), 8 volumes, in The Clarissa Project, AMS Press, 1990. The work of fiction alluded to here, usually given as *Dorastus and Fawnia* when not called by its chief title *Pandosto*, is a work of prose fiction by Robert Greene, published in 1588; it supplied the plot for Shakespeare's *The Winter's Tale*.

4. See the Preface of 1715 to a new translation of Pierre Daniel Huet's *Traité de l'origine des romans*, a work first published as a preface to Mme. De La Fayette's *Zaïde* (1670), then issued in amplified form in French and in Latin. Stephen Lewis, the translator, remarks: "I have no great Reason to fear its being well received in *English*: Especially since *Romance* has of late convey'd it self very far into the Esteem of this Nation, and become the principal Diversion of the Retirement of People of all Conditions.

"And (tho' we have been hitherto, for the most part, supply'd with Translations from the *French*) it is to be hoped, that we *won't* any longer subsist upon *Reverse*: but that some *English Genius* will *dare* to *Naturalize Romance* into our Soil." Preface to *The History of Romance*, "an inquiry into their Original; Instructions for Composing them; an Account of the most Eminent Authors. . . . Written in Latin by Huetius, Made English by Mr. STEPHEN LEWIS" (London: J. Hooke and I. Caldecott, 1715).

5. "Dedication" to *The Adventures of Theagenes and Chariclia, A Romance. Being the Rise, Progress, Tryals, and happy Success of the HEROIC LOVES of those Two illustrious Persons* (London: W. Taylor, E. Curll, *et al.*, 1717), I, xxvi.

6. Marjorie Hope Nicolson, *Voyages to the Moon* (New York: Macmillan, 1948).

7. Lucian of Samosata, "A True History," trans. Lionel Casson in *Selected Satires of Lucian*, ed. and trans. Lionel Casson (New York and London: W. W. Norton, 1962), 13–54. All other references are to this version.

8. Apuleius, *Metamorphoseon sive Asinus Aureus* (*Metamorphoses*, or *The Golden Ass*) in *The Golden Ass*, Loeb edition, 2 vols., ed. and trans. J. Arthur Hanson (Cambridge, Mass.: Harvard University Press, 1989). Although I have consulted various translations including that in the Loeb, passages are given in my own version.

9. *Pensarán vuestras mercedes ahora que es poco trabajo hinchar un perro?*—The meaningless performance is, Cervantes indicates, a parallel to writing:—*Pensará vuestra merced ahora que es poco trabajo hacer un libro?*—"Does your worship think now that it is little labor to make a book?"

Miguel de Cervantes, *Don Quijote de la Mancha*, ed. Martin de Riquer (Barcelona; Editorial Juventud, S. A., 1968), 537. All references are to this edition, with my translation unless otherwise indicated.

10. John J. Winkler, *Auctor & Actor: A Narratological Reading of Apuleius's the Golden Ass* (Berkeley and London: University of California Press, 1985), 313–16.

11. Plutarch, *de Iside*, as quoted by John J. Winkler, *Auctor & Actor*, 314.

12. Laurence Sterne, *The Life and Opinions of Tristram Shandy, Gentleman*, ed. Ian Watt (Boston: Houghton Mifflin, 1965), Bk. VII, chap. xxxii, 398–99.

13. In Giovanni Boccaccio's *Filocolo* (a novel written c. 1336–38), the hero after shipwreck exclaims aggrievedly: "And thou, O highest Aeolus, merciless father of Canace, temper your wrath, unjustly raised against me. Open thine eyes, and know that I am not Aeneas, the great enemy of holy Juno: I am a young man who loves, just as thou hast loved before" (my translation).

14. *Ibrahim, or the Illustrious Bassa*. An Excellent New Romance. The Whole book. In Five Parts. Written in French by Monsieur de Scudery, and Now Englished By Henry Cogan, Gent. (London: Humphry Moseley, William Bentley & Thomas Heath, 1652). Although Monsieur de Scudéry lent his name to the title pages of the novels, the real author is generally agreed to have been his sister Madeleine de Scudéry. *Ibrahim* (published 1641) was one of her early novels.

15. Alexander Pope, *The Dunciad Variorum*, I, 1. 19; see *The Poems of Alexander Pope*, ed. John Butt (New Haven: Yale University Press, 1965), 351.

16. *The History of Persiles and Fayre Sigismunda* (London, 1620), Bk. I, chap. 6, p. 30. All further quotations are taken from this edition. There were later translations of this novel, including *Persiles and Sigismunda: A Celebrated Novel*, published in 2 volumes in 1741, prefaced with an extract from Bayle's "General Historical Dictionary" in praise of the novel, concluding "Briefly, this Performance is of a better Invention, more artificial Contrivance, and of a more sublime Stile than that of *Don Quixote de la Mancha.*"

17. Longus, *Daphnis and Chloe*, Loeb edition (Cambridge, Mass: Harvard University Press, 1988) [rpt. of 1916 edition], Bk. II, chap. 6, p. 70. My translation is assisted by that supplied in the Loeb (a revision of George Thornley's translation of 1657) and by several other translations, but it is not a reproduction of any of them.

18. Henry Fielding, *The History of Tom Jones, A Foundling*, as *Tom Jones*, ed. Sheridan Baker (New York: W. W. Norton, 1973), 340.

19. James Fenimore Cooper, *The Pioneers, or the Sources of the Susquehanna. A Descriptive Tale*, ed. James Franklin Beard (Albany, N.Y.: State University of New York Press, 1980), 23.

20. See Aphra Behn, *Oroonoko: Or, The Royal Slave*. With an Introduction by Lore Metzger (New York and London: W. W. Norton, 1973): Oroonoko, now named "Caesar," as a slave in South America, according to the female narrator needed activity: "and though all Endeavours were us'd to exercise himself in such Actions and Sports as this World afforded, as . . . Killing *Tygers* of a monstrous size, which this Continent affords in abundance; and wonderful *Snakes*, such as *Alexander* is reported to have encounter'd at the River of *Amazons*, and which *Caesar* took great delight to overcome; yet these were not actions great enough for his large Soul, which was still panting after more renown'd Actions" (47).

This passage recaptures some of the excitements of the adventures and geography of the traditional *Alexander Romance*, and in doing so emphasizes resemblances between Oroonoko and Alexander. Not the least of their resemblances appears to be that both are fictional characters based on factual persons.

21. *The Greek Alexander Romance*, translated with an Introduction and Notes by Richard Stoneman (Harmondsworth, Middlesex: Penguin Books, 1991). All further quotations refer to this edition. This is not, however, the only modern English version available. An Armenian version was translated by A. Wolohojian as *The Romance of Alexander the Great, By Pseudo-Callisthenes* (New York and London: Columbia University Press, 1969). The *Alexander Romance* also appears translated by Ken Dowden in *Collected Ancient Greek Novels*, ed. B. P. Reardon (Berkeley, Los Angeles and London: University of California Press, 1989), 650–735.

22. See Voltaire, *Candide, ou l'Optimisme* (1759), chap. 16; in *Voltaire: Romans et Contes*, ed. René Pomeau (Paris, Garnier-Flammarion, 1966), 211–14.

23. Heliodorus, *Aithiopika*, translated by John Morgan as *An Ethiopian Story* in *Collected Ancient Greek Novels*, 349–588; see p. 514.

24. For the Greek text of Heliodorus' novel I follow the dual-language version *Les Éthiopiques*, 3 vols., ed. R. M. Rattenbury and T. W. Lumb, trans. J. Maillon (Paris: Budé, "Les Belles Lettres," 1960). The passages here referred to are to be found in Bk. VII, chap. 12, chap. 13, chap. 17; see vol. 2: 135, 136, 142.

25. Garci Rodríguez de Montalvo, *Amadis of Gaul, Books I and II*, translated by Edwin B. Place and Herbert C. Behm (Lexington: University Press of Kentucky, 1974), Bk. I, p. 34. All further quotations are from this translation. Quotations in Spanish are taken from *Amadis de Gaula*, ed. Juan Manuel Cacho Blecua, 2 vols. (Madrid: Catedra Letras Hispanicas, 1987), 1: 246; 253.

Laetitia Pilkington on Swift:
How Reliable Is She?

A. C. ELIAS, JR.

Sometime during 1739 or early 1740, not too long after the newly-divorced Laetitia Pilkington had fled her native Dublin for London, she received an invitation to have breakfast with the elderly Colley Cibber, the playwright and former theatrical manager. Cibber had recently met her and learned that she had known Swift. "Accordingly I waited on him," she wrote years later,

> and wonderfully was he delighted with my Account of Doctor *Swift.* He had the Patience to listen to me three Hours, without ever once interrupting me, a most uncommon Instance of good Breeding, especially from a Person of his Years, who usually dictate to the Company, and engross all the Talk to themselves.

As she went on with her story, she tells us, Cibber "at last, in flowing Spirits, cried, 'Zounds! write it out, just as you relate it, and I'll engage it will sell' " (3:68, 71).[1] Write it out she did, some years later, and eventually published it in her autobiography, *The Memoirs of Laetitia Pilkington.* It provides the liveliest and most realistic firsthand glimpse of Swift that we have. Swift scholars have either been using it, or turning up their noses at it, ever since.

One who used it extensively was Swift's last full-dress biographer, the late Irvin Ehrenpreis. Ehrenpreis said that he was vastly impressed with Mrs. Pilkington's memory—I seem to recollect that he had checked the accuracy of the many Shakespeare snippets which she quotes from memory. He also reported finding her reliable on Swift wherever he could check her facts.[2] In contrast I remember the late Louis Landa, an equally serious scholar for whom (a good many years ago) I wrote an undergraduate thesis on *Gulliver*. When I tried to quote Mrs. Pilkington in a draft he took me aside and made it clear that this was just not done, that I simply could not rely on her. More than most Swiftians, Landa hated controversy. More than most, he also had worked in mid-century fiction and knew just how racy and dubious a figure Mrs. Pilkington appeared to respectable bourgeois contemporaries like Samuel Richardson and his bluestocking friends. In their day, after all, a woman could only be divorced for adultery, a shocking act in itself. It was made doubly shocking when the injured husband was a clergyman and when, instead of retiring penitent to the country, the divorcée came to London, lived by her wits, and seemed to know half the rakes and other aristocrats who gambled the night away at that most exclusive of clubs, White's.

Just how reliable is Mrs. Pilkington? For more than five years, I have been preparing an annotated critical edition of her *Memoirs*—all three volumes' worth—for the University of Georgia Press. By now I have checked all the anecdotes I could about other people and have begun to make some inroads on those concerning Swift. If an overall pattern emerges, it is this: When she introduces dream-sequences or recounts stories told to her by others—especially mysterious strangers whose experiences she could not possibly have verified—we encounter the techniques of fiction and are just as likely to find her sources in literature as in life. When she recounts her own experiences, we may find a good deal which has been distorted—chronology confused, similar occasions conflated, personalities exaggerated one way or another, complications smoothed over, pertinent facts left out. At the same time, I do not think that I have ever encountered a story which she made up out of whole cloth. There always seems to be some basis in fact.

In her second volume, for instance, she tells us about going to a London lending-library and meeting a politician named Rooke who announces that he is a Member of Parliament for Canterbury. He recounts a number of anti-Walpole stories but dies the next day. I have identified Rooke and find that he was *not* an M.P. for Canterbury but was only preparing to contest the seat. Some of his stories are too late for him to have told, besides being garbled in themselves. It is also possible that he and Mrs. Pilkington met up to five or six weeks before he died in 1739.[3] At the other extreme is her account of the illness and death of her father, Dr. John Van Lewen, a leading physician and man-midwife in Dublin. I have been able to verify the main points to almost the last detail. She claimed that the whole town followed his case, and indeed contemporary newspapers gave him an unprecedented amount of attention for a private citizen.[4]

If Rooke and Van Lewen represent the two ends of the spectrum in Mrs. Pilkington's *Memoirs*, where should we place her various anecdotes of Swift? My work so far suggests that they cover nearly as wide a range. To help us account for it—to help us understand what to expect at each stage in her autobiography— it will be useful to see how the *Memoirs*, all three volumes' worth, took shape.

Between her divorce in Dublin, early in 1738, and the appearance of volume 1 in Dublin ten years later, Mrs. Pilkington spent most of her time as an exile in London, living as best she could. For illiterate noblemen, prostitutes, and others she wrote love letters and hackney verse; during one brief period she turned out political pamphlets; for a while, later on, she kept a print and pamphlet shop; and for much of the time she collected advance subscriptions to publish her own writings, at first a projected collection of her poems and eventually her projected memoirs, which included the poems. It may have been Colley Cibber, as we have seen, who gave her the idea for writing her memoirs down: "Write it out just as you relate it, and I'll engage it will sell." What we should notice here is that much of the *Memoirs* started as spoken anecdotes, part of her conversation, and that, from the very beginning, they featured stories about Swift. Indeed it was principally through her conversation—her ability to engage and hold the interest of potential patrons and subscribers—that she kept herself alive through her eight or nine years in London and her last three in Dublin.[5] This emphasis on spoken anecdote and on entertainment tells us quite a bit. Even humdrum individuals are complex and inconsistent enough in real life. Even the simplest of human actions often prove complex on closer analysis. If writing about them is hard enough without

exaggerating and oversimplifying, talking clearly and engagingly
about them is almost impossible. The speaker must be willing
to sweep unnecessary complications under the rug, heighten
muted colors, stretch or squeeze chronology, seize upon the
colorful detail and ignore the rest. When other people enter
the narrative and have something to say—they usually do—the
anecdotalist must know how to slide from paraphrase to indirect
quotation to direct quotation and back again, with just the right
timing and phrasing for the conversational punch line. We can
see this at work especially strongly early in volume 1, in the long
account of Mrs. Pilkington's first meeting with Swift. After Sunday
services at St. Patrick's, she and her parson husband, Matthew,
humbly follow Swift back to the Deanery House, preceded by the
cathedral verger bearing the Dean's silver-tipped staff of office.
"When we came into the Parlour," she proceeds,

> the Dean kindly saluted me, and without allowing me Time
> to sit down, bade me come and see his Study; Mr. *Pilkington*
> was for following us, but the Dean told him merrily, He did
> not desire his Company; and so he ventur'd to trust me with
> him into the Library: "Well," says he, "I have brought you
> here to show you all the Money I got when I was in the
> Ministry, but don't steal any of it." "I won't indeed, Sir,"
> says I; so he opened a Cabinet, and shewed me a whole
> Parcel of empty Drawers; "Bless me," says he, "the Money is
> flown." (1:44)

Without an independent witness, we are hardly in a position
to controvert Mrs. Pilkington. But here as elsewhere through
her seamless fifteen-page account of that Sunday—dinner in the
Deanery, Swift squabbling amusingly with the servants; then coffee accompanied by his imitation of a prude; then a quiet after-
noon which she passed reading his *Four Last Years of the Queen*
out loud to him; then supper with other guests, including the
Dean's old friend Charles Ford—there is so much anecdotal
artistry that, without dismissing the basic truth of each part, we
may reasonably suspect at least a little conflation, simplification,
or rearrangement of details.[6]

A successful anecdote requires the speaker to pay attention
to his audience as well as to his presentation. By the late 1740s

most of Swift's works were in print and his public image firmly fixed—in England, as the great 'original genius' whose wit and eccentricity set him apart from all other writers; in Ireland, as the same original genius plus paradigm of Irish patriotism, a man of wisdom and public virtue.[7] We can see Mrs. Pilkington trading on her readers' expectations all through the *Memoirs*. When she tells us about visiting Naboth's Garden, in volume 1, she depicts Swift briskly "trolling" along, walking as briskly as a horse. She smiles to think that "he had written so much in Praise of Horses"—Houyhnhnms, in the fourth book of *Gulliver*—"that he was resolved to imitate them as nearly as he could." Later in the same interview Swift calls her husband a fool for marrying her, when for the same expenditure he could have kept a horse which "would have given him better Exercise and more Pleasure than a Wife" (1:64–65). This is wonderful material—though not to be taken *too* seriously. Everyone in those days had read *Gulliver*, and the tradition of laughing about his supposed preference for horses had become so well established that even Swift's friends had fun with the notion, as in Pope's Scriblerian poem "Mary Gulliver, to Capt. Lemuel Gulliver," in which the spurned wife tries to lure Gulliver back from the stables to her bed. That Swift appreciated the jest as much as anyone is suggested by the poem's inclusion in the *Gulliver* volume of his authorized Dublin *Works*. His joke about Matthew Pilkington's mistake is entirely in character. As for his walking like a horse, we may chalk it up to allowable poetic license. Swift was a man of average height who was in the habit of taking long brisk walks, while Mrs. Pilkington was in her own words, "one of the most diminutive Mortals you ever saw who was not a Dwarf."[8] In her account, she also happens to be pregnant at the time. It is fair to guess that any gait faster than waddling would have seemed like 'trolling' to her.

Saying that much of her *Memoirs* began as conversation only partly explains the quality of the Swift anecdotes which appear all through them. The major concentrations are in volumes 1 and 3 but a sprinkling appear in volume 2 as well. Which of her three volumes are we dealing with—indeed, which part of which volume? Sometimes it can make a difference. Her first volume, which appeared in February or March 1748, covers the entire period that she knew Swift—in Ireland, up to the time of her separation and divorce in 1737 and 1738. Her second volume, published in December 1748, carries her story from her landing in England late in 1738 up to her return to Ireland in mid-1747, a year and a half before publication date. This leaves her third volume, unfinished at her death in 1750 but published by her son Jack four years later, with only the last few months of her life to cover—or more accurately, to be filled up with whatever she could lay her hands on that she had not already narrated in its proper place.

Besides the increasing pressure of finding things to write about, Mrs. Pilkington increasingly came under the pressure of publishing deadlines. We do not know how soon she promised to publish in her printed *Proposals*, of which I can trace no surviving copies, but contemporary newspapers show her advertising her second and third volumes as "In the Press" when she was in fact still writing them down. The third volume, which she never finished, was "In the Press" at least eight months before she died. Her second volume was "Ready for the Press" a full year before its appearance—and at least seven months before a number of happenings which she eventually described in it.[9] Indeed, the final hundred pages of volume 2 read like hastily composed filler material, padding to fill the book out to its promised length.[10]

As a result of all this, we may reasonably expect to find her first volume (at least partly composed before she returned to Ireland) more polished than its successors. Similarly we can predict that in volume 3 and the final portion of volume 2, there will be more that seems forced or inconsequential. In a very general sense—with an inevitable number of exceptions—I have been finding that this pattern holds true. But especially where Swift is concerned, there are a number of complicating factors.

The most important is the metamorphosis which Mrs. Pilkington underwent after her first volume appeared, from nonentity to celebrity. Part of the charm in volume 1 comes from its author's modesty, the recognition that she owed the time she had spent with Swift to "my being a Person *sans* Consequence"— someone whom he could boss around, order to speak up, and otherwise be himself with as he grew older, deafer, and crankier (1:38, 58–59). This is an appealing stance. It helped to make volume 1 a success and its author a public personage. Conscious of her new-found power to revenge the insults which she had received over the years, in volume 2 she began to strut and threaten exposure to all and sundry who had abused her, unless of course they mended their ways and politely subscribed to the *Memoirs.* "Whom have I defrauded or belied?" she asks late in volume 2, after exclaiming over the years of wrong that she has borne:

> Nay, indeed, of whom have I spoke half the Evil, which it was in my Power to do? There are few Characters immaculate, and had I an Inclination to retaliate Injuries, I am, I believe, able enough to do it.
>
> And sometimes one has so strong an Inclination to it, that it is hard to resist, especially when a Lady of Quality, that is by Marriage, for her Grandfather was a Blacksmith at *Gowran,* and kept the Sign of the Horse-Shoe there as I have frequently heard the late Lord *Mountgarret* relate, could—because I presumed to beg she would do me the Honour of being a Subscriber to me, a Privilege I thought a long Acquaintance might have entitled me to take—order my Maid to be kicked; and as I am really ashamed to use her Ladyship's Words on the Occasion, being much too indecent for a Repetition, methinks she might have spared them, especially to one who knew her, too,
>
> > *When she was a Maid, if she e'er was a Maid,*
> > *When afraid of a Man, if she e'er was afraid.*
> > (2:238)

This kind of scandal-mongering lost Mrs. Pilkington many of the admirers which her first volume had made.[11] Through much of the next and final volume, where she often lashes out with abandon, it is not surprising to hear a note of desperation or defiance sometimes creeping in.

With anecdotes of Swift, there is a comparable change in emphasis. Increasingly Mrs. Pilkington seems more eager to shock her readers than to amuse them. At the same time—perhaps because she has no narrative framework to allow her structure—she seems much readier to draw conclusions about Swift's character, even to subordinate or custom-fit her anecdotes to the analysis.

Let us have a look at two anecdotes of Swift losing his temper at Mrs. Pilkington, one from volume 1 and the other from volume 3.

In the first volume, Mrs. Pilkington tells a series of anecdotes about Swift's relations with his old friend Alexander Pope, at just the period when we know from other sources they were somewhat strained. Considering her own friendship with Cibber, whom Pope had enthroned in the *New Dunciad*, it is hardly a surprise to find her mining this vein and, wherever possible, putting Pope in the wrong. She writes of the autumn of 1732 when her husband Matthew has recently left for London to begin a term as chaplain to the new Lord Mayor, John Barber. Matthew writes back that Pope had him out to Twickenham as a houseguest and literally showered him with civilities there. Thinking that this would please Swift, she goes to the Deanery and lets Swift read the letter. In turn she is given a letter to Swift in which Pope complains that Matthew is "a most forward, shallow, conceited Fellow" whose "Impertinence" Pope is sick of and whom he "heartily repented" inviting to Twickenham. When Mrs. Pilkington observes that it is ungenerous in Pope to caress and abuse Matthew at the same time,

> the Dean lost all Patience, and flew into such a Rage that he quite terrify'd me; he ask'd me, Why did I not swear that my Husband [*who was as short as she*] was six Foot high? and, Did I think myself a better Judge than Mr. *Pope?* or, Did I presume to give him the Lie? and a thousand other Extravagancies. As I durst not venture to speak a Word more, my heart swell'd so that I burst into Tears, which, he attributing to Pride and Resentment, made him, if possible, ten Times more angry, and I am not sure he would not have beat me; but that, fortunately for me, a Gentleman came to visit him [*—and she makes her escape*].

Eventually, after receiving an apology, Swift calms down and gives Mrs. Pilkington some thoughtful advice about keeping Pope's letter secret, lest her husband find out, complain, and make an active enemy of the poet (1:105–8). We are left with the sense that Swift acted arbitrarily, perhaps even a little frighteningly when he exploded. We may also suspect that he had reasons which our author simply did not know about.

In the third volume, where Mrs. Pilkington affects a more omniscient tone, we see another kind of temper tantrum. At first by implication and then more directly, she now works a theme which her Irish readers in particular would have found shocking, that their great and beloved Hibernian Patriot had begun to show signs of lunacy many years before his mind failed. "One Morning," she says—we are not given any other context or occasion, although an unrelated incident which supposedly followed it can be dated to 1730—she goes early to the Deanery on Swift's invitation to eat breakfast with him. Instead she is forced to sit for two or three hours while he holds forth about his arrangements for managing his household. Finally he explains that he eats a breakfast of rum and gingerbread while walking from the Deanery to the Cathedral to say morning prayers. When she has trouble opening the drawer where he keeps the rum—he thinks she is trying to pull out the drawer by its key—he beats her "most immoderately." And when she declines to accept his odd breakfast, because of her heartburn, he finally "threw me down, forced the Bottle into my Mouth, and pour'd some of the Liquor down my Throat, which I thought would have set my very Stomach on Fire" (3:57–60).

To the same degree that Swift's first tantrum sounds more plausible than the second, it has a stronger demonstrable basis in fact. Whether or not Mrs. Pilkington knew about it—and considering her husband's deviousness, she may have been in the dark—Swift had privately empowered Matthew Pilkington, when in London, to explore the possibilities with the publisher William Bowyer of bringing out a collected English edition of his own miscellaneous works. Swift had been increasingly dissatisfied with the mixed Pope-Swift *Miscellanies* series (containing three pieces by Swift for every one by Pope) which Pope, with Swift's assent, had been bringing out in London. Another such volume, he knew, was in the offing, but his own collection might gracefully forestall it. Meanwhile Pope had recently been embarrassed by Swift's lavish praise of him in a favorite poem of Swift's, *A Libel on Dr. Delany,* which celebrated Pope's scorn of ministers and courts at just the time that Pope was making an effort to mend his fences with them. Matthew's commission was a ticklish one. Despite their private differences, Pope and Swift remained close friends, bent on presenting a united face to the world. From surviving correspondence it is clear that Pilkington handled things badly. On or before 4 October 1732, more than ten days before Matthew was able to visit Twickenham, Pope rushed into print with the fourth volume of *Miscellanies,* full of Swift's verse but minus Swift's favorite *Libel on Delany.* Although it was now pointless to press on with a collected Swift *Works* in London, Matthew did exactly that. He even approached Pope, as someone who could influence the various copyright-holders whose cooperation would have been needed for the scheme. In a surviving letter to Matthew, Pope feigns support but makes it clear that he will do nothing. Privately he must have been furious.

That Pope actually wrote down that Matthew was "a most forward, shallow, conceited Fellow," or flatly stated that he "heartily repented" inviting him to Twickenham, is another question entirely. Pope's surviving letters to Swift, both published and unpublished, show that this was simply not his way of expressing himself. Tact and indirection were his stock in trade. It is almost certain that Mrs. Pilkington has taken liberties, exaggerating Pope's displeasure in order to blacken his character. In all other respects, though, this first tantrum of Swift's make perfect sense. Indeed, if Pope had only *hinted* displeasure over Matthew—which was almost certainly the case—any spirited complaint by Mrs. Pilkington would have seemed out of line. Matthew's pointless and inexcusable forwardness had already placed Swift in an awkward position with Pope. To have Pilkington's wife offering her own commentary, on a point so embarrassing to Swift, would only have added salt to his wound.

With the rum-and-gingerbread incident, by contrast, we are given so little context that it is impossible to know how far to credit it. Probably Swift at some point or points *did* beat Mrs. Pilkington, though perhaps not so "immoderately" as she claims, and more in the spirit of the pinchings and thwackings that we know he distributed among young women friends who committed crimes against spelling and English usage.[12] Conceivably, at some point or points, Swift may even have physically forced her to eat or drink something she disliked. But we have no way of knowing which the point or points, what the circumstances, or even, I suspect, what the kinds of food and physical force—except that, then or later, it allowed her to question Swift's sanity. Meanwhile there are reasons to think that Mrs. Pilkington has left something out, cobbled disparate occasions together, and otherwise exaggerated a good deal. For instance I have not been able to find anything in Swift to suggest a special interest in rum or gingerbread. Indeed, in her first volume Mrs. Pilkington goes out of her way to remark how temperate Swift was with alcohol, that at meals he "never drank above half a Pint of Wine, in every Glass of which, he mix'd Water and Sugar" (1:35). It is hard to imagine him swigging rum out of the bottle at breakfast or expecting anyone else to do so. Mrs. Pilkington's fear of heartburn from gingerbread may also puzzle us. Towards the beginning of volume 2, when she travels to London a year after her last possible contact with Swift, we see her receiving a "Ginger-bread-nut" from a love-struck Welsh parson—not with the remark that it is the last thing she could eat, but merely with a joke about the giver (2:3–4). It is only during her last months of life, the very time when she was writing this anecdote, that I can document any digestive complaints. According to her son's Appendix in volume 3, she suffered from "an extreme bad Stomach and Digestion" towards the end, so much so that it surprised and delighted him when she could eat some ham with a couple of glasses of white wine (3:224, 229–30).

That we need to check Mrs. Pilkington's facts before using them, against outside sources and against the *Memoirs* themselves, should not prejudice us against her. To some extent we need to check the facts in all the other early biographical accounts which we have of Swift, not to mention the accounts written since. Following the lead of Sir Harold Williams,[13] most of us naturally gravitate to the late eighteenth-century *Life* of Swift written by his godson Thomas Sheridan, the former actor and theater manager, who was a son of Swift's closest crony, the elder Thomas Sheridan. Here we have anecdote, dialogue, and corroborating detail in plenty. But as Philip Sun first observed in his unpublished dissertation, here we also have a number of unacknowledged liftings from earlier published accounts. Let us consider Swift's squabbling with the cook–maid during dinner at the Deanery, on Mrs. Pilkington's first visit, when the beef was overcooked. "The Dean called for the cook–maid," Mrs. Pilkington tells us, "and ordered her to take it down Stairs and do it less; the Maid

answer'd, very innocently, 'That she could not.' 'Why, what Sort
of a Creature are you,' says he, 'to commit a Fault which cannot be amended?' " (1:45). Although Mrs. Pilkington may have
polished this story in the telling,[14] we have no reason to doubt
she had witnessed some sort of wrangle between Swift and the
cook–maid. In Sheridan we get the same story and punch line,
with the dialogue extended a few lines longer and a few details
added to increase its air of verisimilitude. The cook–maid is now
"a woman of a large size, robust constitution, and coarse features;
her face very much seamed with the small-pox, and furrowed by
age; this woman he [Swift] always distinguished by the name of
Sweetheart"—a nickname, incidentally, which anyone could have
looked up in Swift's poem about her, *Mary the Cookmaid's Letter*, in
print since 1732. But hold, let us not accuse Sheridan of decking
out Mrs. Pilkington's story with borrowed plumage. It was Patrick
Delany in his *Observations on Swift*, published four years after
she died, who had already done this. Dialogue and all, Sheridan
merely borrows wholesale from Delany, down to the description
of Sweetheart as, in Delany's words, "a cook–maid of a large size
and very robust constitution," with a face "much roughed with the
small-pox, and furrowed by age."[15] The difference between Mrs.
Pilkington and Sheridan is that her first-person stories, however
polished as anecdotes, point to her own firsthand experience,
while Sheridan's too often point to somebody else's. We should
be grateful for what she gives us.

APPENDIX

Laetitia Pilkington's *Memoirs*: contents, dates, and publication.

Volume 1: The Memoirs of Mrs. Laetitia Pilkington, Wife to the Rev. Mr.
Matth. Pilkington. Written by Herself. Wherein are occasionally
interspersed, All her Poems, With Anecdotes of several eminent
Persons, Living and Dead. In Two Volumes. Vol. I. Dublin: [by
S. Powell] for the Author, 1748. 8°.
Contents: Life in Ireland up through divorce, February 1737/8, and
departure for London, fall or winter 1738. Central figure: Swift.
Publication: Printed *Proposals* (none now extant) available by June 1747,
following author's return to Ireland; book "In the Press and speedily will be published" December 1747; actually published February
or early March 1747/8.

Composition: At least partly written in London before author returned to Ireland in mid May 1747.

Volume 2: The Memoirs of Mrs. Laetitia Pilkington . . . Wherein are Occasionally interspersed, Her Poems, With Variety of Secret Transactions of some Eminent Persons. Vol. 2. Dublin: [by S. Powell] for the Author, 1748. 8°.

Contents: London exile from arrival in England late in 1738 through trip back to Ireland, May 1747; adds various quarrels of author in Dublin during the spring, summer, and fall of 1748. Central figure: Cibber.

Publication: Printed *Proposals* (also covering vol 1.) available by June 1747; "ready for the Press" in December 1747; book actually published December 1748.

Composition: Last third of book, covering incidents of 1748, written as late as November or December of that year.

Volume 3: The Third and last Volume of the Memoirs of Mrs. Laetitia Pilkington, Written by Herself. Wherein are occasionally interspersed, Variety of Poems: As also the Letters of several Persons of Distinction: With the Conclusive Part of the Life of the Inimitable Dean Swift. London: [by G. Woodfall?] for R. Griffiths, 1754. 12°.

Contents: Unfinished. Supposedly covers author's life in Dublin after her arrival in May 1747; in fact, mainly made up of digressions introducing material from the period covered by the first two volumes. Her son John Carteret Pilkington supplies an Appendix (pp. 224–68) which describes her last illness and death, sketches in his own life since, and otherwise fills out the volume to a respectable length.

Publication: An 8vo edition was advertised in Dublin as early as November 1749 ("In the Press, and will speedily be published"), but nothing appeared until this 12°, published in London during June 1754, after Jack Pilkington had recovered the MS from Powell and taken it to England in 1753.

Composition: Author's text seemingly abandoned because of ill health towards the end of 1749 or beginning of 1750. She died on 29 July 1750. Jack Pilkington's dedication is dated 31 January 1754.

NOTES

1. Volume and page numbers in parentheses refer to the preferred editions of Mrs. Pilkington's *Memoirs,* summarized in the Appendix. Quotations, however, are from my own critical text, in preparation.

2. Ehrenpreis, *Swift: The Man, His Works, and the Age*, 3 vols. (Cambridge, Mass.: Harvard University Press, 1962–83), 3:637–38n., 707n. He excepts "natural evasions concerning her shady liaisons."

3. For Mrs. Pilkington's account of George Rooke, son of the Tory naval hero Admiral Sir George Rooke, see 2:92–103. Rooke takes an interest in her after reading her anonymous anti-Walpole pamphlet *An Apology for the Minister*, in print by late September 1739 (*Daily Post*, 27/29 September). For his preparations to stand for Parliament for the city of Canterbury, see his obituary two months later in the *London Evening Post*, 24/27 November 1739. One story put in his mouth (2:99) allegedly concerns Walpole's mistress Maria Skerrett, George II's mistress Lady Yarmouth, and the royal backside. For its original, featuring Lady Yarmouth, a second royal mistress and the backside in October 1742, nearly three years after Rooke's death, see Horace Walpole's report in *The Yale Edition of Horace Walpole's Correspondence*, ed. Wilmarth S. Lewis et al., 48 vols. (New Haven: Yale University Press, 1937–1983), 18:71.

4. Compare her account in 1:149–58 to the coverage in the *Dublin News-Letter, Pue's Occurrences, Dublin Evening Post, Dublin Weekly Journal, Dublin Daily Advertiser*, and the official *Dublin Gazette* between Monday 18 October 1736, the day after Van Lewen accidentally slipped and fell on one of his surgical knives, and 8 January 1736/7, a week after he died. The newspapers suggest that his initial crisis came on the third night, rather than the fourth as Mrs. Pilkington remembers. Overall she also engages in some telescoping about the rally he mounted, which the newspapers report underway in early December. If Van Lewen's fashionable clientele and many charity cases made him a man of note in Dublin, I suspect that it was the freakishness of his case and suspicions of a bungled suicide attempt which attracted so much public notice. By 11 December Lord Orrery was grumbling to Bishop Robert Clayton that the town "is now quite tir'd of curing and killing, and killing and curing Doctor *Vanleuen*." See Harvard MS Eng 218.2, 7:52, printed in *The Orrery Papers*, ed. Emily De Burgh Canning Boyle, Countess of Cork and Orrery, 2 vols. (London: Duckworth, 1903) 1:178.

5. When she returned to Dublin and began seeking subscribers there as well, she wrote Cibber that she entertained them "in the same manner I have had the honour of amusing you, with a particular account of Dr. Swift." See *The Correspondence of Samuel Richardson*, ed. Anna Laetitia Barbauld, 6 vols. (London: for Richard Phillips, 1804), 2:160, dated 18 June 1747, a month after her arrival back in Dublin.

6. It is probable that the artistry in Mrs. Pilkington's anecdotes evolved from retelling them in conversation, rather than from any special care she took in writing them down. Early in her first volume

she boasted that she was "too volatile" to revise or take pains over her writing (1:95). What she really valued, she later added, was irregularity or spontaneity (3:33). The claim is born out by a general absence of authorial changes in successive editions of the volumes which appeared in her lifetime—in marked contrast, for example, to Lord Orrery, who published the first book-length study of Swift a year after her death, with constant textual tinkering (most of it quite petty) from one edition to the next.

7. See for example the poem by young Edmund Burke's friend Beaumont Brenan about this time, "To the Memory of Doctor Swift," prefixed to John Hawkesworth's *Life of the Revd. Jonathan Swift, D.D.* (Dublin: for S. Cotter, 1755), iii–viii. We see Swift as the repository of every public virtue, now hymning with the angels in heaven while patriots below defend his earthly reputation:

> All worthy Minds, whom Love of Merit sways,
> Shou'd shade from Slander his respected Bayes;
> And bid that Fame his useful Labours won,
> Pure and untainted through all Ages run.

8. Bernard Clarke, *A Collection of Poems Upon Various Occasions,* Numb. I[-IV] (Dublin: by S. Powell for the Author, 1751), 62.

9. At one point when she was stalling her subscribers with advertisements claiming that not enough money had come in to print the volume, she had to break off a private letter with the explanation, "Here's the Printer wants more Copy." See Clarke, *Collection of Poems,* 63, datable to summer 1748.

10. She may even have been finishing the first volume when advertising that it was "In the Press," especially if we credit her later claim, published in vol. 3, that she only had written forty pages' worth when she first returned to Dublin and started advertising it (3:198). Previously she implied that she had written *all* of it before returning to Ireland in 1747—hence, she says in the preface, her explanations of Irish customs not familiar to English readers (1:vii). But there are not many such explanations, and they seem to cluster towards the first quarter of the book (e.g., 1:56, on the affection of Irish wet nurses for the babies they tend). Nothing is explained later on for such customs as the "Diversions of the Season at *Mallow,*" Co. Cork (1:144), which all Irishmen but few enough English would recognize as the Irish equivalent of the spa at Bath.

11. Including the young country schoolmaster Bernard Clarke, from whose correspondence with her I have previously quoted. It was Clarke, then a stranger, who sent in the celebratory verses printed in the

preface of her vol. 2. He corresponded with her until shortly before the book's appearance. By the time she embarked on vol. 3 she had also lost her chief backer in Ireland, the generous young Lord Kingsborough. In a letter of January 1752, three years after vol. 2 came out, Mrs. Delany records an epigram being handed about on another uncomplimentary account of Swift, Lord Orrery's *Remarks*:

> A sore disease this scribbling itch is,
> His Lordship of his Pliny vain,
> Turns Madam Pilkington in britches,
> And now attacks the Irish Dean.

See Mary Granville Delany, *The Autobiography and Correspondence*, ed. Lady Llanover, 6 vols. (London: Richard Bentley, 1861–62), 3:79. Orrery had published a translation of Pliny's letters early in 1751.

12. In her vol. 1 Mrs. Pilkington reported receiving the same kind of chastisement "whenever I made use of an inelegant Phrase" (1:87). After a long visit in Dublin early in the 1730s, the lively young widow Mary Pendarves (no fool or masochist when it came to men) wrote back to Swift to say how much she missed him: "And since I have not now an opportunity of receiving your favours of pinching and beating," she says, "make me amends by chiding me for every word that is false spelt, and for my bad *English*" in this letter. See *The Correspondence of Jonathan Swift*, ed. Sir Harold Williams, 5 vols. (Oxford, 1963–65; rpt. corr. Oxford: Clarendon, 1965–72), 4:180 (21 July 1733).

13. Williams, "Swift's Early Biographers," in James L. Clifford and Louis A. Landa, *Pope and His Contemporaries: Essays presented to George Sherburn* (New York: Oxford University Press, 1949), 114–28.

14. The popularity of Swift's *Directions to Servants*, published less than three years before this volume of *Memoirs*, may also have influenced Mrs. Pilkington. Certainly it prepared her readers for accounts of Swift squabbling with his servants.

15. Phillip S. Y. Sun, "Swift's Eighteenth-Century Biographies" (Diss., Yale, 1963), 145–60; Sheridan, *The Life of the Rev. Dr. Jonathan Swift* (London: for C. Bathurst et al., 1784), 460; Delany, *Observations upon Lord Orrery's Remarks on the Life and Writings of Dr. Jonathan Swift* (London: by W. Reeve and A. Linde, 1754), 186–87.

The Humors of Quilca:
Swift, Sheridan, and County Cavan

JOSEPH McMINN

Thomas Sheridan's ancestral home in Quilca, county Cavan, seems to have provoked and attracted those aspects of Swift's personality and temperament which medieval doctors would have called the cardinal humors—blood, phlegm, choler, and melancholy.[1] A seventeenth-century definition of "humor" indicates a faculty for perceiving and expressing the ludicrous and the absurd in human affairs,[2] one fully exercised by Swift in his visits to this rural hideaway.[3] Traditional Irish music uses another, plural form of the term which might suggest something of the fanciful and spontaneous character of Swift's time at Quilca, a world seemingly unfit for the saturnine Dean, but one which allowed him to indulge his contradictory and playful sense of humour.[4]

Swift enjoyed hating Quilca. For him, the anarchic condition of the place was inseparable from the personality of its owner, so much so that the logical relation between cause and effect, house and host, was somewhat blurred. The domestic chaos at Quilca was usually attributed to Sheridan's spectacular incompetence, but often Swift would suggest that no civilized man could prosper in such a slum. Despite everything, it remained the home of one whom James Woolley calls "Swift's closest Irish friend."[5] Carole Fabricant refers to Swift's "love-hate relationship" with Quilca, and interprets much of his literary version of the place in terms of a radical anti-pastoral, a grotesque version of English Augustan poesy.[6] We might add that Quilca was an important literary retreat for the Dean, a place where he finished and transcribed *Gulliver's Travels*, and where he completed his campaign as Drapier. The wilds of Cavan also allowed Swift to indulge his favorite and obsessive practical arts, plantation and gardening, the ordering of rural chaos.

In trying to appreciate the nature and value of Swift's association with Sheridan and Quilca, we may benefit from some historical and geographical sense of the place. Some gesture towards this kind of reconstruction is not only of biographical or historical interest, but also in keeping with Swift's strong, observant, and critical sense of physicality and landscape. Like those medieval doctors, Swift explains most disorders by tracing them to their physical or material foundations. The image of a constitution, in matters political, is one obvious and recurrent example in his writings, especially in his Irish pamphlets.[7] Quilca is indeed "a country of the mind" (Fabricant 1982, 160), a kind of sportive fiction, but its reality and immediacy also engrossed Swift. To appreciate more fully some of the images and echoes within that fiction, we need to understand something of the cultural context in which it made its appearance.

Quilca is a townland four miles northwest of the plantation town of Virginia, in the parish of Mullagh in southeast Cavan, a region formerly known as East Breffni.[8] In Swift's day, it lay just outside the English-speaking Pale, one of whose outposts was the ancient cathedral town of Kells, in the neighboring county of Meath. Kells, which lay eight Irish miles from Quilca was, according to Swift, "the nearest habitable place" (*Correspondence* 3:61), and the nearest town for sending and receiving letters. "Quilca" derives from the original Gaelic name, the adjectival "cúilceach," meaning "abounding in reeds," most likely because of the small lake in the townland. In Petty's map of 1685, *Hiberniae Delineatio*, and in subsequent maps by Henry Pratt (1708) and Hermann Moll (1728), half the parish is represented by the blunt appellation "The Great Bog," an area wholly unsuited to tillage. Bogs were always a feature of the Irish landscape which frustrated Swift's ideal of a self-sufficient form of economy, a geological distortion which he hoped to reform out of existence.[9]

The Sheridans in the parish had been native Catholics until around 1600 when Denis Sheridan, Thomas's grandfather, converted to Protestantism, and later helped the Bishop of Kilmore, William Bedell, translate the Bible into Irish.[10] This conversion helped the Sheridans to obtain possession of the lands of Quilca after the Restoration of Charles II. What is most striking about Thomas Sheridan's background is the uncertain and unpredictable nature of land ownership and religious-political loyalty. Sheridan's disastrous sermon on 1 August 1725, in Rincurran, county Cork (a living which Swift helped him obtain), when he seemed to declare Jacobite sympathies, had unfortunate precedents in the family. Two of his paternal uncles had been Jacobites; William, also Bishop of Kilmore, was deprived of his see for refusing to take the oaths of allegiance on the accession of William and Mary, and Thomas, who served as a Privy Counsellor to James II, fled to France after King William's victory. In his "History of the Second Solomon," an ironic tribute to Sheridan's maladroit behavior, Swift mentions that it was well known that his close friend was "famous for a high Tory" (*PW* 5:223). After the scandal in Cork, Swift defended Sheridan's innocence and integrity, and dismissed his detractors as Yahoos. He never expressed any discomfort with the Jacobite tradition in Sheridan's family. I suspect that he secretly admired such principled stubbornness.

Swift's fixation about Sheridan's tenure at Quilca was more than a simple version of his fatherly impatience with this feckless junior. Because of their Jacobite loyalties, the Sheridans had been dispossessed of Quilca after the defeat of James, when it came into the hands of a neighboring family, the McFaddens. Only by marrying Elizabeth, the daughter of that family, did Thomas repossess Quilca. Legal and secure ownership of landed property was vital to Protestant Ireland in the early decades of the eighteenth century, when fears of yet another rebellion were still very much alive. In June 1725, while staying at Quilca, Swift realized that Sheridan had not properly surveyed the nature and extent of his lands, and undertook to employ a competent surveyor out of his own pocket.[11] Sheridan's mismanagement of his property affronted everything in Swift's political and emotional outlook, an example of slovenliness perhaps natural to the natives, but inexcusable in a settler. And yet, Sheridan was of native Irish stock and had never been out of Ireland. Swift, on the other hand, was the first of his family to be born in Ireland and always felt a sense of strangeness and novelty about the place.

Compared with his many other friends in the country, Sheridan seems closest to, and most at ease with, what we may call "native" Ireland, and moved easily between the two cultures. In 1735, when he had moved to Cavan town, twenty miles northwest of Quilca, to take up his new position at the Royal School, Sheridan wrote to Swift, including a lengthy account of a local incident which seemed to him typically Irish and which would tickle the Dean's fancy. He related how a man called Mackay, from the neighboring county of Armagh, had been brought to the public gallows in the town, whereupon he had entertained his audience for two hours with stories and jests, all the while perfectly sober, before fearlessly asking the hangman to proceed. Sheridan then challenged Swift, "Match me this with any of your *Englishmen,* if you can" (*Correspondence* 4:376). He later told another tale of two gigantic millstones being stolen from the Quilca area, the thieves chased as far as Killeshandra, about ten miles away, on the other side of Lough Oughter, then vanishing, and he concluded, "I do believe this dexterity may challenge history to match it. It has made all our country merry, but the poor miller that lost them" (*Correspondence* 4:543). In the arts of thievery, as well as in its inability to prosper, Ireland did indeed seem perversely unique. Politically, this comic lawlessness could not have amused the Dean: artistically, however, it often suited his literary humor.

Situated on the borderlands between Planter and Gael, Quilca was one of those many islands of potential order with which Swift was familiar in his extensive travels throughout the country. Like a boy playing truant from the discipline of school, Swift enjoyed an invigorating kind of personal, intimate liberty while staying at Quilca. This thrilling sense of forbidden pleasure is conveyed in a breathless passage of a letter to Sheridan after Swift's very first visit, in the summer of 1722. Swift confides that the letter was written during a break from a game of cards with friends, the Dean stealing out "like a lover writing to his Mistress" (*Correspondence* 3:441). In this letter, he recalls their summer escapades together, ironically sympathizing with Sheridan's present loneliness:

You will find Quilca not the Thing it was last *August*; nobody to relish the Lake; nobody to ride over the Downs; no Trout to be caught; no dining over a Well; no night Heroics, no Morning Epics; no stollen Hour when the Wife is gone; no Creature to call you Names. Poor miserable Master *Sheridan*! no journies to *Rantavan*! (*Correspondence* 3:441)

Most intriguing about this catalogue of country delights is the sense that Sheridan introduced Swift into the "Hidden Ireland," the world of Carolan, the most celebrated musician of Gaelic Ireland, a native of the neighboring county Leitrim and a contemporary of Swift. The definitive work on Swift's contact with that other culture and language has been done by Alan Harrison and Andrew Carpenter in their close study of the text and context of *Pléaráca na Ruarcach*, a poem set to music by Carolan.[12] Yet Swift's mention of "journies to Rantavan" conjures up another possible link with that other culture.

Rantavan House lay only five miles southeast of Quilca, on the shores of Mullagh Lake, and was the home of Henry Brooke, a student in Sheridan's school and a close friend of the family.[13] Brooke himself became an enthusiastic antiquarian and collected Gaelic poems from some of his field-laborers. Some of these were passed down to his more famous daughter, Charlotte, whose *Historical Memoirs of the Irish Bards* (1786) included two poems by Carolan and whose *Reliques of Ancient Irish Poetry* (1789) was a landmark in the translation of Gaelic verse. Brooke himself had his early education from a Catholic scholar in the parish, Felix Comerford, who earned his living in the area through introducing young men to classical literature. The disconcerting blend of cultural sophistication and domestic ruination which Swift saw in Sheridan suggests something of this wandering-scholar type, a hedge-school master practicing his art in the city of Dublin.

Swift's literary image of Quilca is, predictably, a satirical version of rural bliss. In his letters, verse, and prose he represented the place as a perfect parody of a gentleman's retreat, a grotesque idyll, a way of life that beggared civilized belief. Its vast potential for farce was signaled in the author's subtitle to his prose-catalogue, "The Blunders, Deficiencies, Distresses and Misfortunes of Quilca," which promised, confidently, "one and twenty Volumes in Quarto" on the subject (*PW* 5:219).

On Sheridan's estate, Nature and servants conspire together to torment and confuse all expectations of order and normality. The hapless guest endures December weather in May and is forced to gather up wet turf while the menials, delighted with such unseasonal inclemency, stay abed. Travel and holidays were inconceivable without servants, but at Quilca the usual hierarchy of service is turned upside down. To complete this account of barbaric infection, Swift records "The Ladies and Dean's Servants growing fast into the Manners and Thieveries of the Natives" (*PW* 5:220), a final humiliation which forces masters into self-reliant servitude. As Irvin Ehrenpreis has noted, life at Quilca is an early prototype of the absurdist version of Big House fiction such as we find later in the century in Maria Edgeworth's *Castle Rackrent* (1800).[14]

To more fully appreciate the humors of Quilca, we should always keep in mind places like Moor Park in Surrey, where Swift was utterly domesticated, without any opportunity or need to impose himself on either company or landscape. The uncultivated terrain of Quilca became a kind of productive paradise for Swift, a place where he could test his energies against the stubborn and lawless elements and inhabitants. Never a passive or relaxing guest, he found the disorder most congenial to his humor for "improvement." As was his custom wherever he visited, he began to tame, redesign, and cultivate the landscape, playing the role of a pioneering farmer whose duty was to transform the wilderness into a garden. In May 1725, he wrote to Knightley Chetwode from Quilca:

> [I] . . . have been forced for amusement to set Irish fellows to work, and to oversee them. I live in a cabin and in a very wild country; yet there are some agreeablenesses in it, or at least I fancy so, and am levelling mountains and raising stones, and fencing against inconveniencies of a scanty lodging, want of victuals, and a thievish race of people. (*Correspondence* 3:60)

This image of a middle-aged, city churchman stomping around the hills of Quilca, assuming the role of frontier developer, should not be confused with, or likened to, someone like Marie Antoinette acting out playful fantasies of pastoral life. Swift was deadly serious. Since Sheridan, like his servants, could not be trusted to secure, let alone attend to, his property, Swift, for the sake of his health as much as for the pleasure of bossing people, assumed the stewardship of Quilca.

When Sheridan was down in Cork preparing for his calamitious sermon, Swift spent the summer at Quilca with Stella and Rebecca Dingley, and enjoyed absolute sovereignty in the place. He wrote to Charles Ford:

> We live here among a Million of wants, and where everybody is a Thief. I am amusing my self in the Quality of Bayliff to Sheridan, among Bogs and Rocks, overseeing and ranting at Irish Laborers, reading Books twice over for want of fresh ones, and fairly correcting and transcribing my Travels, for the Publick. Any thing rather than the Complaint of being Deaf in Dublin. (*Correspondence* 3:89)

Such a barbarous landscape allowed Squire Swift to play out many fantasies of status and identity. Ehrenpreis suggests that the Dean's industry at Quilca was born out of a real desire to identify with "the whole people of Ireland in their productive functions."[15]

It also, of course, gave him the firsthand knowledge and experience of rural economy which authenticated the rhetoric of so many of his pamphlets. His final pamphlet on Wood's halfpence, *An Humble Address to Both Houses of the Irish Parliament*, composed at Quilca and brought down to Dublin by Sheridan, contrasted the practical virtues of the yeoman-farmer with the speculative vices of the urban politician.[16] *A Short View of the State of Ireland* (1728) deplored the ruinous waste of so much natural potential on the land,[17] and one of his contributions to *The Intelligencer*, No. 19 (1728), is spoken in the guise of an outraged county Down M.P. lamenting the emigration of so many Protestants from the land to the colonies in America, thereby abandoning Ireland to even greater ruin, if such a thing were possible.[18]

Quilca became a perfect example of much that was wrong with Ireland, a microcosm of national illness, curable only through discipline and industry. Whether in his fictions about Quilca, or in his pamphlets on Ireland, Swift showed virtually

no aesthetic interest in landscape or place, preferring to empha-
size the workings of its inhabitants. Landscape was territory not
scenery, an investment to be protected and enriched, not a place
for fanciful yearning. (When he did indulge his humor for the
sublime, as in "Carberiae Rupes," a poem about the wild splendor
of the coastline of West Cork, the result is quite forgetable).[19]
This is why Swift never really described the color and texture of
Quilca, keeping instead to its essential features, such as "cabin,"
"bog," and "lake," preferring to see it as both health-farm and
industrial site for its visitors.

Swift enjoyed the organization of compulsory recreation for
the ladies, noting that Stella's health always improved with the
rigors of Quilca but that Rebecca Dingley, being an "absolute
corrupted city lady" does not know "the pleasures of the country, even of this place, with all its millions of inconveniences"
(*Correspondence* 3:91). Like a peeved scoutmaster, he conceded
that Mrs. Dingley "would rather live in a *Dublin* cellar, than a
country palace." Compared to his summer breaks on the estates
of the rural squirearchy, such as the Rochforts of Gaulstown,
county Westmeath, the Chetwodes of Woodbrooke, county Laois,
the Achesons of Markethill or the Copes of Loughgall, in county
Armagh, Swift's time at Quilca was all the more enjoyable for
being all the less refined. The absence of, and the need for,
civility and order excited his imagination and gave it something
to combat, to engage with, and to protect. This, of course, is as
much a way of describing his relationship with Sheridan as that
with Quilca.

By way of a historical postscript, a few words should be said
about the literary legacy of Quilca. Thomas Sheridan, twenty
years Swift's junior, died in 1738, seven years before the Dean.
His son, also called Thomas, continued to reside at Quilca, when
he was not engaged with the Smock Alley Theatre in Dublin.
In 1758, due to a financial crisis, he sold off the house and
lands by public auction. In a way which recalled his father's lucky
repossession of the property at the beginning of the century, the
new owners turned out to be relations of the family, named Le
Fanu.[20] In 1852, Quilca was owned by Joseph Sheridan Le Fanu,

Gothic novelist and author of *Uncle Silas* (1864). It is through this succession that Swift makes a curious and important reappearance. In 1927, a descendant of the Sheridan Le Fanu family presented to the world an original catalogue of Swift's library, drawn up in 1715 by the Dean himself.[21] This catalogue had been passed down to the Le Fanu family by Thomas Sheridan junior, the Dean's godson and biographer.

Coincidentally, in the same year that Joseph Sheridan Le Fanu took over Quilca, a descendant of the Brooke family contributed a colorful, if highly pedantic, memoir of the place to the *Dublin University Magazine*, entitled "A Pilgrimage to Quilca."[22] In the leisurely style of a gentleman-antiquarian resurrecting the ghosts of the area, the writer tries to account for Thomas Sheridan's corrupted potential and attributes it to two simple causes, his "intimacy with Swift" and "his ancient Irish lineage." The latter, he contends, explains Sheridan's "wasteful, reckless, and over-hospitable mode of living." Clearly, Sheridan's Protestantism did not go back far enough.

The misalliance with Swift is full of the same kind of stereotyping, but especially that of the Dean as monstrous egotist, a "horse-leech friend" who bullied Sheridan into frivolity, keeping him "in a perpetual whirl of excitement and levity, frequently descending to buffoonery, or deviating into schoolboy folly." Such an utterly humorless account of the friendship between the two men is part of a nineteenth-century bias against a demented Dean, one derived from Samuel Johnson.[23] It also exemplifies a rare sense of the word "humor," denoting a state of mind having no apparent ground or reason, a capricious or wholly fanciful understanding. Nothing in the evidence from the relationship between Swift and Sheridan supports such a bilious view; on the contrary, it was a rich fusion of background and temperament, age and rank, seriousness and serendipity.

NOTES

1. Such medicinal lore survived well into the seventeenth century; see Robert Burton's *The Anatomy of Melancholy* [1621], ed. and intro. Holbrook Jackson (London and Toronto: Dent, 1977), esp. 147ff.

2. *Oxford English Dictionary* (2nd edition, 1989).

3. Swift made three lengthy visits to Quilca: the first, in the summer of 1722, the second during the winter of 1723–24, and the third in the summer of 1725. For the second and third visits, he was accompanied by Stella and Rebecca Dingley.

4. In the Irish language, "fonn" refers to humor, fancy, or inclination: it is also a term for a tune or musical air.

5. James Woolley, "Thomas Sheridan and Swift," *Studies in Eighteenth Century Culture* 9 (1979): 93–114.

6. Carole Fabricant, *Swift's Landscape* (Baltimore and London: Johns Hopkins University Press, 1982), 156–60.

7. As in the opening lines of the Drapier's fourth pamphlet, *To the Whole People of Ireland*: " . . . I find that Cordials must be frequently applied to weak Constitutions Political as well as Natural" in Swift, *Prose Works*, ed. Herbert Davis et al., 14 vols. (Oxford: Blackwell, 1939–1968), 10:53.

8. Most of the topographical and historical detail concerning Quilca is taken from *Portrait of a Parish: A History of the Parish of Mullagh* (Cavan: Cavan Historical Society, 1988), 22–36.

9. See, for example, Swift's seventh and final Drapier's pamphlet, *An Humble Address to Both Houses of the Irish Parliament* in *Prose Works* 10:139–40.

10. On the Sheridan family, see Woolley, 93, *Portrait of a Parish*, 139, and Sara Cullen, "In the Sheridan Country," *Drumlin: Journal of Cavan, Leitrim and Monaghan* 1 (1978):43–48.

11. In a letter to a Mr. Sheridan (possibly a relation of Swift's friend) in the employment of William Fitzherbert of Shercock, county Cavan, in *The Correspondence of Jonathan Swift*, ed. Harold Williams, 5 vols. (Oxford: Clarendon, 1963–1965), 3:65–66.

12. Alan Harrison and Andrew Carpenter, "Swift's 'O'Rourke's Feast' and Sheridan's 'Letter': Early Transcripts by Anthony Raymond," *Proceedings of the First Münster Symposium on Jonathan Swift*, eds. Hermann J. Real and Heinz J. Vienken (Munich: W. Fink, 1985), 27–46.

13. *Portrait of a Parish*, 134–38. On Brooke's later role in the revival of interest in Gaelic literature, see *A New History of Ireland*, vol. 4 of *Eighteenth Century Ireland 1691–1800*, eds. T. W. Moody and W. E. Vaughan (Oxford: Clarendon, Oxford University Press, 1986), 468–69.

14. Irvin Ehrenpreis, *Swift: The Man, His Works, and the Age*, 3 vols. (London: Methuen, 1962–1983), 3:377.

15. Ehrenpreis, 3:379.

16. *Prose Works*, 10:119–41.

17. *Prose Works*, 12:5–12.

18. *Prose Works*, 12:54–61. See *The Intelligencer*, ed. James Woolley (Oxford: Clarendon, Oxford University Press, 1992), 20–26, for Swift's literary collaboration with Sheridan.

19. *The Poems of Jonathan Swift*, ed. Harold Williams, 3 vols., 2nd ed. (Oxford: Clarendon, 1958), 1:315–19.

20. The Le Fanu family were descendants of French Huguenots who had settled in Ireland in the early eighteenth century. Alicia Sheridan, a sister of the dramatist Richard Brinsley Sheridan, married Joseph Le Fanu in 1776. Their grandson, called Joseph Sheridan Le Fanu, was the popular nineteenth-century novelist.

21. T. P. Le Fanu, "Catalogue of Dean Swift's Library in 1715, With an Inventory of his Personal Property in 1742," *Proceedings of the Royal Irish Academy* 37 (1927): 263–75.

22. No. 239 (November, 1852): 509–26.

23. Johnson's portrait of Swift's personality is well known for its harshness, epitomized in the lines, "He had a countenance sour and severe, which he seldom softened by any appearance of gaiety. He stubbornly resisted any tendency to laughter" in *Lives of the Poets*, intro. Arthur Waugh, 2 vols. (Oxford: Oxford University Press, 1956), 2:212.

Jonathan Swift's Library,
His Reading, and His Critics

HEINZ J. VIENKEN

In view of the fact that we have Swift's 1697/8 reading list, his 1715 inventory, and Lyon's autograph list of 1742, it would be sheer sciamachy were one to try and find out why Sir Harold Williams chose to reprint the sale catalogue of Swift's library in facsimile, thus forgoing the possibility of actually establishing the contents of the 657 volumes sold, including broken sets.[1] Although we are given a rough description of the subject matter and authors of these approximately two hundred folios, one hundred quartos, and the remaining octavos and smaller sizes, we are told nothing about the fact that here are represented some 1,961 authors. Of these, 336 travel writers can be found in Hakluyt, 272 in Purchas, 144 humanists, antiquaries, and polymaths in the anthologies of Graevius, 116 in that of Gronovius, 73 in Michael Maittaire's copious *Opera et fragmenta veterum poetarum latinorum profanorum & ecclesiasticorum* (London, 1713) and even 46 minor authors in Ralph Winterton's anthology. To sample further, the library contains 358 historians, 120 theologians, 43 medical writers, 33 legal authors, and 29 diplomats.

By comparison, Swift's library may have been small; however, there is more here than meets the eye, and Williams's statement needs amending when he claims: "It is rather surprising . . . to find among the Dean's books only two editions of Horace."[2] In reality, there are five: an Elzevier (1629), James Talbot's edition (Cambridge, 1699), Carthy's translation of the second book of the *Epistles* (Dublin, 1731), Pine's two-volume edition (1733–37), and the *Opera* in Maittaire's anthology (1:442–93). Also, it

154

does not seem appropriate to say that there "are two indifferent editions of Ovid in the catalogue,"[3] when Swift had Edward Lovett Pearce's gift of Raphael Regius's incunable (Venice, 1493), Nicolaus Heinsius's Elzevier edition (Amsterdam, 1676), Maittaire's edition of *Opera* (1:534–753; 2:1582–83), Marot's translation of *Metamorphoses*, books I and II, and Congreve's translation of the third book of the *Art of Love*. Nor does the following sentence stand up: "Lucretius, Claudian, Juvenal, and Persius are represented by an edition apiece."[4] Swift's Lucretius (Amsterdam, 1631) is now at the Pierpont Morgan Library; furthermore he had the Cambridge 1675 edition and again Maittaire's "De rerum natura libri sex" (1:293–341). Claudian is present with Colinaeus's edition (Paris, 1530), Nicolaus Heinsius's edition (Amsterdam, 1650), and further nineteen titles in Maittaire. Juvenal's sixteen satires are reprinted in Maittaire (2:1142–67) and in Joseph Lang's edition (Freiburg, 1608). There is also an additional Persius by way of Sheridan's translation (Dublin, 1728). Where Williams counts four editions or translations of Lucian, seven editions or translations of the *Pharsalia* can be counted.[5] Further light can be shed on Williams's somewhat garbled description of the Plautus situation.[6] Prior's present of Robert Estienne's edition (1530), "Given me by my most ingenious Friend Mat. Prior Esq. 1710–11 Jonath. Swift." appeared on the market twice in 1990 and 1991;[7] then there is Lambin's (Paris, 1576) edition,[8] a further Lambin (Paris, 1588), printed from the sheets of the 1576 edition with a fresh title, an (Amsterdam, 1619) edition given to Dan Jackson, and Johann Friedrich Gronovius's 1669 edition "ex officina Hackiana." Swift's copy of this edition is at Abbotsford House,[9] a gift from St. George Ashe, whose name appears in the top right-hand corner of volume 1, "St. Geo: Clogher." To this Swift has added "given by St. Geo: Clogher to J.S." In addition to these, there are "Comoediae" printed by Maittaire (1:1–224) and "Fragmenta" (2:1470–73).

These remarks are not intended to excoriate Williams's work, they merely point to the necessity of looking at each imprint in the Dean's library again, especially when it comes to the contents of each volume. There may be 120 French volumes in the library, "not far from one-fifth of the whole library,"[10] yet these at the same time represent 229 authors. As regards "books on Ireland"[11] Williams only finds Samuel Madden, Sir William Fownes, Sir John Browne, Sir John Temple, Carte's *Life of Ormonde*, and Nicholson's *Irish Historical Library*, whereas a computer count yields some 34 Irish authors in the library proper, not taking into account all the Irish authors we come across in Swift's reading, or those he may have come across in Dublin.

Williams also claims that, "Apart from English and French the modern languages were virtually unrepresented in Swift's library."[12] This may be true; however, one will find some 158 Italian authors, some 67 Spanish, 50 Dutch, 8 Belgian, and 7 Danish writers, especially in the major anthologies, who would in those days, of course, either write in Latin or be translated from the vernacular for the sake of being universally understood.

While we would expect to find a large number of classical, British, and French authors and a plethora of humanist writers, by now anthologized and no longer individually present as, say, in the days of Robert Burton, we find it at times hard to understand why Swift had some books on his shelves that are completely forgotten today. A case in point is Friedrich Hoffmann's *Poeticum cum musis colludium* (Amsterdam, 1663), several centuries of hilarious epigrams in Latin, mixed with German and Greek snippets. For lovers of Anglo-Latin games like Swift and Sheridan, this collection would have been right up their street, with epigrams like "Dactyli sunt fructus Palmae arboris: die Datteln," or "Unter-Roecke sind Appetit-Roecke," or the amusing advice to the teacher to call badly behaved boys Stifel, which he explains as an acronym of the words "Schlingel, Tölpel, Igel, Flegel, Esel, Lümmel."[13]

Of even greater satirical value is the most celebrated satire of the sixteenth century, the *Epistolae obscurorum virorum ad Dn. M. Ortvinum Gratium. Nova et accurata editio . . .* (Frankfurt, 1643), coarse, scurrilous, irreverent, but uproariously funny, Aristophanic in the freedom and audacity of its humor.[14] This edition not only contains the two volumes of the epistles but also a "Conciliabulum theologistarum adversus Germaniae et bonarum literarum studiosos," the dialogue "Huttenus captivus," a dialogue between Hutten and *veritas* "Huttenus illustris," the Menippean satire "De generibus ebriosorum, et ebrietate vitanda. Cui adiecimus: De meretricum in suos amatores, et concubinarum in sacerdotes fide: quaestiones salibus et faceris plenae, laxandi animi, iocique suscitandi causa, nuper editae," followed by a medley in verse and prose both in Latin and German, "De fide concubinarum, in sacerdotes, quaestio accessoria, causa ioci et urbanitatis, in quodlibeto Heydelbergensi determinata a magistro Paulo Oleario, Heydelbergensi"; then follow fifteen pages of "Prognostica, alioquin barbare practica perpetua nuncupata. Ab Andrea Gartnero." From the German vagrant literature are then printed Latin translations of "Monopolium philosophum, vulgo, Die Schelmenzunfft," "Marcolphus hoc est: Disputationes, quas dicuntur habuisse inter se mutuo rex Salomon sapientissimus, et Marcolphus, facie deformis et turpissimus, tamen, ut fertur, eloquentissimus," and finally, "Disputatio de Cornelio et eiusdem natura ac proprietate." The interpretative potential of these highly satirical texts for the study of Swift has never been considered.

Examples like these can be multiplied and seem to me of great moment for scholarship on the Dean's works. Another case in point where an author is hidden behind a different text is Swift's copy of Herodian's eight books of history, in the translation of Angelo Poliziano, printed by Henri Estienne in 1581. The work is dedicated to Sir Philip Sidney, whom Estienne had met in Heidelberg. What is important is that this edition contains the *editio princeps* of the first two books of the Greek historian Zosimus, a history in four books of the Roman Empire from Augustus to A.D. 410, published in full by Leunclavius in 1590. For a lover of books of history like Swift this seems an addition to the library of some importance.

A further point worth discussing when we look at authors from Swift's library is the contemporary authority of texts and authors that are either completely forgotten today or have lost their reputation in the meanwhile. If we take Claudian as an example, we note that he enjoyed a continuous *Nachleben* from the Middle Ages through the eighteenth century. He had been translated into Middle English as early as 1445, earlier than any other classical writer. Among the authors who knew, translated, or alluded to the poet were Chaucer, Leonard Digges, Thomas Elyot, Thomas Lodge, William Webbe, Henry Peacham, and Edmund Spenser. Ben Jonson, John Milton, Abraham Cowley, John Dryden, and many others can be shown to have been familiar with Claudian's work. Thomas Pope Blount included a long chapter on Claudian with the opinions of, among others, Scaliger and Rapin in his *De re poetica* of 1694. Many of Swift's acquaintances and personal friends quoted from Claudian or translated him. Addison translated excerpts from numerous poems of Claudian in his *Remarks on Italy* and the second *Dialogue on Medals* and frequently referred to Claudian in the *Spectator*. Tickell contributed a translation of *Phoenix* to the Tonson *Miscellany* of 1709, and Steele included some of Eusden's translations of Claudian in *Guardians* nos. 127 and 164.

Claudian's works also played a significant role in the Mirror-of-Princes tradition. A famous passage from *Stilico*, bk. iii, ll. 114–15, became commonplace with the supporters of absolute monarchy in the seventeenth century: "Numquam libertas gratior extat/ quam sub rege pio." Filmer chose this passage in a mutilated form as a motto for the title page of *Patriarcha* (1680), and Pope turned this sentence into its reverse in a passage of the *Dunciad* concluding with the lines, "May you, may Cam, and Isis preach it long!/ 'The RIGHT DIVINE of Kings to govern wrong.' "

In the eighteenth century it was the figure of Claudian's Rufinus who became the subject and victim of three different political pamphlets of the period. It is most likely that Swift knew about William King's *Rufinus* pamphlet and the use his friend had made of Claudian. Swift himself had read his Claudian well. In a letter to Harley of 11 October 1722 he mentions a motto from Claudian to be inscribed under his portrait of the Earl. In a later letter to Harley's son, he mentions the motto again. In view of the immense popularity of Claudian in the Augustan period of English literature, it is surprising that no further traces of the last great Roman poet have been discovered so far in Swift's work.

On the other hand, there are many vestiges of authors not in his library whom Swift can be shown to have read. From his works one can expiscate some 464 authors or anonymous texts, of whom some loom large while others are merely represented by a marginal note. Thus, Gilbert Burnet, whom Swift regarded as "the worst qualified for an historian," was obviously not an author the Dean wanted to gaze at on his shelves but rather borrowed John Lyon's copy of the *History of His Own Times,* 2 vols. (Dublin, 1724–34), added many pencil crosses and some furious marginalia.[15] Furthermore, from the Dean's works we can prove that he knew at least eight further titles by Burnet, among them, *A Vindication of . . . the Church and State of Scotland; Some Letters; A Discourse of Pastoral Care,* and the *History of the Reformation.* Similarly, John Dryden can be included with some eight titles in this reading list, with titles like *Sir Martin Mar-all, The Hind and the Panther,* Juvenal's satires, and Dryden's translation of Virgil. Authors like Defoe, Dunkin, Dunton, Leslie, Manley, Oldmixon, or Philips would also be found, again with several titles. In the case of La Rochefoucauld we simply lack the imprint Swift must have owned at some stage, and therefore include him in the reading list.

Strange bedfellows in this list are authors like Lorenzo Ramirez de Prado and his *Pentekontarchos* (Antwerp, 1612) or Joseph Justus Scaliger's *Epistolae* (Frankfurt, 1625), who occur as ink marginalia in Swift's copy of Tonson's Horace (Cambridge, 1699). Although not in Swift's library, both titles had been in Marsh's Library since 1705.[16]

We move in a grey area when we approach, for example, what Herbert Davis has called "Later Activities of the Drapier." Here it is difficult to determine whether Swift could have been the author, whether his understrappers were at work, or whether he even read what was printed before his very eyes.[17] And is one to believe the title of John Ballard's poem "Honour . . . Humbly inscrib'd to, and friendly recommended by the rev. Dr. Swift, D.S.P.D. (Dublin . . . 1739)," to which Foxon adds: "A note on p. 22 records that Swift corrected this poem, but the whole publication appears to be fraudulent"?[18]

Instances like these necessitate, in addition to Swift's library and his reading, a third section which might be called "Indirect references." Here belong items of a very different kidney, and while a count must be indefinite, some 1,416 authors and anonymous items have to be reckoned with. There are authors inferred by critics Swift is supposed to have known, such as John Abernethy's *Nature and Consequences of the Sacramental Test considered* (1731).[19] Then there are items of possible interest for the interpretation of Swift's works, such as "The prophesy: or

M[asha]m's lamentation for H[arle]y. Translated from the Greek of Homer. [London] Printed for Abel Roper, 1710."[20] In addition, there are authors of Swiftian and generally Scriblerian interest, like Ulisse Aldrovandi, Abu Bakr's *Improvement of human reason* in the translation of Simon Ockley (1711), Alexander of Ales, or Caelius Aurelianus, as they can be gleaned from either Swift's works or, for that matter, *The Memoirs of Martinus Scriblerus*.[21] Swift might have noticed much material or it might have been brought to his attention, such as "An Account of the State of Learning in the Empire of Lilliput" (1728), recorded in Teerink's section of "Biography, Criticism,"[22] while other texts have been rejected over the years as uncanonical, such as "Actaeon; or the Original of the Horn Fair,"[23] or "The Alderman's Guide," which is accepted by Ball, rejected by Williams, and given to James Sterling by Foxon.[24] Other authors must be mentioned because of their friendship and collaboration with Swift, or, for that matter, because of their enmity or malevolence. We know that Swift liked, befriended, or admired people like Constantia Grierson, James Maculla, William Maple, George Rooke, and Thomas Sheridan, or had his under spur-leathers Robert Ashton and Samuel Owens, but that he also disliked and antagonized people like James Arbuckle, Charles Carthy, Charles Coffee, Andrew Cumpsty, that "arrant rascal" Fairbrother, Henry Nelson, Ambrose Philips, Jonathan Smedley, James Sterling, William Tisdall, and John Whalley.[25]

During his stay in London we would assume that Swift took notice of or registered journalistic and literary activities that he either provoked himself, or which he himself reported on. Thus he possessed Stephen Poyntz's "The Barrier-Treaty Vindicated" (1712), and he may have known pamphlets like "The Examiner Examin'd" (1713), or "The Negociations for a Treaty of Peace" (1711), where the postscript reads: "The Examiner is extremely mistaken, if he thinks I shall enter the Lists with so prostitute a Writer, who can neither speak Truth, nor knows when he hears it."

And might not Swift, on the occasion of the failure of the South Sea Project, have taken notice of other versifications, like "The hubble bubbles" (1720), or "The hue and cry after the South-Sea, or, a new ballad call'd the Hubble bubbles" (Dublin,

1720)? And he cannot have missed much of what was going on under his very eyes concerning the Wood affair: pamphlets by Bindon or John Browne, pamphlets like "Advice to the Roman Catholics of Ireland. Concerning Wood's Halfpence" (1724), "An Epigram on Wood's Brass-Money," or "The Drapier Anatomiz'd" (1724), "The Drapier Demolished," or "The Drapier Dissected."

Another cluster of texts centers around the publication of *Gulliver's Travels*, concoctions like "Seasonable Reflections Address'd To the Citizens of Dublin" (1727), "The Anatomist Dissected . . . By Lemuel Gulliver" (1727), "An Account of the State of Learning In the Empire of Lilliput" (1728), or the various fabrications under the pseudonym of "Martin Gulliver."

To this section also belong those publications in which Swift's texts were part and parcel of a collection of various authors. Thus the first part of *The Bee* (1715) contains "Mrs. Harris's Petition." *Four Poems* (1725–26), in addition to poems by Roscommon, Rochester, and Ormond, contains also Swift's "Baucis and Philemon"; and James Ralph's nonce collection *Miscellaneous Poems* of 1729 contains, among other previously published poems, two riddles by Swift.

Finally, there are the various addresses to Swift, which the Dean may have ignored, but of which he may also have been informed. Thus he did retort to an attack on Sheridan and himself as joint writers of the *Intelligencer*, called "The true Character of the Intelligencer," with "On Paddy's Character of the Intelligencer." There are the various "epistles" on behalf of the Irish poets, on preferment, to a certain dean, to Dean Swift by a gentleman in the army, or an epistle in answer to a libel on Doctor Delany. Similarly, the "letters" from Aminadab Firebrass praising the Drapier's letters; from a young lady, praising Swift for his public spirit and call to action; a letter to the drapier signed Misoxulos, referring to the rights and liberties of the Irish; a letter against the brewers addressed to M.B. for their raising the price of malt liquors. Last but not least, there are many poems inscribed to Swift, such as Usher Gahagan's "Palaemon," Edward Davys's "Poem delivered to the Reverend Doctor Swift," a birthday poem for 1725 and, again, for St. Andrew's Day 1726 by an anonymous author.

To conclude, it needs pointing out that many a modern critic has drawn attention to the fact that Swift must or could have known a variety of authors, who are neither present in his library nor mentioned in his works. Reasons for these attributions are heterogeneous; they may lie in the affinity of contents and ideas or motifs and sources. Typical examples that spring to mind in this connection are François de Callières, Descartes, or Cyrano de Bergerac.

NOTES

I gratefully acknowledge the cooperation of Dirk F. Passmann in the preparation of this paper.

1. Harold Williams, *Dean Swift's Library, with a Facsimile of the Original Sale Catalogue and Some Account of Two Manuscript Lists of His Books* (Cambridge: Cambridge University Press, 1932); quoted hereafter as *SL.*

2. *SL*, 42.

3. *SL*, 43.

4. *SL*, 43.

5. *SL*, 43–44.

6. *SL*, 44.

7. At Sotheby's on 19 July 1990 and in Sokol's Catalogue XVI (1991).

8. *SL*, no. 593.

9. Pressmark Study K.3.

10. *SL*, 64.

11. *SL*, 70.

12. *SL*, 69.

13. For Hoffmann, see, among others, Curt von Faber du Faur, *German Baroque Literature: A Catalogue of the Collection in the Yale University Library*, vol. 1 of 2 (New Haven: Yale University Press, 1958), 155–56.

14. See F. A. Wright and T. A. Sinclair, *A History of Later Latin Literature from the Middle of the Fourth to the End of the Seventeenth Century* (London, 1969 [1931]), 371–74. Swift's copy was sold at the Anderson sale in 1919, bearing the signatures of both Pope and Swift. The literature on the *Eov* is vast; see particularly Eduard Böcking, ed., *Ulrichi Hutteni equitis operum supplementum*, 2 vols. (Leipzig, 1864–69); Aloys Bömer, ed., *Epistolae obscurorum virorum*, 2 vols. (Heidelberg, 1924); Francis Griffin Stokes, trans., *On the Eve of the Reformation: "Letters of Obscure Men": Ulrich von Hutten et al.*, new intro. by Hajo Holborn (New York, Evanston, London, 1964 [1909]).

15. See *Miscellaneous and Autobiographical Pieces: Fragments and Marginalia*, ed. Herbert Davis (Oxford: Blackwell, 1962), xxxvi-xxxvii, 183–84, 266–94; *SL*, 61–62.

16. See E. J. W. McCann, "Jonathan Swift's Library," *Book Collector* 34 (1985), 336.

17. *The Drapier's Letters to the People of Ireland* (Oxford: Clarendon, Oxford University Press, 1965 [1935]), 323–51.

18. D. F. Foxon, *English Verse, 1701–1750*, vol. 1 of 2 (Cambridge: Cambridge University Press, 1975), 41 (B43).

19. *Irish Tracts, 1728–1733*, ed. Herbert Davis (Oxford: Blackwell, 1971 [1955]), xliii.

20. Foxon, op. cit., vol. 1, 1 (A4).

21. See the edition of Charles Kerby-Miller (New York and Oxford, 1988 [1950]).

22. H. Teerink, *A Bibliography of the Writings in Prose and Verse of Jonathan Swift, D. D.* (The Hague: Martinus Nijhoff, 1937), 366 (1234).

23. *The Poems of Jonathan Swift*, ed. Harold Williams, 2nd ed., vol. 3 (Oxford: Clarendon, Oxford University Press, 1966), 1073 (20).

24. See F. Elrington Ball, *Swift's Verse* (London: John Murray, 1929), 280–81; Williams, op. cit., vol. 3, 1131 (17); Foxon, op. cit., vol. 1, 758 (S752).

25. See Bryan Coleborne, *Jonathan Swift and the Dunces of Dublin* (Diss., Dublin, 1982), 318–35.

Sarah Harding as Swift's Printer

JAMES WOOLLEY

Sarah Harding's unimpressive printing might lead one to ask why she, of all Dublin printers and booksellers, should have been chosen to issue such works as *A Short View of the State of Ireland* (1728), the *Intelligencer* papers (1728–29), or *A Modest Proposal* (1729). This question is answered only in part by the fact that Sarah succeeded her husband John as Swift's printer: why indeed was John Harding Swift's printer?

But in discussing Swift and *any* of his Dublin printers and booksellers, the first problem is to say in just what sense they were "his." Leaving aside the Faulkner period—post-1729[1]—one may consider and rapidly dismiss the notion that whatever was published in Dublin by a prominent Dublin author must have been published with his cooperation or contrivance if not at his direct request. In fact a considerable number of Swift's writings issued during Queen Anne's reign by such Dublin booksellers as John Henly, Edward Waters, Cornelius Carter, and John Hyde were mere reprints of London publications, and there is as a general rule no reason to suppose that Swift had anything to do with such reprints.

In a world where title pages often concealed the identity of authors and booksellers alike, evidence confirming or opposing such a general rule will ordinarily derive from textual collation. Thus, contrary to this general rule, there are significant authorial variants in *The Conduct of the Allies* as issued in Dublin by John Hyde in 1712, as Herbert Davis shows in volume 6 of the *Prose Writings*, and more importantly there are significant authorial variants in Hyde's edition of *Gulliver's Travels* published in 1726, as David Woolley shows in his article on the Armagh *Gulliver*.[2] To summarize, Dublin reprints probably lack textual significance, but on the other hand they *may* be textually significant, and only textual collation can settle the question. Inasmuch as Swift entrusted to Hyde the management of the Dublin subscription for Matthew Prior's works, 1719–21,[3] it would certainly seem worthwhile to look closely at any Hyde printings of works by Swift, although this was not done consistently by Herbert Davis.

Why, then, should Swift not have used John Hyde rather than Edward Waters in 1720 to publish *A Letter . . . to a Gentleman, Designing for Holy Orders* and *A Proposal for the Universal Use of Irish Manufacture*? For printing this latter piece, it will be remembered, Waters was taken into custody, requiring Swift's lobbying to get the charges dropped.[4] There are at least two differences between Hyde's publications of 1712 and Waters's of 1720. Waters was issuing works not previously published, and second, Waters was a printer as well as a bookseller. In sending new material to the public, Swift evidently valued deniability (if I may use a Watergate term), which meant a) avoiding direct contact with the bookseller; b) giving the bookseller no assurances as to authorship; and c) expecting that the bookseller would absorb the risks of prosecution or other legal harassment rather than passing such risks back to him. It is likely, indeed, that Swift's *Intelligencer* papers were copied by an "unknown hand" before being sent to the printer, as were his Drapier's Letters and as he ordered done with *The Journal of a Dublin Lady*, intended for the *Intelligencer*.[5] As Swift on a later occasion explained to the London bookseller Benjamin Motte about his Dublin publications, "I have writ some things that would make people angry. I always sent them by unknown hands, the Printer might guess, but he could not accuse me, he ran the whole risk, and well deserved the property."[6]

In such circumstances Swift is likely to have preferred dealing with a bookseller who did his own printing—with Waters, say, rather than Hyde, who was at that time only a bookseller.[7] In this way he could more efficiently control production and could limit the circle of those who had even indirect knowledge of the source of what was being published.

It is not certain why Swift, having used Waters in 1720, moved to John Harding, Sarah's husband, to print the Drapier's

Letters in 1724, but it is easy to believe that Waters had by this point had his fill of prison and was not eager to incur new risks.[8] Harding meanwhile had printed the prologue and epilogue for the weavers' benefit in 1721 and Swift's *Last Speech and Dying Words of Ebenezor Elliston* in 1722; more importantly, he had been very active in printing the bank tracts, some of them by Swift, in 1722.

John Harding did not, however, represent a step up the ladder of bookselling prestige for Swift. Perhaps Harding, primarily a printer rather than a bookseller, seemed like the sort of printer a draper would engage; after all, a cloth merchant advertised regularly in Harding's *Dublin Impartial News Letter.*[9] Whatever may have been the case with Hyde and Waters, Harding was not highly literate or cultivated, not like John Barber or Ben Tooke, or Motte, or Faulkner. With what exaggeration I am not sure, Swift described Harding in *Seasonable Advice* as a "poor Man" and "Ignorant."[10] In 1721 John Harding found it necessary to protest that while he would do job printing "at Rates as Reasonable as any Printer in Dublin can afford," he would "not undertake to force Trade or become a porter by pasting up Bills and advertisements in the Coffee-houses."[11]

A printer this near the bottom of his trade could be useful to Swift "as a convenient screen."[12] It might have been significant that John Harding had no apparent ties with the London book trade; he was not systematically sending material to London or reprinting material from London; for the most part he was not a bookseller, strictly speaking, but only a publisher of pamphlets and newspapers, not forgetting his halfsheet elegies,[13] and thus his operations were unlikely to be a significant target of the cultural establishment's surveillance.

John Harding had, moreover, demonstrated a willingness to take risks. By the time he began printing the Drapier's Letters, he had been threatened with arrest for printing a Jacobite proclamation (1719),[14] and he had been taken into custody for robbery (1720, acquitted),[15] for unauthorized printing of the Lord Lieutenant's speech (1721),[16] for falsely reporting that the value of gold coin would be raised,[17] and for libel (1723/24, apparently).[18] All these arrests he publicized in his own newspapers.

Harding must have looked to Swift like an appropriate person to issue ephemeral, adventuresome, even dangerous papers of controversy.

Like her husband, Sarah Harding was a Dublin pamphlet printer distinguished neither for typography nor for business success. But she was John's widow, and they had both been imprisoned for printing the fourth Drapier's Letter, *A Letter to the Whole People of Ireland* (1724).[19]

John died on 19 April 1725, before the Wood's halfpence controversy was resolved.[20] In 1726 there appeared a halfsheet poem seeking charitable donations for Sarah Harding, John's "poor Widow . . . who, by the Death of her Husband, is reduc'd to a helpless Condition; but might, by a small assistance, from each well-wisher of *Ireland*, be enabled to [print] again for her Country's Service, if it shou'd ever be in Need."[21] The poem includes these lines:

> To hearten him, the DRAPIER sent to him in Jail,
>   To tell him, he'd quickly get home to his Wife;
> But, scarce cou'd he find one, to stand for his *Bail*,
>   Which struck to his Heart, and depriv'd him of Life.
>
> He left with his Widow, two Children behind,
>   And little, God help her, to keep them from
>   Starving;
> But hoped, for the DRAPIER's Sake friends she wou'd
>   find,
>   Or, for his own merit, they'd think her deserving.
>
> But, alas, She's forgot! there's not one among all,
>   That ever thinks on her, or, her Childrens Case,
> Tho' her Husband helped to hinder their Fall,
>   And she suffer'd by it much shame, and Disgrace.

Clearly John was viewed as a martyr for the Drapier's cause. Had the Wood's halfpence controversy continued, Sarah would have continued printing for the Drapier.[22] That her suffering for his cause continued to be a mark of distinction is suggested by Sheridan's *Intelligencer* advertisement late in 1728, asking "that the Widdow, the PRINTER of these *Papers*, who did likewise *Print* the DRAPIER's Letters, may be enabled by Charitable Encouragements to keep a *merry Christmass*; for She, and her Family, were ruined by Iniquitous *Imprisonments*, and *hardships*, for *Printing* those *Papers*, which were to the Advantage of this Kingdom in General."[23]

Lest it be thought that Sarah was merely a printer's widow and not knowledgeable about printing, there is some evidence that she was the daughter of Elizabeth Sadleir,[24] a Dublin printer, bookseller, and typefounder, and it seems possible that she was related through her mother to other Dublin printers and typefounders, Francis Sadleir, Sarah Sadleir, and Ralph Sadleir. In short, John Harding may have married into the printing business.[25] Certainly Sarah issued at least one publication over her own name, presumably while John was in prison, in 1721.[26]

The frequent but erroneous claim that Sarah herself was imprisoned in 1728 for printing a satiric poem seems to have originated with E. R. McClintock Dix;[27] she *was* arrested for printing *On Wisdom's Defeat in a Learned Debate* (1725), a satiric poem that Swift may have written.[28] Much of her important printing, satiric and otherwise, was for Swift or Sheridan. She issued Swift's *A Short View of the State of Ireland* and *An Answer to a Paper, Called A Memorial* as well as the *Intelligencer* in 1728 and *The Journal of a Dublin Lady* and *A Modest Proposal* in 1729.[29] Altogether, she was active as a printer only from 1725 to 1729, however, and during this period her total output was small (see Appendix).

The *Intelligencer* was her biggest single project. Typical of her work for Swift and Sheridan, the *Intelligencer* was badly printed in small octavo halfsheets using old battered ornaments. Crude typography, cheap paper, shabby makeready, and at times careless proofreading were standard in the Harding shop. William Bowyer's London reprint of the *Intelligencer* accurately describes Sarah Harding's pamphlets as "straggling in a mean Condition."[30] It might be supposed that the *Intelligencer* was deliberately sent into the world in shabby guise—that the authors were masquerading, like Swift as the Drapier. What argues against this supposition is the relatively careful typography of the first edition of *Intelligencer* 1, with a split title-page layout that took some trouble to produce, running heads, spacing between paragraphs, and the first word of each paragraph raised to all caps.[31] Subsequent numbers and editions did not attempt such niceties, but I assume the first number more nearly reflects authorial intentions and that relaxed standards later were tolerated. This is not to say that Swift and Sheridan were ever greatly concerned about typography or that Mrs. Harding's printing was the worst that Dublin could produce. In fact, the *Intelligencers* for all their shabbiness are well within the normal range of contemporary Dublin ephemeral printing.

For book publishing Swift and Sheridan turned elsewhere, however—to James Carson, who printed Sheridan's *Ars Pun-ica* (1719), to John Hyde and E. Dobson, who issued Sheridan's translation of Sophocles' *Philoctetes* (1725), and to George Grierson, who published his translation of Persius (1728); Swift cooperated with John Hyde's Dublin edition of *Gulliver's Travels* (1726).[32] I think that because of Mrs. Harding's background, political affiliation, loyalty, and known association with them, Swift and Sheridan wanted to give the *Intelligencer* to her and thought her work would be adequate.

Sarah Harding, then, recommended by her suffering and her husband's, was chosen to print the *Intelligencer*. Her original printings, rare today, offer the best text of it, despite their occasional corruption. In an attempt to reconstruct the text as it was intended to appear in those printings, I collated every copy of the Sarah Harding printings known to me. This comparison led to the discovery of numerous concealed editions and impressions among the Harding printings (and accordingly the discovery of numerous unsuspected textual variants). Apparently Mrs. Harding found it desirable to print and reprint small batches, perhaps because she was too poor to buy paper in large quantities.[33]

During most of the *Intelligencer's* run—that is, during 1728—Sarah Harding's address was "next Door to the *Crown* in *Copper-Alley*."[34] In *A Modest Proposal*, published in October 1729, the imprint gives her address as "opposite the *Hand and Pen* near *Fishamble-Street*, on the *Blind Key*." After *A Modest Proposal* she drops from sight, and George Faulkner becomes Swift's regular printer. Barry Slepian has surmised that Swift made the change because she died.[35] A contemporary halfsheet suggests rather that she remarried, to another printer, Nicholas Hussey, whose address was also "opposite the Hand and Pen near Fishamble-Street, on the Blind Key."[36] The new alliance seems to have formed early in 1729. It may be that Sarah fades from the bibliographical scene in 1729 because she had become Mrs. Hussey, and it may be also that Swift felt freer to turn to Faulkner, as he did in 1730, knowing that she was no longer alone.

Among Swift's Dublin printers, John and Sarah Harding should be of strong interest to Swift scholars. Fuller inquiry is needed into works from the Harding shop—the Drapier's Letters, say, or *A Modest Proposal.* The collation of multiple copies—a labor not undertaken by Herbert Davis—promises to reveal new textual variants and new information about the publication and revision of these works as well.

APPENDIX:
A CHECKLIST OF SARAH HARDING IMPRINTS

These items are gathered primarily from the on-line Eighteenth-Century Short Title Catalogue,[37] Foxon, and Teerink.[38] Otherwise I have provided the location of a copy, and except as noted, these latter items as well as most others are based on my personal examination. Unsigned imprints are sometimes (if fallibly)[39] attributed to Harding on the evidence of printer's ornaments, using the index of Dublin printer's ornaments compiled in the Department of Early Printed Books, Trinity College Dublin, under the direction of M. Pollard.[40] The hiatus in 1726 is unexplained, although it was perhaps a consequence of Harding's imprisonment for printing *On Wisdom's Defeat* in 1725; a cessation of business seems to be referred to in the *Poem to the Whole People of Ireland* (1726), quoted above.

SH = Sarah Harding
TCD = Trinity College Dublin

1721

S., J. *The Present Miserable State of Ireland. In a Letter from a Gentleman in Dublin to His Friend in London.* ESTC n020957; Teerink 1583, p. 310. Herbert Davis rejects the attribution to Swift, though without explicit discussion of the SH imprint; see *Prose Writings,* 12:xv–xvi.

1725

[Barber, Mary]. *To His Excellency the Lord Carteret, Occasion'd by Seeing a Poem Intituled, The Birth of Manly Virtue.* ESTC t005242; Foxon

B78; Teerink 1200, p. 324. The typography is much above SH's
usual style; I am grateful to M. Pollard for the observation that on
the evidence of ornaments this pamphlet appears to have been
printed by Pressick Rider and Thomas Harbin.

*A Funeral Elegy on the Much Lamented Death of Robert Lord Viscount
Molesworth. Who Departed This Life, on Sunday the 23d of May, 1725.*
Dublin, printed by the Widow Harding, 1725. ESTC t040335.

[?Swift, Jonathan]. *On Wisdom's Defeat in a Learned Debate.* ESTC t005236;
Foxon O230; *Poems,* ed. Williams, 3:1117–18.

[?Sheridan, Thomas]. *To the Honourable Mr. D. T. Great Pattern of Piety,
Charity, Learning, Humanity, Good Nature, Wisdom, Good Breeding,
Affability, and One Most Eminently Distinguished for His Conjugal Af-
fection.* ESTC t005244; Foxon T373.

[?Sheridan, Thomas]. *Numb. II. The Following Fable Is Most Humbly Inscribed to the Honourable Mr. D.T. . . . The Sick Lyon and the Ass.* ESTC
t005245; Foxon T374.

*The Virtuous and Pious Life of His Holiness Peter Francis Ursini, the Presen
Pope.* Dublin, printed by S. H. on the Blind-Key. Copy: TCD Press
A.7.4/158. Not seen; I am grateful to M. Pollard for information
about this item. Ursini was Pope Benedict XIII from May/June
1724 till February 1730, and Pollard dates this publication "ca.
1725" on the assumption that it would have appeared not long
after Ursini became pope. Harding ornament.

1727

Advice to the Electors of the City of Dublin. ESTC t217201, supplying the
erroneous dating "1747." Teerink 935, p. 329. Attributed to SH on
the evidence of a printer's ornament. See *Drapier's Letters,* 339–43.

La Boissiere, Peter. *The Starry Interpreter: or, A Most Useful and Compleat
Almanack for the Year of our Lord, 1728.* ESTC t160401. Probably
issued in 1727 for 1728. Edward Evans reports an edition of this
almanac for 1729—just possibly an erroneous report of the edition
for 1728: *Historical and Bibliographical Account of Almanacks, Direc-
tories, etc., etc., Published in Ireland from the Sixteenth Century* (1897;
reprinted Blackrock: Carraig Books, 1976), 56.

*A Letter to the Freemen and Freeholders of the City of Dublin, Who Are Protestants
of the Church of Ireland as by Law Established.* ESTC t169748, dating it
"[1725?]"; Teerink 934, p. 329. Attributed to SH on the evidence
of a printer's ornament. See *Drapier's Letters,* 336–38.

[?Sheridan, Thomas]. *To the Gentleman Freeholders, and Freemen of the
City; A Few Words Concerning the Alderman and Squire.* Attributed
to Sheridan by Davis in *Drapier's Letters,* 328, and to SH on the

evidence of the printer's ornament, ibid., 331. Copy: TCD Press A.7.4/180.

[Sheridan, Thomas]. *To the Right Honourable the Lord Viscount Mont-Cassel: This Fable Is Most Humbly Dedicated by a Person Who Had Some Share in His Education.* ESTC t128290; Foxon S417.

A Short History of the Eight Philosophers of the Island Cos. Attributed to SH on the evidence of a printer's ornament. Copy: TCD Press A.7.2/114.

1728

[?Abercorn, James Hamilton, 6th Earl of]. *The Speech of a Noble Peer: Made in the House of Lords in Ireland, When the Priviledge-Bill Was in Debate There.* ESTC t001989; for the attribution, see *Intelligencer*, 115.

[Audouin, John]. *The Last Speech Confession and Dying Words of Surgeon John Odwin, Who Is to Be Executed near St. Stephen's-Green: on Wednesday Being the 5th of June, 1728. For the Murder of His Servant Maid Margaret Kees.* ESTC t205303.

Butler, Isaac. *Advice from the Stars: or, An Almanack and Ephemeris for the Year of our Lord, 1729.* Printed by S. Harding . . . for Mary Whalley, 1729. ESTC n060760. Probably issued in 1728 for 1729; preface is dated 20 August 1728. I am grateful to Máire Kennedy of the Gilbert Library (Dublin Public Libraries) for supplying me with a photocopy and description of this item.

An Humble Remonstrance in the Name of the Lads in All the Schools of Ireland, where Latin and Greek Are Taught: and of the Young Students Now in the University of Dublin, Together with a Protest of All the Senior Fellows in Trinity College, Dublin, (except One) against the Provost. ESTC t190885.

A Letter to the Intelligencer. Written by a Young Gentleman, of Fourteen Years Old. See *Intelligencer*, 337. Copy: Beinecke.

Savage, Richard. *The Bastard. A Poem. Inscribed with All Due Reverence to Mrs. Bret, Once Countess of Macclesfield.* ESTC t021391; Foxon S95.

[Swift, Jonathan]. *An Answer to a Paper, Called A Memorial of the Poor Inhabitants, Tradesmen and Labourers of the Kingdom of Ireland. By the Author of The Short View of the State of Ireland.* ESTC t021996; *Prose Writings*, 12:324–25; Teerink 665, p. 330.

[Swift, Jonathan]. *A Short View of the State of Ireland.* ESTC t001868; *Intelligencer*, 326–27; *Prose Writings*, 12:323; Teerink 663, p. 329.

[Swift, Jonathan, and Thomas Sheridan]. *The Intelligencer*, Nos. 1–19. *Intelligencer*, ed. Woolley, 299–335; *Prose Writings*, 12:325–29; Teerink 666, p. 330. Nos. 4, 6, 8, 12, and 16 are attributed to SH on the evidence of typography and because she advertised them for sale (*Intelligencer,* 31); the other numbers are signed.

1729

[?Barber, Rupert]. *An Answre to the Christmass-Box. In Defence of Docter D–n–y.* By *R–t B–r.* ESTC n004305; Foxon A246. Attributed to SH (or alternatively to Nicholas Hussey) on evidence of ornaments.

MacDaniell, Alexander, and Philip A-Thoush. *The Last and True Speech Confession and Dying Words of Alexander Mac-Daniell, and Philip A-Thoush (alias Malone,) Who Is to Be Executed near St Stephen's-Green, This Present Saturday Being the 24th Day of January, 1728–9.* ESTC t213941.

Ross, Daniel. *The Last and True Speech Confession and Dying Words of Daniel Ross, Who Is to Be Executed near St Stephen's-Green, This Present Saturday, Being the 15th of This Instant February 1728–9.* ESTC t212316.

A Satyr on the Taylors Procession, July the 28th, 1729. ESTC t213698; Foxon S66. Attributed to SH (or alternatively to Nicholas Hussey) on evidence of ornaments.

Sheridan, Thomas. An *Ode, to Be Performed at the Castle of Dublin, March the 1st, 1728–9. Being the Birth-Day of Her Most Serene Majesty Queen Caroline. . . . The Musick Compos'd by Matthew Dubourg.* Foxon S411. Attributed to SH (or alternatively to Nicholas Hussey) on evidence of ornaments.

[Swift, Jonathan]. *The Journal of a Dublin Lady; In a Letter to a Person of Quality.* ESTC t124769; Foxon S863; *Poems,* ed. Williams, 2:443–44; Teerink 669, p. 333.

[Swift, Jonathan]. *A Modest Proposal for Preventing the Children of Poor People from Being a Burthen to Their Parents, or the Country, and for Making Them Beneficial to the Publick.* ESTC n005335; *Prose Writings,* 12:335–36; Teerink 676, p. 336.

[Swift, Jonathan]. *The Intelligencer, No. 20. Intelligencer,* ed. Woolley, 335; *Poems,* ed. Williams, 2:454; Teerink 666, p. 330. Attributed to SH (or alternatively to Nicholas Hussey) on evidence of ornaments.

NOTES

This paper revises certain portions of the textual introduction to my edition of Swift and Sheridan's *Intelligencer* (Oxford: Clarendon, 1992; © James Woolley 1992). The new information added here relies heavily upon the Eighteenth-Century Short Title Catalogue and upon the holdings and catalogues of the National Library of Ireland, the Royal Irish Academy, Trinity College, Dublin, and other libraries strong in eighteenth-century Irish imprints. I am indebted to A. C. Elias, Jr., and M. Pollard for generously shared findings from their unpublished research.

1. James Woolley, "Arbuckle's 'Panegyric' and Swift's Scrub Libel: The Documentary Evidence," in *Contemporary Studies of Swift's Poetry*, ed. John Irwin Fischer and Donald C. Mell, Jr. (Newark: University of Delaware Press, 1981), 208n.

2. Swift, *Prose Writings*, ed. Davis et al., 14 vols. (Oxford: Blackwell, 1939–1968), 6 (1951, 1964): 205–9; David Woolley, "Swift's Copy of *Gulliver's Travels*: The Armagh *Gulliver*, Hyde's Edition, and Swift's Earliest Corrections," in *The Art of Jonathan Swift*, ed. Clive T. Probyn (London: Vision, 1978), 141–44, 148.

3. Swift, *Correspondence*, ed. Harold Williams, rev. David Woolley, 5 vols. (Oxford: Clarendon, 1965–72), 2:313, 318, 322, 324, 329, 347, 379.

4. Irvin Ehrenpreis, *Swift: The Man, His Works, and the Age*, 3 vols. (London: Methuen, 1962–83), 3:128–30.

5. Swift, *The Drapier's Letters to the People of Ireland against Receiving Wood's Halfpence*, ed. Herbert Davis (Oxford: Clarendon, 1935; corrected impression 1965), 99; *Correspondence*, 3:308; compare 4:82.

6. 4 November 1732, *Correspondence*, 4:82.

7. David Woolley, "Swift's Copy," 142.

8. Robert Munter believes that "from 1716 to 1720 [Harding] operated out of the shop of Edward Waters" (*A Dictionary of the Print Trade in Ireland, 1550–1775* [New York: Fordham University Press, 1988], s.v. John Harding). Whether Harding was in some sense Waters's partner or only his tenant is less than clear.

9. And other newspapers: *Harding's Dublin Impartial News Letter, The Flying-Post, Harding's Impartial News-Letter*, and briefly *The Dublin Journal*. These may all be found in the University Microfilms series Irish Newspapers Prior to 1750 in Dublin Libraries.

10. *Drapier's Letters*, 92. Robert L. Munter, in *The History of the Irish Newspaper, 1685–1760* (Cambridge: University Press, 1967), calls Harding "a strange, distant, and generally unpopular publisher," and says that Swift "was forced to choose such disreputable printers [as Waters and Harding] because they were the only ones sufficiently desperate to risk prosecution" (106, 133–34). The first comment is, to the best of my knowledge, unsubstantiated, beyond the expected gibes of his competitors; the second comment is speculation. See also Munter, *Dictionary*, s.v. John Harding, Abraham Thiboust, and John Whalley.

11. *Harding's Weekly Impartial News Letter*, 11 April 1721.

12. David Woolley, "Swift's Copy," 143.

13. These are the three kinds of fare mentioned in the poem "Harding's Resurrection. From Hell upon Earth," *Harding's Weekly Impartial News Letter*, 18 February 1723/24.

14. Oliver W. Ferguson, *Jonathan Swift and Ireland* (Urbana: University of Illinois Press, 1962), 125; Ferguson offers a valuable discussion of Harding's risk-taking.

15. *Dublin Impartial News Letter*, 6 February 1719/20.

16. Munter, *History*, 144.

17. Munter, *History*, 148. Munter considers this and the "libel" next referred to to be the same incident, and he may be right.

18. This last he announced by the publication of the poem "Harding's Resurrection"; it says he had been "Trencht" "for LIBELS."

19. *Drapier's Letters*, 99, 201.

20. *Elegy on the Much-Lamented Death of John Harding Printer, Who Departed This Transitory Life, This Present Monday Being the 19th of This Instant April 1725* ([Dublin, 1725]; BL 11602.i.1/11); *Correspondence*, 3:93. The claim that John died in prison is, I believe, erroneous *(Intelligencer*, 35).

21. John T. Gilbert, *A History of the City of Dublin*, 3 vols. (1854; reprinted Dublin, Gill and Macmillan, 1978), 1:59–60; *A Poem to the Whole People of Ireland, Relating to M. B. Drapier, by A. R. Hosier* ([Dublin]: Elizabeth Sadleir, 1726; Trinity College Dublin, Press A.7.4/47). The poem is here quoted from the halfsheet.

22. *Correspondence*, 3:93.

23. *Intelligencer*, 201.

24. A Dublin quack and newspaper publisher, John Whalley, was John Harding's rival in business. *Whalley's News Letter* for 22 December 1721 claimed that the anti-Whalley publication *Doctor Whalley's Prophecy* had been published by Harding's "mother-in-law" the previous week. Elizabeth Sadleir seems to have been the only woman bookseller or printer in Dublin at this time; she frequently advertised in Harding's newspapers, and it was she who published the *Poem to the Whole People of Ireland* seeking sympathy for Sarah Harding after John's death. John Harding printed *The Last Farewell of Ebenezor Elliston to This Transitory World* for Elizabeth Sadlier (the spelling varies) in 1722. On Elizabeth and Ralph Sadleir as typefounders, see Munter, *History*, 44; Munter, *Dictionary*, s.v. Sadlier; and M. Pollard, *Dublin's Trade in Books, 1550–1800* (Oxford: Clarendon, 1989), 120. On women in the Dublin book trade, see Munter, *History*, 34.

25. Because Harding was not a member of the Guild of St. Luke the Evangelist (the Dublin stationers' guild), we lack information about his apprenticeship. At this period there were a number of printers,

including some prominent ones, who were not members of the Guild. See Munter, *History*, 26; and Munter, *Dictionary*, 2–6.

26. See Appendix.

27. H. R. Plomer et al., *Dictionaries of the Printers and Booksellers Who Were at Work in England, Scotland, and Ireland, 1557–1775 . . . Reprinted in Compact Form* (London: Bibliographical Society, 1977), s.v. Sarah Harding; Munter, *Dictionary*, s.v. Sarah Harding.

28. Irvin Ehrenpreis believes he did (3:314–16); see also *Drapier's Letters*, lxvi; *The Poems of Jonathan Swift*, ed. Harold Williams, 2nd ed. (Oxford: Clarendon, 1958), 3:1117–18; Swift, *Poetical Works*, ed. Herbert Davis (London: Oxford, 1967), xiv (one "of the more likely Attributions"); Swift, *The Complete Poems*, ed. Pat Rogers (Harmondsworth, Middlesex: Penguin, 1983), 751.

29. Swift also refers to her in "The Furniture of a Woman's Mind" (which Faulkner dates 1727 but which may date from Swift's visit to Market Hill in 1728). See *Poems*, ed. Williams, 2:417.

30. *Intelligencer*, ed. Woolley, 267.

31. For the title page see the photograph in *Prose Writings*, vol. 12, facing p. 29, showing the National Library of Ireland copy (the implication, p. 325, that this is a Trinity College Dublin copy is erroneous).

32. See David Woolley, "Swift's Copy," 141–44, 148.

33. *Intelligencer*, 43 n.27.

34. This was—is—a narrow walkway just north of the Castle. She had used the address "on the Blind-Key" in 1725—e.g., in *On Wisdom's Defeat* and in ?Sheridan's *To the Honourable Mr. D. T.* (D. F. Foxon, *English Verse, 1701–1750*, 2 vols. [London: Cambridge University Press, 1975], T373).

35. Barry Slepian, "When Swift First Employed George Faulkner," *Papers of the Bibliographical Society of America* 56 (1962): 354–56.

36. *A Hue and Cry after the Letter to the Lord-Mayor of the City of Dublin* (Dublin: E. Waters, 1729) reprints *A Letter from a Country Gentleman, to the Honourable the Lord-Mayor of the City of Dublin* with this note: "N. B. That I have taken the above scurvy Letter, exactly from Mrs. Hussey, alias Harding's Print." BL C.121.g.8/171. See also Munter, *Dictionary*, s.v. Nicholas Hussey; and *Fog's Weekly Journal*, 16 August 1729, quoted in Jeremy Black, *The English Press in the Eighteenth Century* (Philadelphia: University of Pennsylvania Press, 1987), 157.

37. Searched 4 July 1994.

38. H. Teerink, *A Bibliography of the Writings of Jonathan Swift*, 2nd ed., ed. Arthur H. Scouten (Philadelphia: University of Pennsylvania Press, 1963).

39. Printers may have borrowed or otherwise acquired ornaments from one another on occasion. There is also the possibility of shared printing, in which different printers printed different sheets of a job, although shared printing is presumably not a factor in any of the unsigned publications listed here: none of them occupies more than a single sheet. As detailed study of eighteenth-century Dublin typography progresses, more reliable attribution of unsigned printing may become possible. Most Harding ornaments are reproduced in *Intelligencer*, pp. 290–91.

40. I have systematically excluded unsigned imprints with Harding ornaments if they were issued before John's death 19 April 1725, on the assumption that they were printed by John.

Swift and Catholic Ireland

ROBERT MAHONY

Hic depositum est Corpus
JONATHAN SWIFT S. T. D.
Hujus Ecclesiae Cathedralis
Decani,
Ubi saeva Indignatio
Ulterius
Cor lacerare nequit.
Abi Viator
Et imitare, si poteris,
Strenuum pro virili
Libertatis Vindicatorem.

The Latin epitaph Jonathan Swift composed for himself invites the onlooker, without respect to nationality, to emulate his defense of human liberty. In Ireland, however, his reputation has long had a distinctly local significance, for Swift's *Drapier's Letters* in 1724 articulated the popular—and successful—opposition to the London government's award of a patent to the Englishman, William Wood, to mint copper coinage for Ireland. "Wood's halfpence" might seem a comparatively trifling example of English oppression in Ireland, but the resistance to it was a rare victory of public opinion over governmental fiat. Swift gained instant and enormous popularity, and was credited with drawing support for his efforts from all quarters:

> At the sound of the DRAPIER'S trumpet, a spirit arose among the people. . . . The Papist, the Fanatic, the Tory, the Whig, all listed themselves under the banner of M.B. DRAPIER, and were equally zealous to serve the common cause.[1]

Still, contemporary Irish Catholics themselves left very little evidence that they admired Swift; in the penal era, prudence would

have counseled their discretion on political topics. Thus a broad-
side poem of 1726, complaining of Swift's lengthy visit to England
that year, hints delicately at its Catholic provenance by carrying
into English the mixture of eros and millenarian anticipation of
the hero's return that is a common feature of Jacobite patriotic
poetry in Irish:

> Will *Cadenus* longer stay?
> Come *Cadenus*, come away;
> Come with all the haste of Love,
> Come unto thy Turtle Dove;
> The rip'ned Cherry on the Tree
> Hangs and only hangs for thee,
> Luscious Peaches mellow Pears,
>
> *Ceres* with her yellow Ears,
> And the Grape both red and white
> Grape inspiring just Delight,
> All are ripe and courting sue
> To be pluck'd and press'd by you;
> . . . .
> Come *Cadenus*, bless once more,
> Bless again thy native Shore,
> Bless again this drooping Isle,
> Make it's weeping Beauties smile,
> Beauties that thine absence mourn,
> Beauties wishing thy Return.[2]

But even so indirect a record of Catholic appreciation of Swift
is rare for the time. Indeed, Catholics remained generally silent
about the Dean for almost a century after his death, well beyond
the penal years, and their attitudes for decades later were often
hostile towards him. Most glowing notices of Swift's patriotism in
the eighteenth and early nineteenth century come, like Orrery's,
from Protestant writers; and it is not until the twentieth century
that Catholic Ireland could accept Swift as a patriot without
equivocation.

Swift, of course, was equivocal about Catholics, rarely ex-
hibiting overt anti-Catholicism but also never disputing the necessity of the penal laws or otherwise adopting the cause of

Catholics specifically, as distinct from that of Ireland. Hence it is not remarkable that Catholic writers in the eighteenth century should generally have kept silent about Swift as a patriot, even as Irish Protestants hailed his efforts and inspiration. What few positive references occur appear in the context of Catholic appeals to the good nature and patriotic spirit of Irish Protestants; curiously, these could cite Swift tangentially to support arguments for the expedience of relaxing the penal laws.[3] Such sparse eighteenth-century references hardly indicate that Irish Catholics had adopted Swift posthumously as their champion, but his patriotic reputation did gain some ground among Catholics at the beginning of the nineteenth century. *An Historical Review of the State of Ireland*, by Francis Plowden, an English Catholic, celebrated Swift in 1803 as a pioneer of civil liberty and freedom of the press in the face of a malevolent government.[4] A few years later, the Irish controversialist Denis Taafe drew attention to Swift's sympathy for the rural poor, casting the Dean as "a patriotic genius . . . like lightning illuminating the gloom of a clouded night."[5] Less lyrically, Matthew O'Conor in 1813 maintained that Swift's opposition to Wood's halfpence united Catholics and Protestants and "infused into his countrymen a portion of the spirit and patriotism with which his own soul was animated."[6]

Irish Catholic praise of Swift was short-lived, however. Donal MacCartney has suggested that from the enactment of the Union until about 1808, such historical writers had made "a wholehearted effort . . . to prove their steadfast loyalty" to the new settlement and their willingness to embrace Swift as a patriotic hero fits this pattern. But that cooperative spirit gave way fairly soon thereafter to "a historiographical counterattack," once it became clear that the government would make no further concessions to Catholic claims, especially Emancipation,[7] and after the bouquets of admiration thrown his way by Plowden and Taafe, he was again all but ignored by Catholic writers. While they were silent, Swift was accused of complicity in the oppression of their forebears by the Scottish critic Francis Jeffrey, commenting on Walter Scott's 1814 edition of Swift's *Works*. For Jeffrey, Swift was a political turncoat whose insincerity in this respect matched that of his social and personal treatment of women, while his disappointed

ambition for advancement in England made him ultimately a
misanthropist. The judgment dismissed his Irish patriotism as a
means simply of embarrassing Walpole's government, offering as
proof Swift's obliviousness to the situation of Catholics:

> A single fact is decisive upon this point. While his friends
> were in power, we hear nothing of the grievances of Ireland;
> and to the last we hear nothing of its radical grievance,
> the oppression of its Catholic population. His object was,
> not to do good to Ireland, but to vex and to annoy the
> English ministry. To do this, however, with effect, it was
> necessary that he should speak to the interests and the
> feelings of some party who possessed a certain degree of
> power and influence. This unfortunately was not the case in
> that day with the Catholics; and though this gave them only
> a stronger title to the services of a truly brave or generous
> advocate, it was sufficient to silence Swift.[8]

To an Irish Protestant defender of Swift, Edward Berwick,
such an observation revealed Jeffrey's ignorance of Irish history.
Given the widespread hostility and contempt toward "Papists" in
the governing circles of Swift's day, Berwick wondered rhetorically "what would they have said to Swift, had he proposed to
them the emancipation of those Papists? And Swift's not having
alluded to the oppression of [Ireland's] Catholic population, is
set down amongst the crimes with which he is charged."[9] But
Berwick was even more insistent that during the Wood's coinage
affair in 1724 Swift had touched a chord of resentment against
British arrogance and misgovernment that united Protestants
and Catholics:

> He taught his country to protest against her grievances, and
> gave her spirit by which she redressed them. . . . You will say,
> he had the Irish People. There was no People; he was to
> create a People, by whom he was defended.[10]

That Swift had effectively created an Irish People reflects a view
increasingly appealing to nineteenth-century Irish Protestants.
For it accorded them an identity that was much more than colonially British, one in which Catholics and Protestants both could

share, based upon a historical antipathy to characteristics of British governance in Ireland, however differently those characteristics might be seen by the two communities.

That difference in perception, nonetheless, amounted to an obstacle all but insuperable for Irish Catholics, whose antipathy to those characteristics of British rule in Ireland was not only historical but current. Thus, in an exception to the Catholic near silence about Swift in these years, Thomas Moore in 1824 responded sharply to the kind of thinking Berwick represents: "Swift's own patriotism was little more than a graft of English faction upon an Irish stock—fructifying, it is true, into such splendid produce, as makes us proud to think it indigenous to the soil." What compounds the impurity of Swift's motives, for Moore as for Jeffrey, is that "for the misery and degradation of his Roman Catholic countrymen (who constituted, even then, four-fifths of the population of Ireland) he seems to have cared very little more than his own Gulliver would for the sufferings of so many disenfranchised Yahoos."[11] At best, Moore ironically concedes the historical value of "the affair of Wood's halfpence, upon which so much of Swift's wit was lavished," for this "though magnified at the time into more than its due importance, is interesting, even now, as having been the first national cause, round which the people of Ireland had ever been induced to rally. What neither Christian charity nor the dictates of sound policy could effect, an influx of brass halfpence brought about at once."[12]

Still, there is evidence that Swift was gaining some acceptance as a "character" among Catholics on a different social level from that of writers and political leaders. The Dean features in a number of folktales collected in the 1930s by the Irish Folklore Commission, mostly in Irish and dating to as much as a century before.[13] In these "Jack and the Dane" stories, Swift and a servant trick each other verbally or physically, and some few even present Swift as a covert or death-bed Catholic; they demonstrate that as an engaging character Swift could be absorbed into Gaelic oral culture in the 1830s and 40s. It is significant, however, that other Protestants remain outsiders, regarded, if at all, with contempt or hostility, and that Swift's patriotism goes unmentioned. Of course, Catholic peasants hardly needed a Protestant hero in the

1820s and 30s when Gaelic Ireland had a pre-eminent one of its own in Daniel O'Connell.

O'Connell's patriotism admitted no inspiration from Swift. Instead, he used history selectively to foreground Catholic grievances as Ireland's. To Protestants, O'Connell's loyalist rhetoric could seem undercut by his evoking for Catholic audiences long-standing vexations like the position of the established church and the attendant issue of tithe rectification, or ancient dispossessions of the Gael—and hinting that Emancipation, or Repeal later, would redress them.[14] It is thus remarkable that an Irish Catholic, Francis Sylvester Mahony, should have attempted in turn to foreground Swift as an ancestral figure for Irish national identity by marginalizing O'Connell. A former priest in Cork, Mahony began in 1834 to write whimsically erudite essays for *Fraser's Magazine* as "Father Prout," taking the name of an actual deceased priest. In the fourth of these, Mahony celebrated Swift as "the first, the best, the mightiest" of Irishmen who would be recognized as such in his own country only "when the frenzied hour of strife shall have passed away, and the turbulence of parties shall have subsided."[15] The frenzy and turbulence are, of course, the work of O'Connell, whom Mahony despised as a hypocritical manipulator; his genuine admiration for Swift is also a vehicle for denigrating the Liberator.[16] Thus Mahony holds that while Swift's passionate love of country drove him to madness, the self-seeking O'Connell simply drove the country mad. O'Connell's "Catholic rent" to support Emancipation efforts is even likened to Wood's halfpence.[17] And while Mahony, like Berwick, locates the unifying force of Swift's patriotism in resentment at English misgovernment, the recent instances he cites of the latter—which the Tory *Fraser's* audience would appreciate—are London's concessions to O'Connell. But Mahony's promotion of Swift, so couched, had virtually no effect on the Dean's reputation among Irish Catholics.

What did have effect, perceptibly altering their general silence or antipathy to Swift, was Thomas Davis's tactic, in the early 1840s, of establishing a line or genealogy of Irish patriots, part of the Young Ireland program of uniting Catholics and Protestants in the cause of Repeal and national identity. When Davis founded *The Nation* in 1842 with two Catholics, Charles Gavan Duffy and

John Blake Dillon, he used it at least as much to address those of his own Protestant tradition as to reach the Catholic majority. Exhorting his readership to recognize, value, and strengthen their Irish identity, he turned often to history for examples, even a kind of genealogy of Protestant patriots, among whom Swift usually figured. One of the earliest instances is a lengthy list of the Irish "intellectual wares" which have been appropriated by the "mind monopoly, and mind robbery, of England," namely "Irish Ussher, Boyle and Berkeley, Swift, Sterne and Goldsmith, Lucas, Burke and O'Leary, Flood, Grattan and Curran."[18] Similar lists of eminent Protestants continued to appear in *The Nation* thereafter, though usually limited to the major eighteenth-century patriots. In 1843, indeed, O'Connell's "Repeal Year," *The Nation* frequently drew parallels between the long struggle for legislative independence in the eighteenth century and the contemporary struggle to restore it through Repeal. One of the better-known instances extended the parallel to include the act of the Jacobite "Patriot Parliament" of 1689, declaring that the English parliament had no right to legislate for Ireland; this anticipated the exertions of Molyneux, Swift, and Lucas, which Flood and Grattan brought to fulfillment.[19]

This patriot genealogy had a unifying purpose, manifesting the nationalist heritage of Irish Protestants while at the same time supplying a pedigree for O'Connell's overwhelmingly Catholic movement. But even singly, Swift could be put to unitive effect. In the same issue of the *The Nation* that celebrated the Jacobite parliament, Davis continued in the spirit of appealing to Catholics by promoting the Irish language, concluding "Had Swift known Irish, he would have sowed its seed by the side of that nationality which he planted. . . . Had Ireland used Irish in 1782, would it not have impeded England's re-conquest of us?"[20] And later the same month *The Nation* denounced the government's issuing a contract to an Englishman named Croal for coaches to be used in Ireland, a case regarded as trifling; but such a trifle was Wood's patent:

> . . . and against this "trifle" SWIFT shouted aloud, and called the nation together. How funny these Irishmen are—they are in a passion now about a Coach Contract, as they were

long ago about brass halfpence. Aye, but read the whole story, and you will find that a conviction had then grown up in Ireland that England was a selfish and monopolizing tyrant, who amused the Protestants with an anti-Catholic yell, while she plundered them of wealth, fame and freedom. WOODS' [*sic*] patent was the trifling occasion, SWIFT saw it, and . . . rallied the Protestants. As his voice resounded, even the chained Catholic raised his head and blessed the intolerant patriot, and the British government bent before his demand. He set the precedent for an Irish party—he pioneered the road to success. 'England's fear'—it was his spell; 'Ireland's union'—it was his talisman.[21]

Though an "intolerant patriot"—the editorial refers to him later as "the great Protestant patriot"—Swift is yet enlisted as an ancestor, not only for Protestants "malcontent at being treated as the spurious and degraded offspring of England,"[22] but also for Catholics, by the implicit admonition that only unity between them and Irish Protestants could bring about Repeal.

Swift provided Davis, of course, not simply an ancestor for his own nationalism, but a model of purpose and effect. Davis was the first Protestant Irish nationalist who was, like Swift himself, not a politician but a publicist. In the repeated invocations of the patriot line and of Swift himself, there is the hint that nationalist Ireland, led for over twenty years by O'Connell, was in need of a new, disinterested, Protestant voice, which Davis was providing. The parallel is personal as much as national, or collectively Protestant. Thus, declaiming in 1844 against a proposal that the lord lieutenancy be abolished and Ireland centrally administered, *The Nation* invokes the patriot line to recall the successful efforts of the previous century and then strikes the parallel between this present spur to indignation and that which provoked the Dean—"What a subject for SWIFT!"[23]

Whatever the personal impetus that underlay it, Davis's enlisting Swift in the cause of *The Nation* and even Davis's genealogy of Protestant patriotism did not succeed in drawing Protestants from their allegiance to the Union or support for the government's measures to preserve it. Other advocates of Repeal besides Davis nonetheless sought to use Swift's presumed high standing among Protestants to weaken that support. In late January 1844, during the sedition trial of O'Connell and his lieutenants arising from their Repeal Year agitations, Richard Lalor Shiel, counsel for O'Connell's son John, likened the defendants to Swift, who in 1720 had published "a proposal for the use of Irish manufacture, and was charged with having endeavoured to create hostility between different classes of his majesty's subjects—one of the charges preferred in this very indictment." In the *Drapier's Letters*, furthermore, "Swift addressed the people of Ireland . . . in language as strong as any that Daniel O'Connell has employed."[24] A few days later, James Whiteside, defending *The Nation's* Gavan Duffy, pushed the tactic further, contrasting the unarmed "moral force" of the Repeal movement with the armed Volunteers of 1782: "All that the genius of Swift, the learning to Molyneux, and the patriotism of Lucas failed to obtain—all that was denied to justice was yielded to men with arms in their hands."[25] But such rhetoric was unavailing: the jury returned a verdict of guilty, though this was later set aside by the House of Lords on appeal. As *The Nation* recognized with some bitterness early in 1845, Irish Protestants would not be swayed from Unionism by recollections of their ancestors' patriotism:

> Poor deluded Irish Protestants! brave! fierce! impotent! You have denied the country for which a race of Protestant patriots—DANIEL O'NEILL, MOLYNEUX, SWIFT, LUCAS, FLOOD, GRATTAN, TONE and SAURIN—fought and spoke.[26]

While most Protestants seemed deaf to invocations of Swift, *The Nation* continued to forward him as an ancestral patriot for the advanced nationalists of Young Ireland. During Davis's lifetime, however, and even after his death in September 1845, the paper laid little stress on Swift's literary eminence, partly because it could be taken for granted, partly because the patriot-publicist aspect of Swift's reputation seemed most amenable to nationalist absorption. It was left to the Young Ireland poet Denis Florence MacCarthy, a Catholic, to enshrine Swift the next year in a literary pantheon built to nationalist specifications. MacCarthy celebrates Swift as "unquestionably the greatest [name] in our literature," and places him at the beginning of a genealogy of Irish nationalist writers, though with a slight hedge as to his motives: "He was the first great Anglo-Irish writer who felt that he was an Irishman, and that his injured and despised country was worthy even of the affectation of patriotism."[27] Implicitly rebuking the ambivalence of those like Thomas Moore, for whom Swift's own personal motives and circumstances devalued his patriotism, MacCarthy certainly promotes the respectability of Swift as a patriotic ancestor even for Catholics. But MacCarthy went beyond praising the writer as patriot: through the works he discerns a tragic, frustrated, maddened man, connecting those factors to his patriotism. He constructs Swift as a sufferer—the more appealing to Catholics for that—and if not specifically like Robert Emmet or the martyrs of 1798 a sufferer in Ireland's cause, yet one whose suffering is integral to his Irishness, rendering him part of the nation and one in whom the nation can see itself.

Considered from a political perspective, then, patriotic achievement could transcend inadequacies of attitude or motive, while from a sufficiently nationalized literary viewpoint, even Swift's character defects could be valorized as the stigmata of Ireland's own oppression. And in a more activist political context, when Young Ireland patriots broke away from O'Connell's Repeal association and formed the Irish Confederation, Swift could be included in a patriotic genealogy more Catholic than Davis's. At the inaugural meeting of the Confederation, T. F. Meagher identified its spirit as that which "made the walls of Limerick impregnable . . . dictated the letters of Swift . . . sanctified the scaffold of the Geraldine, and made the lyre of Moore vibrate through the world," and prompted the Volunteers, Grattan and Davis, and O'Connell himself in his more defiant days.[28] True to their Young Ireland roots and their abandonment of O'Connell's emphasis on "moral force," the Confederation constructed an Irish history from examples less of grievance than of boldness and inspiration. It was organized into clubs named for great patriots and published documents from patriotic history in pamphlet form. One of the first clubs in Dublin was named for Swift, with John Mitchel as a vice president, and Mitchel edited the first pamphlet, *Irish Political Economy*, which included Swift's *Short View of the State of Ireland* (1727) and *Proposal for the Universal Use of Irish Manufactures* (1720). This was quickly reviewed in *The Nation* with the comment that Swift had first articulated that "distrust of foreigners and reliance on ourselves" characteristic of Irish economic patriotism. The review also noted, echoing Mitchel's own Preface to the pamphlet, that the condition of the Irish countryside Swift described was unchanged, showing "how little of political advancement has taken place here for the last one hundred years."[29]

Swift's prominence in Young Ireland's stridently nationalistic genealogy of patriotism drew Catholics gradually to share the longstanding Protestant admiration of the Dean. The forward role of contemporary Protestants like Mitchel and William Smith O'Brien in the Confederation and the abortive 1848 Rising doubtless abetted the progress of this consensus favoring an earlier Protestant hero. Yet the view of Swift as a misanthropist driven by disappointed ambition to a specious Irish patriotism remained strong in Britain, promoted the more by W. M. Thackeray's popular lecture on Swift in 1851–52.[30] And for Irish Catholics, his obliviousness to their ancestors' rights could still be a thorn. The range of animosities is acknowledged in an 1849 government-sanctioned account of Swift, designed for use in the national schools:

> A difference of opinion has always existed with regard to the motives by which Swift was actuated in deserting the political party with which he first connected himself; and it is a matter of fact which admits of no dispute, that although he advocated, with unyielding firmness and unrivalled powers of wit and sarcasm popular rights and constitutional freedom in Ireland, yet he was the inveterate opponent of the claims of Roman Catholics and Dissenters to an equality of political power. The important services he rendered to Ireland, at a very critical period of her history, are admitted by Irishmen of every party and every creed.[31]

Straining to accommodate strong reservations, this passage yet comes to a conclusion on Swift as patriot which essentially reflects that of Young Ireland, though without the further validation of a succeeding patriotic genealogy. A decade later a Catholic school text indicates a growing acceptance of the Dean in its brief and restrained notice of the success of the *Drapier's Letters* in the face of English corruption, simply avoiding any reference to Catholic reservations about the purity of Swift's patriotism.[32] And in the 1860s the outlines of the Young Ireland position on Swift were echoed and developed by both English and Irish commentators, Catholics and Protestants, political and literary historians, from W. E. H. Lecky to James Whiteside (Gavan Duffy's counsel in the 1844 sedition trial), and the surviving Young Irelander D'Arcy McGee.[33]

The Young Ireland position could attract such a common front to maintain Swift's patriotic eminence because it was by nature functional: the Dean had been hailed in his own time as a great patriot and was complemented by virtue of a line of nationalist successors. G. L. Craik's comment in 1861 on the Wood's halfpence affair is typical:

> Swift was universally regarded by his countrymen as the champion of the independence of Ireland—the preserver of whatever they had most to value or to be proud of as a people. And perhaps, the birth of political and patriotic spirit in Ireland as a general sentiment, may be traced with some truth to this affair of Wood's halfpence and to these letters of Swift's.[34]

Beyond that, his achievements could be privileged over his motives or defects of character, as J. F. Waller demonstrates:

> his political sins, his faults of temper, his imperious bearing, and his caprices, were almost forgotten in the general sentiment of gratitude and veneration, and to this day men remember not so much his failings and his errors, as his services, his power, and his genius.[35]

Swift's detractors, by contrast, stood upon the narrower ground afforded by his character defects, impugning his motives and, like Thomas Moore forty years earlier, wondering at his reputation. The most outspoken of them, like many of Swift's defenders, were Protestants, even English, but would not have lacked some influence upon Catholic opinion in Ireland. To Goldwin Smith, for instance, Swift was a self-interested agitator; to W. F. Collier, one prompted by a lifetime of bitter disappointments; to W. H. Flood, a descendant of the patriot Henry Flood,

Swift was simply a derivative propagandist.[36] Considered apart from the genealogy of patriotism, Swift's character might at best seem "gigantic," as the British literary historian Charles Grant put it, but with "the grandeur of a fallen angel."[37]

Such criticism, however, did not address the functional attractiveness of the nationalist consensus on Swift derived from Young Ireland. Hence the most noteworthy of Swift's detractors in this minor controversy of the 1860s was a former Young Irelander himself, John Mitchel, whose conversion from espousing Swift as patriot in his Irish Confederation days can be traced from the mildly derogatory references to the Dean in his *Jail Journal* to his sharp denigration of Swift in *The History of Ireland* (1869), where Mitchel's irony approaches a Swiftian level. He renews Thomas Moore's complaint that Swift neglected the plight of Catholics but was moved to furious activity by the trivialities of Wood's halfpence scheme; Mitchel judges from Swift's choice of such "an occasion, no matter how silly," that the Dean was more a satirist than a patriot. Instead of complementing his patriotism, his literary gifts actually undermine his claim to it: "any peg would do, to hang his essays upon."[38] And since "he opposed English domination over Ireland, yet equally opposed the union of Irishmen to resist it" by ignoring Catholics and persecuting Dissenters, "the verdict of history must forever be, that he was neither an English patriot nor an Irish one."[39]

Mitchel's rejection of Swift's Irish patriotism was soon echoed by Father Thomas Burke, a popular Dominican preacher who championed Irish nationalism against the imperialist bias of the historian J. A. Froude. Froude's *The English in Ireland in the Eighteenth Century* was a wide-ranging assault upon the nationalist historical program; it acknowledged the constant English misgovernment of Ireland but provokingly laid this to a policy not of oppression but concession, both to Catholic backwardness and criminality and to Anglo-Irish Protestant patriotic posturing. To Froude, very few of the Irish acted disinterestedly, but Swift did, becoming "in the best and noblest sense, an Irish patriot."[40] Froude's antipathy to Catholicism and Irishness in general inflamed nationalists, and in voicing their indignation categorically Father Burke briefly targeted Swift, extending Mitchel's criticism by denying Swift's Irish nationality altogether.[41] Yet Burke focused insufficiently upon Swift to alter immediately the course of his reputation in Ireland; while Froude's positive view could not shift the British perception of Swift as mainly a literary figure, his character represented in terms of misanthropy and madness—such was Thackeray's influence—and his Irish patriotism slighted. Attempting to redress such English neglect, Stanley Lane-Poole in 1881 did not even mention Froude but outlined instead the nationalist consensus favoring Swift.[42] Throughout the 1880s and 90s, indeed, that consensus achieved a currency in both Britain and Ireland, without any such controversy as marked its emergence in Ireland in the 1860s. Promoting it in *A Bird's-Eye View of Irish History* (1882), Gavan Duffy clarified its indebtedness to the Young Ireland position on Swift of four decades earlier, and as nationalist history was adopted by the Home Rule movement, the Dean was praised as prophet by John Redmond and even W. E. Gladstone, who was clearly influenced by Duffy's *History*.[43]

The nationalist consensus on Swift was even shared by the Unionist W. E. H. Lecky, whose *History of Ireland in the Eighteenth Century* (1892) was drawn from his *History of England* (1878–90) and designed to refute Froude.[44] Lecky's *History* promoted eighteenth-century Anglo-Irish patriotism and the zenith of its achievement, the settlement of 1782, which Froude had considered ludicrous.[45] But though Lecky's account provided Irish nationalists with very considerable evidence of poor British government, he supported the Union in nineteenth-century circumstances because he was deeply opposed to the democratic trend of contemporary nationalism. Swift is thus fitted into a program emphasizing Protestant patriotic guidance. By the later 1890s, however, some could regard such a program as itself all but synonymous with the genealogy of patriotism that the general nationalist consensus had long maintained, for this, too, privileged Anglo-Ireland (at least in retrospect) to the detriment of the Gaelic nation that the language revival movement was assiduously rediscovering. Numerous works focusing on Swift in the 1880s and 90s elaborated upon the notion of Swift as the wellspring of Irish patriotism and at least implicitly the ancestor of a race of nationalists.[46] But this seemed to diminish the Irish

identity of the bulk of the Irish people, the Gaelic and Catholic
Ireland with which Swift never identified himself.

The inevitable reaction came at the end of the decade in an
attack on Anglo-Irish patriotism by D. P. Moran, focusing largely
on Swift and his influence, which had nearly extinguished the
Gaelic soul of Ireland:

> The spirit of Molyneux and Swift . . . the spirit which 99 out
> of every 100 of us still look up to as our polar star, was the
> death of those elements of the Irish race that could have
> defied the attacks that were to come. It started the spirit of
> English civilization and English progress in our midst, and
> the Irish race, ceasing to think for itself, has persistently
> mistaken this for the spirit of the Irish nation.[47]

Swift himself stands as a particular irritant:

> . . . that great Irishman, as we love to call him, who had not
> a drop of Irish blood in his veins, no Irish characteristics,
> and an utter contempt for the entire pack of us . . . This
> Englishman, whom, with characteristic latter-day Irish cringe
> we claim for ourselves, became a popular hero of the Irish
> people.[48]

Moran anticipates, to reject, the charge of racism, expressing
pride in those Protestants "who dreamt and worked for an independent country," even while stressing their proper subordina-
tion to those of Gaelic stock, for "the foundation of Ireland is
the Gael, and the Gael must be the element that absorbs."[49] The
thrust of Moran's Irish-Ireland concept is not so much crudely
racist, however, as anti-cosmopolitan, with some affinity with the
language revival movement, for both sought a bulwark against the
absorptiveness of anglicization. But the Gaelic League in these
years fostered a cultural principle for uniting the Irish people,
with the language and its associated customs as that bulwark. It
could attract Protestants, even Unionists, because it addressed
social and political issues covertly at best. Moran's principle, on
the other hand, promotes the Gael as a sociological construct,
latently more powerful than a cultural one, to counter the urban-
based, cosmopolitan thrust of a patriotic genealogy sprung from

Protestant ancestors. Unity or synthesis in the face of anglicization is eschewed in favor of the Gael's counter-absorptiveness.

Despite Moran's all-but-overt sectarian appeal, however,
Swift had proven of value to the nationalist cause for too long to
be discarded easily. Not only the mainstream Home Rule coali-
tion, but on its fringes, the advocates of cultural revival found
him useful. The cultural movement, of course, had both Gaelic
and Anglo-Irish aspects, often acting in tandem in the 1890s,
and while W. B. Yeats was to take an active interest in Swift only
much later, lesser lights found inspiration in him during those
years. Moran could complain of Swift's enduring popularity in
1899, for instance, though William Rooney as a boy ten years
earlier had lamented the nation's neglect of him and other Irish
writers.[50] A tireless promoter of the cultural revival in his brief
career, Rooney praised Swift for his putative interest in Gaelic
literature as well as for his patriotism.[51] Rooney's friend and
colleague Arthur Griffith was even more laudatory, exalting Swift
in the paper they founded, *The United Irishman*, from its opening
issue, 4 March 1899. Griffith continued to cite the Dean in this
paper and its successor, *Sinn Fein*, as a precursor for his view that
Ireland should share a monarch with Britain while preserving
her essential independence, and maintained in the latter that
between Shane O'Neill and Parnell, "England thoroughly feared"
only two Irish patriots, Swift and Davis.[52]

Griffith so identified Swift with the ideals of Sinn Fein that
the historian and critic D. J. O'Donoghue was tempted to title
his 1912 article on the Dean "Jonathan Swift, Sinn Feiner and
Cattle Driver." While Griffith had been content with frequent
allusions to Swift, O'Donoghue provides an extensive updating
of the old nationalist consensus, emphasizing—in an oblique but
palpable rebuttal of Moran's criticisms—that "Swift was fanatically
anti-English and an out-and-out Irish Irelander."[53] For "to stand
by Ireland whenever the question is one between this country
and England is not a bad definition of an Irishman," and Swift
certainly meets that test; furthermore, considering that "there
were only two classes in Ireland in his day—the people and
their oppressors[,] Swift was with the people and against their
oppressors all the time."[54] O'Donoghue's forthrightly advanced-
nationalist judgment was echoed in a pamphlet distributed by

Cumann na mBan in 1915,[55] and the next year even Padraig Pearse's significantly titled pamphlet *Ghosts*, adopting a version of the patriotic genealogy that Moran had despised, considered Swift with some favor. Pearse stressed the greater utility to modern nationalists of such "authentic" patriots as Tone, Davis, and Mitchel, yet numbered Swift, with Berkeley and Burke, among those "who have thought most wisely about Ireland."[56] In 1917, finally, P. J. Lennox presented a view of Swift for an American Catholic intellectual readership that was largely indebted to O'Donoghue.[57]

At the threshold of Irish autonomy, therefore, Swift's longstanding adoption by Irish nationalism had been claimed by those of its most vigorous wing, which would soon become the new establishment. Some continued to demur at that adoption; the Irish-Ireland influence on popular historiography is clear from the dismissive treatment of Swift as merely a Protestant, "colonist" patriot in the 1916 edition of the standard Christian Brothers' history and another student-oriented work in 1920.[58] But by this time, even as a new Irish polity was emerging, an awareness of Ireland's literary history was becoming more general, prompted by the "Renaissance" of Irish literature in English.[59] As literary history itself often follows a genealogical model, the contemporary prominence of Anglo-Irish writers drew attention to their precursors. Opposing this trend, Daniel Corkery argued in *The Hidden Ireland* (1924) and *Synge and Anglo-Irish Literature* (1931) against endowing Anglo-Ireland with a retrospective, or even current, Irish nationality. In 1934, reviewing three works on Swift, he clarified the particular incongruity of the Dean's genealogical position. His rhetoric lacks Moran's bitterness, and he underpins his argument with the simple fact that in his own time Swift had nothing in common with such Irish contemporaries as Carolan, Ó'Rahilly and Ó Doirnín:

> The dominant factor, the scale of values, native to the minds of these poets was a "glow" transmitted from the Gaelic past. The "glow" in Swift's mind came to him from the past of the English nation; the dominant factor in his mind was English.[60]

Proceeding carefully from this premise, Corkery allows that Swift sympathized with the downtrodden Irish, but as a humanitarian rather than as a patriot; nor were his exertions for liberty patriotic, for liberty meant to him simply the "freedom of the ascendancy from British interference."[61] In a later article the same year, Corkery asserted that a Protestant could only be "an Irish nationalist *sans phrase* if his purpose was to conserve the national mind."[62] And of course Swift had no such objective.

Corkery's was the most studied, temperate, even commanding statement in Swift's posthumous career against his acceptance as an Irish patriot. Appropriately, it appeared in a learned journal, but this also blunted its impact upon a popular view that had, simply from repetition over ninety years, gained the force and the aura of tradition. As such it had contributed to a genealogically oriented patriotic historiography of significant value to the new state and the nationalist movement from which that state emerged. Moreover, among the Anglophone realities of Ireland's cultural condition by the 1930s was unblinkably an Anglo-Irish literature, increasingly Catholic (or, perhaps, lapsed Catholic) in its progress but largely Protestant in its roots. And to the tradition of that literature, as D. F. MacCarthy had noted as early as 1846, Swift was fundamental. If earlier critics of Swift's place in the patriotic and literary traditions had possessed Corkery's clarity of mind, the Dean might not still have figured so large in them. But as they stood, these traditions made Corkery's voice seem singular, even cranky. Thus Swift's bicentenary in 1945 called forth an appreciation by J. J. Hogan, who held that Swift was a true nationalist simply because in all his Irish writings he had the good of the nation at heart, whether in a humanitarian and social sense (as when attacking the shortsightedness of the Irish gentry) or in a political one (as when holding for Irish independence). "Swift was no colonial patriot, if by that is meant the patriot of a class; he had no notion of erecting an Anglo-Irish freedom upon native helotry."[63] In keeping with what had become the trend of twentieth-century criticism, Hogan's celebration of Swift is mostly concerned with his qualities as a writer; admiration for his patriotism serves mainly to introduce this stronger focus, and Swift's value as an ancestor in Ireland's nationalist and literary traditions is largely implicit. Yet that value has often emerged in commentaries since Hogan's time; as Seamus Deane has recently pointed out, for instance, "Anglo-Irish writing does not begin with Swift, but Anglo-Irish literature does."[64] An Irish nationalist and literary genealogy, giving Swift pride (or a share of pride) of place, remains valuable, and validated, because of what followed after him, which was ultimately successful in breaking the political link with Britain while retaining a cultural association, not least in that Ireland has developed as a modern, Anglophone nation. Contemporary Ireland is almost certainly not what Swift anticipated, nor necessarily what other patriots looked for, but in each generation since Davis's time these have not only espoused a cause but sought to validate it by invoking a tradition. Or, perhaps more accurately, by inventing one. It is in this way that they could be said to have hearkened to the injunction Swift himself gave in his epitaph: imitate him, if you can.

NOTES

1. John Boyle, Earl of Orrery, *Remarks on the Life and Writings of Dr. Jonathan Swift* (London: A. Millar, 1752), 73.

2. "A Young Lady's Complaint for the Stay of Dean *SWIFT* in *England*" (Dublin: G. Faulkner, 1726).

3. For example, John Curry, *Observations on the Popery Laws* (Dublin: T. Ewing, 1771), 50; Charles O'Conor, introducing Curry, *The State of the Catholics of Ireland*, appended to *An Historical and Critical Review of the Civil Wars in Ireland* (Dublin: L. White, 1786), 2:iii–iv <second pagination>. A quotation from the fourth *Drapier's Letter* was also used as epigraph for *Proceedings of the Catholic Meeting in Dublin . . . October 31, 1792* (Dublin: H. Fitzpatrick, 1792), t.-p.

4. Francis Plowden, *An Historical Review of the State of Ireland* (London: T. Egerton, 1803), 1:389–91.

5. Denis Taafe, *An Impartial Review of the State of Ireland*, 4 vols. (Dublin: J. Christie, 1809–11), 4:21.

6. Matthew O'Conor, *The History of the Irish Catholics* (Dublin: J. Stockdale, 1813), 194.

7. Donal MacCartney, "The Writing of History in Ireland, 1800–30," *Irish Historical Studies* 10 (1957): 355.

8. Francis Jeffrey, "Jonathan Swift," *Edinburgh Review* 27 (September 1816): 22.

9. Edward Berwick, *A Defence of Dr. Jonathan Swift* (London: Nichols & Son, 1819), 35.

10. Berwick, 38–40.

11. Thomas Moore, *Memoirs of Captain Rock* (London: Longmans, 1824), 123.

12. Moore, 126–27.

13. See Mackie L. Jarrell, " 'Jack and the Dane': Swift Traditions in Ireland," in *"Fair Liberty was all His Cry"*: *A Tercentenary Tribute to Jonathan Swift*, ed. A. Norman Jeffares (London: Macmillan, 1967), 311–41; also D. O hÓgain, *The Hero in Irish Folk History* (Dublin: Gill and Macmillan, 1985), 87–99.

14. See Gearoid O Tuathaigh, "Gaelic Ireland, Popular Politics and Daniel O'Connell," *Galway Archeological and Historical Society Journal* 34 (1974-75): 27–33.

15. Francis Mahony, "Dean Swift's Madness: The Tale of a Churn," *Fraser's Magazine* 10 (July 1834): 20.

16. Mahony's antipathy to O'Connell is a recurrent theme in Ethel Mannin, *Two Studies in Integrity: Gerald Griffin and the Rev. Francis Mahony (Father Prout)* (New York: Putnam's, 1954), esp. 140–41, 165.

17. Mahony, 20.

18. "English Appropriation of Irish Intellect," *The Nation*, 26 Nov. 1842, 106.

19. "A Patriot Parliament," *The Nation*, 1 Apr. 1843, 392.

20. "Our National Language," *The Nation*, 1 Apr. 1843, 394.

21. "An Irish Party," *The Nation*, 15 Apr. 1843, 424.

22. "An Irish Party," 424.

23. "Abolition of the Lord Lieutenant," *The Nation*, 18 May 1844, 504.

24. [Address to the jury, 27 Jan. 1844], *Dublin Evening Post*, 27 Jan. 1844, 2.

25. [Address to the jury, 1 Feb. 1844], *Dublin Evening Post*, 3 Feb. 1844.

26. "The Betrayed Protestants," *The Nation*, 25 Jan. 1845, 248.

27. Denis Florence MacCarthy, *The Poets and Dramatists of Ireland*, 2 vols. (Dublin: James Duffy, 1846), 1:130.

28. [Speech of 13 Jan. 1847] *The Nation*, 16 Jan. 1847, 229.

29. *The Nation*, 27 Mar. 1847, 394.

30. Published as "Swift," *The English Humourists of the Eighteenth Century* (London: Smith, Elder, 1853).

31. *Biographical Sketches of Eminent British Poets . . . intended for Teachers, and the Higher Classes in Schools* (Dublin: Commissioners of National Education in Ireland . . . 1849), 235.

32. Christian Brothers, *Historical Class-Book, comprising Outlines of Ancient and Modern History* (Dublin: W. Powell, 1859), 574.

33. W. E. H. Lecky, *Leaders of Public Opinion in Ireland,* (London: Saunders, Otley, 1861), esp. 48–59; Whiteside, "The Life and Death of the Irish Parliament," *Lectures delivered before the Dublin Young Men's Christian Association . . . during the Year 1863* (Dublin: Hayes, Smith, 1864), 81–89; D'Arcy McGee, *A Popular History of Ireland: from the Earliest Period to the Emancipation of the Catholics* (New York: D. & J. Sadlier, 2 vols., 1864), 2:616–622.

34. G. L. Craik, *A Compendious History of English Literature, and of the English Language* (London: Griffin, Bohn, 1861), 2:216.

35. J. F. Waller, "Life of Jonathan Swift," in his edition of *Gulliver's Travels* (London: Cassell, Peter and Galpin, n.d. [1864]), xlii.

36. Goldwin Smith, *Irish History and Irish Character* (Oxford: J. H. and Jas. Parker, 1861), 137–38; W. F. Collier, *A History of English Literature, in a Series of Biographical Sketches* (London: T. Nelson, 1862), 282–87; W. H. Flood, *An Historical Review of the Irish Parliaments* (London: J. Kenny, 1863), 68–71.

37. Charles Grant, *The Last 100 Years of English Literature* (Jena: Fr. Fromman; London: Williams and Norgate, 1866), 7.

38. John Mitchel, *The History of Ireland from the Treaty of Limerick to the Present Time* (Glasgow: Cameron & Ferguson; London: C. Griffin, 1869), 56.

39. Mitchel, 63.

40. J. A. Froude, *The English in Ireland in the Eighteenth Century,* 3 vols. (London: Longmans, Green and Co., 1872), 1:500.

41. Thomas Burke, *English Misrule in Ireland* (New York: Lynch, Cole & Meehan, 1873), 124, 129.

42. Stanley Lane-Poole, "Swift and Ireland," *Fraser's Magazine* n.s. 24 (Sept. 1881): 385–400.

43. Gavan Duffy, *A Bird's-Eye View of Irish History* (Dublin: J. Duffy, 1882), 173–77; John Redmond, "Irish Protestants and Home Rule" [address delivered in the Rotunda, Dublin, 29 Nov. 1886], *Historical and Political Addresses, 1886–1897* (Dublin: Sealy, Bryers & Walker, 1898), 122–24; W. E. Gladstone, *Special Aspects of the Irish Question: A Series of Reflections in and since 1886* (London: J. Murray, 1892), 115.

44. W. E. H. Lecky, *A History of Ireland in the Eighteenth Century,* New Edition (London: Longmans, 1892; New York, D. Appleton, 1893), esp. 456–58.

45. See Anne Wyatt, "Froude, Lecky and 'the humblest Irishman,' " *Irish Historical Studies* 19 (1974–75): 261–85.

46. For example, Henry Craik, *The Life of Jonathan Swift* (London: J. Murray, 1882): 334–66; John Bowles Daly, ed., *Ireland in the Days of Dean Swift*, (London: Chapman and Hall, 1887); Richard Ashe King, *Swift in Ireland*, (London: T. F. Unwin, 1895).

47. D. P. Moran, "The Pale and the Gael," *New Ireland Review* 11, no. 4 (June 1899): 230.

48. Moran, 232.

49. Moran, 233.

50. William Rooney, "Illustrious Irishmen" (lecture to Irish Fireside Club in 1889), quoted by Philip Bradley, introducing Rooney's *Poems and Ballads* (Dublin: M. H. Gill, 1901), xviii.

51. Rooney, *Prose Writings* (Dublin: M. H. Gill, 1909), 2–3, 97.

52. Arthur Griffith, "Parnell," *Sinn Fein*, 7 Oct. 1911, 3.

53. D. J. O'Donoghue, "Swift as an Irishman," *The Irish Review* 2, no. 4 (June 1912): 209.

54. O'Donoghue, 210.

55. Anonymous, *Dean Swift on the Situation* (Dublin: Cumann na mBan [Central Branch], 1915).

56. Padrais Pearse, *Ghosts*, Tracts for the Times, No. 10 (Dublin: Whelan, 1916), 16.

57. P. J. Lennox, "Swift, the Irish Patriot," *Catholic Educational Review* 14 (Nov. 1917): 289–99.

58. Christian Brothers, *Irish History Reader* (Dublin: M. H. Gill, 1916), 243; Mary Hayden and George A. Moonan, *A Short History of the Irish People* (Dublin: Talbot Press, 1921), 384–85.

59. Among the first to consider this concept in depth was Ernest Boyd, *Ireland's Literary Renaissance* (New York: John Lane, 1916).

60. Daniel Corkery, "Ourselves and Dean Swift," *Studies* 23 (1934): 211.

61. Corkery, 213.

62. Corkery, "The Nation that was not a Nation," *Studies* 23 (1934): 612.

63. J. J. Hogan, "Bicentenary of Jonathan Swift," *Studies* 34 (1945): 505.

64. Seamus Deane, *A Short History of Irish Literature* (London: Hutchinson, 1986), 37.

Index